ALSO BY JOHN J. BERGER

Nuclear Power: The Unviable Option. A Critical Look at Our Energy Alternatives (1976)

Restoring the Earth

Restoring the Earth

*How Americans Are Working to Renew
Our Damaged Environment*

John J. Berger

With a Foreword by Morris K. Udall

Alfred A. Knopf   New York   1985

THIS IS A BORZOI BOOK
PUBLISHED BY ALFRED A. KNOPF, INC.

Library of Congress Cataloging-in-Publication Data

Berger, John J.
Restoring the earth, how Americans are working
to renew our damaged environment.

Bibliography: p.
Includes index.
1. Nature conservation—United States.   2. Landscape
protection—United States.   3. Reclamation of land—
United States.   4. Environmental protection—United
States.   I. Title.
QH76.B47   1985   363.7'00973   85-40341
ISBN 0-394-52372-5

Portions of this work were first published in *Audubon, Sierra,* and *Yankee.*

Manufactured in the United States of America
First Edition

Research support for this book was provided by:
The Max and Anna Levinson Foundation; The Evergreen Fund;
The Frank J. Weeden Foundation; The Jewish Endowment Fund;
The Island Foundation; The Foundation for National Progress;
Stanley K. Sheinbaum; Clarence E. Heller;
and others cited in the Acknowledgments.

To Agnes and Laszlo

Men's failures are often as beautiful as men's triumphs,
    but your returnings
Are even more precious than your first presence.
                    —Robinson Jeffers, "Bixby's Landing"

Contents

Foreword

During the past twenty-five years in America we have seen a tremendous explosion of environmental consciousness and activity in almost every sector of society. The public's concern is evident in the extraordinary number of public-interest, civic, and lobbying groups at the national, state, local, and even neighborhood levels, and in the steady growth of such venerable organizations as the Sierra Club and the Wilderness Society.

Environmental research in both industry and academe is now extensive. All major academic institutions offer environmental studies, or have even established separate departments, which did not exist as such before. Whole new profit-making industries have emerged to treat or prevent pollution and degradation. The Federal Government has responded by erecting a formidable legal and regulatory framework with laws such as the Clean Air Act, the Clean Water Act, the Toxic Substances Control Act, the Wilderness Act, the Surface Mining Control and Reclamation Act, and many, many others, as well as with the agencies needed to administer them. Much of this framework is replicated by state and local governments.

This is an exceptional achievement, unmatched anywhere else in the world. It is one sign of a maturing industrial nation. It is, to be sure, far from a perfect achievement: with the many success stories have come many disappointments, many worsening environmental problems, and many new threats. Nonetheless, we clearly have a far better opportunity to deal with our environmental responsibilities today than twenty-five years ago.

Naturally, our earliest efforts were devoted to stopping abuses and preventing their repetition. Now, however, in this important and useful book, John Berger turns our attention to an activity that, with our maturing environmental awareness, we would do well to focus on more intently: restoring the integrity of damaged environments. We can stop the dumping of pollutants into our waterways, but if those ecosystems are not biologically functional and self-sustaining, they are not really healthy. We can set aside some of the dwindling riparian areas that remain, but what then of the much vaster ones man has already crippled? Is there not an enormous challenge and opportunity in the possibilities of revitalizing such areas?

Fortunately, we are beginning the process of restoration. In 1977, for example, the Congress established the Abandoned Mine Land Fund, which allocates billions of dollars generated by current coal production to transform old, devastated strip mines back into useful, productive lands. In this book, you will read of many restoration projects around the country. Still, not enough is being done, and more discussion and more action on returning our abused Earth to its self-sustaining state are clearly needed.

John Berger makes an important statement here not just about our environment but about people. There is much despair and hopelessness about the ability of one or a few people to really accomplish anything in a society as huge, complex, and powerful as ours. In this book we see just what dedicated, determined people—even a single dedicated, determined person— can do and have done. All the successes of the environmental movement to date did not happen through the workings of an ineluctable Fate; these victories required countless people making innumerable decisions. It will take many more people to guarantee that those successes are not lost in the future. John Berger shows us people making those decisions and efforts in areas where there is as yet no great support or recognition. Their stories are an inspiration and a beginning. What follows is up to us.

Morris K. Udall,
Member of Congress

Restoring the Earth

Introduction
New Approaches to a Better Future

Imagine a world where the rivers and streams flow clean again, brilliant and teeming with fish. The air is fresh and crystalline. The earth, once bare and robbed of its topsoil, now is green with healthy vegetation. This vision of Nature thriving and restored can become reality.

In 1976 when I began working on this book, I had no idea whether meaningful environmental restoration was feasible, nor whether it might offer economic as well as aesthetic rewards. But I was concerned by the many ominous signs of environmental crises: the toxic chemicals and groundwater contamination; the clear-cutting of erosion-prone forests; the widespread pollution of freshwater; the acid rain; the buildup of atmospheric CO_2; the loss of open space; the waste of precious topsoil; the filling of wetlands; the solid waste dumps; the destruction of estuaries and coastal marshes; the disappearance of wildlife; and the extinction of endangered species.

I saw widespread examples of "patchy" environmental failure. Many resources had already been destroyed. What if the patches closed, in ever larger arcs of resource destruction? And what if certain destructive trends—such as the progressive damage to forests from long-term air pollution—unexpectedly exceeded biological limits and thus brought irreversible disaster?

These concerns led me to wonder whether citizens and environmentalists could not increase their efforts to protect the natural resources on which our survival rests. Environmental groups were working to conserve resources and to reduce or avert pollution, but few people seemed to be thinking about how to *recover* lost ground. I believed that conservation and pollution abatement were necessary, but I felt these were intrinsically rearguard actions to protect dwindling resources. While they slowed devastation, relentless development pressure was eroding other resources. To counterbalance this attrition, an active program of restoration seemed vital.

Once damage such as desertification and groundwater contamination occurs, it cannot generally be cured by environmental protection. Toxic aquifers and deserts, abandoned mined lands, dead lakes, and eroding clear-cut forests all seemed to *require* restoration. So did the plights of many endangered species.

I therefore wondered if there were people somewhere in the United States who agreed with this conclusion and who were already working to restore damaged ecosystems. My search for resource restorers began by mail, telephone, and visits, often to out-of-the-way places where I had heard about someone trying to heal the Earth.

The quest took eight years of sometimes intense and sometimes intermittent effort. During my journeys and interviews throughout the nation, I sought out people pursuing different approaches to ecosystem restoration of various resources, in hopes of getting a comprehensive understanding of restoration. I hoped to learn who these resource restorers were, what they had in common, why they chose to do restoration, and why they succeeded or failed. This book is the result. Virtually all quoted material, unless otherwise noted, is from my personal interviews.

·   ·   ·

Let me begin by clarifying what restoration means. Natural resource restoration is a process in which a damaged resource or region is renewed. Biologically. Structurally. Functionally.

If the resource is being polluted, the pollution is stopped. If the resource is disappearing, its erosion or extraction is halted. But restoration goes beyond preservation, beyond conservation, beyond traditional environmentalism.

Until now, humanity has been primarily a resource-taker, a simplifier, a destroyer of ecosystems. We cultivated the soil but wiped out varied and intricately interwoven webs of life. By contrast, restoration is an effort to imitate nature in all its artistry and complexity by taking a degraded system and making it more diverse and productive.

In restoration, not only are abuses halted, but the resource itself is physically repaired, and, if necessary, its missing components are replaced. Native seed varieties are sown; plants are used to bandage and rebuild the land. Roots, soil, mosses, and fungi all re-form a dense living mat of soil that nourishes plants, retains moisture, and cleanses water percolating into the ground. Barrens become productive again. Endangered animal populations gradually revive. While certainly no longer in a pristine state, the restored resource becomes healthy, life supporting, and pleasing to the eye. In this condition, the resource provides a sound basis for the creation of new jobs and prosperity.

The world's population will exceed six billion by 2000 A.D., just fifteen years from now. As resources once taken for granted are exhausted or contaminated—and as we thus draw closer to the Earth's carrying capacity—the need for actively restoring damaged resources becomes ever more urgent. "If the creature destroys its environment," said Gregory Bateson, "it destroys itself." The prevalence of cancer from environmental causes is only one sign that we are mistreating the Earth. The contamination of our bodies with traces of carcinogens like DDT and PCBs is another.

Many people have grown fatalistic about our tremendous environmental problems, believing that polluted air, contaminated water, industrial wastes, and despoiled land are acceptable and here to stay.

This book is about a few Americans who fervently believe a blighted environment is not acceptable and who are optimistic about restoring the Earth ecologically. These are people determined to succeed and willing to sacrifice. They have the vision, courage, and creativity to tackle projects of monumental difficulty and scope. They are today repairing American forests, fisheries, croplands, rangelands, prairies, wetlands, mined lands, toxic waste sites, rivers, lakes, and streams. You may never have heard about these people or the particular habitats or species they have struggled to reestablish. These people do not thrust themselves into the limelight. Yet these people are important. They are the beginnings of a national restoration movement that can help us choose survival over environmental destruction.

I

BRIGHT WATERS

1

Mother Nashua

A web of shimmering brooks and lively springs merges west of Fitchburg, in north-central Massachusetts, to form the headwaters of the Nashua River. The countryside through which the river flows is for the most part a land of small old towns, picturesque fields, wetlands, and forests still wild enough for bobcat, mink, and porcupine. As agriculture has declined here for half a century, forests and meadows have taken over old fields to reclaim two-thirds of the rural land.

Before Europeans first settled here, the Nashaway Indians, an Algonkian tribe of the Pennacook Confederacy, inhabited this river valley, hunting game in the virgin forests and fishing for salmon, shad, and alewives in its crystal waters. They called the river Nashua: "river with the beautiful pebbled bottom." But by the early 1960s, you could no longer see those pebbles. Local industry from the seventeenth century on had clustered around the river, drawn by the free hydro power for sawmills and cotton mills, and by the clean water for manufacturing. For over 200 years, industry used the river as a fifty-mile-long sewer. East and north of Fitchburg the Nashua was opaque with decaying organic matter and industrial chemicals. Its color ranged from red-dish brown to red, white, blue, or green, according to the color of the paper being made by the paper manufacturers who poured their dyes and pigments into the river. In the absence of artificial coloration, the Nashua was an evil greenish grayish black. Raw sewage flowed into it carrying typhoid and other diseases. The river gave off a putrid odor so strong that some citizens of Hollis, New Hampshire, claimed it kept them awake at night. (The Nashua crosses into New Hampshire near Hollis on its way to the Merrimack River, which links the Nashua to the Atlantic.)

Within the river, decaying organic material consumed so much oxygen that little or none was left for aquatic life. After a three-year drought, in the summer of 1966, much of the Nashua had no dissolved oxygen, and so no fish.

Local citizens had discussed solutions to the river's pollution problems for years, but somehow the talk had never led to effective action. Paradoxically, by attracting settlers to the area and industry to its banks, the Nashua in a sense had invited its own destruction. The subsequent despoliation, however, made the area so unattractive that it saved much of the riverfront from development, thus preserving its rural character and restoration potential.

Not everyone condoned abuse of the Nashua. A few people even had the audacity to think they could change the situation. Marion R. Stoddart was one such optimist. The youthful, unflappable grandmother, now 56, had been a fair-housing activist, a sponsor of underprivileged children, a teacher, a counselor, and a defender of wetlands, all before taking an interest in the Nashua.

Having grown up on an irrigated alfalfa farm in arid Fernley, Nevada, Stoddart appreciated water resources, and as an adult had helped protect wetlands between the Sudbury and Concord rivers by coordinating a successful citizen campaign for passage of the 1966 Massachusetts Wetlands Act.

Stoddart is a sturdy, cheerful woman of medium height with a fine net of wrinkles that cross ruddy cheeks to join laugh lines around her mouth. On a typical spring morning before work, she

is apt to be up before breakfast jogging a few miles in the remains of an unseasonably late snow. Next day she may be out
canoeing on the Nashua with rain pelting her salt-and-pepper
hair. She also likes to go cross-country skiing, and her interest in
camping led her to cofound Women Outdoors, a national organization.

When Stoddart moved in 1962 to Groton on the banks of the
Nashua near Fitchburg, the Nashua was considered one of the
most polluted rivers in the United States and was getting worse.
"If the Nashua can be cleaned up, *any* river in the country can
be restored," said one cynical observer. The river's nauseating
stench could be smelled two miles away, and it was so full of
paper pulp that birds and small animals allegedly could scamper
across the surface. Local wags deemed the Nashua "too thick to
pour but too thin to plow."

When the high waters of spring receded, the Nashua's banks
were coated with paper sludge the consistency of wet egg cartons. It hung from trees at the water's edge and killed riverbank
vegetation. Pulp and other sludge rose to the river's surface,
buoyed on stinking bubbles of hydrogen sulfide gas. Within the
river practically nothing but a few carp survived, in isolated
stretches. Nearby land had plummeted in value, and, in one case,
the Federal Housing Administration ascribed a value of zero to a
home too close to the river. U.S. Army Corps of Engineers employees who came to look at the Nashua pronounced it dead.
Wildlife and fish could not be replaced, they said.

The river's sinister appearance hurt Fitchburg's economy as
well as its image. The town's mayor, for example, once received
a letter from a businessman who explained bluntly that he had
had every intention of doing business with a Fitchburg concern
until he saw the condition of the Nashua. He had then concluded that the community and its industrialists had so little regard for themselves and their environment that he could not in
good conscience do business with anybody from Fitchburg.

Even in the early sixties, however, Marion Stoddart was
looking at the filthy river and, in her mind's eye, seeing it transformed. "I had a vision," she said, "of the Nashua River being

restored, of a greenway along the whole length of the river, and a comprehensive conservation plan for the whole watershed implemented by all the people who lived, worked, and played in the area."

Why did she act on the vision instead of brushing it aside? Stoddart was sophisticated enough to know that the task she was undertaking was formidable and that success was uncertain. At best, the project would take years to complete. Yet she was going through a period of personal crisis and felt unfulfilled by her role as wife, mother, and small-town citizen. She had an almost desperate need for a more challenging and significant vocation. As her parents had been active in community service, it was natural for her also to think in terms of public service, and, after vacillating for months between social work and conservation, she finally chose the Nashua River, drawn by the excitement of her vision of a "wonderful, cooperative venture by the industrialists, businesspeople, and homemakers [from which] everyone would benefit." Her dream, however, proved easier to visualize than to accomplish.

When Stoddart moved to Groton, one of the first things she did was to find out who the community leaders were. She then got together with them and organized the Nashua River Cleanup Committee, a citizens' group. Next, she began contacting state, regional, and federal agencies to find out what plans, if any, they had for restoring the Nashua. There was little hope, they said, that under existing legislation the river would be restored. Thus, her new group's first project was to help change the laws by gathering support for a bill known as the Massachusetts Clean Water Act.

The bill contained provisions for setting up the Massachusetts Division of Water Pollution Control and for making matching state funds available to localities for assisting with wastewater treatment plant construction. It also contained a system of classifying the state's rivers according to their future intended uses and of assigning them corresponding water quality goals.

By 1965, Stoddart had been in touch with the New England

Interstate Water Pollution Control Commission, an appointed body that had developed its own water quality agenda for New England. But its goals for the Nashua were low indeed. Much of the river—its north branch and part of its main stem—was to be given a "D" water use classification, a standard that would have precluded using these waters for anything but "the transportation of sewage and industrial wastes," and for power and navigation; fishing, swimming, boating, wildlife habitat, and even most industrial uses would have been excluded. Another portion of the river was to be given a "C" rating: suitable for noncontact sports (canoeing, for example), industrial processes, and other uses. When Stoddart learned of these proposals, she went to the commission chairman exclaiming, "My God, that's terrible! People in this area want the Nashua to be suitable for all uses! What can we do?"

"There's nothing you can do," the chairman replied, "unless you can get the governor to change his mind." Stoddart decided to try. "I gave my life to the restoration campaign . . . the watershed association was my whole identity," she said. The newly organized Cleanup Committee gathered more than 6,000 signatures from the small towns along the Nashua on a petition calling on Governor John A. Volpe to do everything in his power to clean up the Nashua.

Simultaneously, the Cleanup Committee asked all key government officials of towns along the river, including state legislators, mayors, and selectmen, to attend a meeting with the governor at his office. The group presented its petition and asked the governor to support a river cleanup and to help pass the Massachusetts Clean Water Act, which knowledgeable political observers thought had little chance of passage that year. The fact that so many small-town officials, especially unpaid selectmen, had left their businesses on a weekday out of concern about the polluted river impressed the governor. These were not just students, environmentalists, or Nature lovers. These were middle-class voters.

The committee presented the governor with a bottle of revoltingly dirty river water. The sample shocked the governor, and he promised to keep it on his desk as a constant reminder until the river was cleaned up. He also pledged to help pass the state's Clean Water Act. The meeting made a media splash, and the Cleanup Committee gained overnight recognition. About this time, Massachusetts Senator Edward Kennedy announced a tour of polluted rivers in the state, not including the Nashua. Stoddart asked him to visit the Nashua, too, and persuaded selectmen and mayors to do likewise. Kennedy agreed and came with then Secretary of the Interior Stewart Udall.

The committee brought more than 500 people, including a busload of senior citizens, to meet Kennedy and Udall at the airport that Labor Day weekend in 1966. Governor Volpe and Lieutenant Governor Elliot Richardson joined the two federal officials. The dignitaries received more water samples. Volpe opened his bottle, smelled the potent brew, and accidentally spilled some on himself. "You didn't get as good a sample as I did," he joked to Kennedy.

The waiting crowd was in high spirits, hopeful that at last something would be done about the river. From the signs, banners, and applause, the officials could feel the crowd's eagerness. Stoddart spoke, urging that the river be restored for fishing, boating, and swimming. The crowd cheered. Later that day in Boston, the governor signed the Clean Water Act of 1966 into law. The *Boston Globe* of September 7 hailed the measure as the nation's first comprehensive water pollution control program. The cleanup campaign was suddenly in high gear.

Businessman Wayne Kimmerlin, chairman of the Hollis Conservation Commission in New Hampshire, and Lee P. (Bill) Farnsworth, a resident of Lancaster, an old town on the Nashua in Massachusetts, both had laid groundwork for the Cleanup Committee's rapid success in environmental politics. Stoddart had assumed a voluntary post on the Groton Conservation Commission in the early sixties in her search for ways to protect the Nashua riverfront from development. While she was serving on that commission, it received a letter from Kimmerlin of nearby Hollis urging citizens to collect signatures on petitions calling for a river cleanup. Kimmerlin had started a citizens' group called Project Purewater in 1966 and had already gathered 600 signatures on a similar petition just in the hamlet of Hollis. Prior to his letter, Stoddart had felt that protection of the riverbanks should come first, while the river was still dirty, and no one had any interest in acquiring that land. State and federal officials had already laughed at her for asking whether their agencies would buy land along the Nashua for open space. We're only interested in purchasing land along *clean* rivers, they said. She therefore decided to adopt Kimmerlin's approach, making water cleanup the first priority. Thereafter, the Massachusetts and New Hampshire branches of the Nashua restoration effort worked in parallel.

The other early pivotal figure in the Nashua cleanup besides Kimmerlin was Bill Farnsworth, a mechanical engineer at Lincoln Laboratories in Lexington, Massachusetts. Farnsworth lives a few minutes' drive from Fitchburg in the Lancaster house in which he grew up, with smallish rooms, antique furniture, and the air of a fine colonial museum. (The Farnsworths have been in Lancaster for about eleven generations, arriving in the 1600s.) Bill Farnsworth is a tall, soft-spoken man with a creased face and a brushy gray crew cut that sticks up in a flattop over receding temples. Whereas his father once swam and fished in the Nashua, Bill, now in his sixties, had never known the river to be unpolluted, even during his boyhood. Before 1962, he recalls, no one in town was trying to clean up the river, even though everyone was complaining about it. That year, however, the city of Leominster got permission from the Massachusetts Department of Public Health to dump 150 million gallons of raw sewage per day into the river during expansion of its sewage plant. Farnsworth was outraged and set up the Nashua River Study Committee in response.

He also became active in Lancaster town planning issues as a selectman, and he began working on a local zoning ordinance to protect the town and the river. He eventually did eight years of night and weekend volunteer work and produced "The Nashua River Greenway Plan." This report was part of a formal *Pre-*

liminary Regional Plan for the Nashua River Greenway. Stoddart's group succeeded in having the state and the Nashua River conservation commissions recognize this document as an official regional plan. This made the riverfront towns eligible for matching state cleanup aid under the Massachusetts Clean Water Act.

As the sixties drew to a close, the patient efforts of Farnsworth, Stoddart, Kimmerlin, and many other citizens began to reinforce each other. "All the key people in the restoration," said Stoddart, "had the same vision. It included cooperation, and it included mutual benefits." Their initial major objective was reclassification of the river upward to a "B" rating—"B" meaning suitable for bathing, fishing, and public water supply. (An "A" classification was not sought because that would have legally restricted the Nashua to drinking-water use only.) The higher the river's rating, the more money and effort polluters would have to spend to reach the standard. More expensive municipal-industrial treatment plants would be needed. Resistance to a "B" classification was not long in coming: One paper company was soon telling its workers they would have to choose between their jobs and clean water. Other companies said, "If we have to clean up, we'll close or move South." Stoddart's group argued that the companies would not be able to evade pollution control responsibilities by moving.

The U.S. Congress had passed a Clean Water Act of its own in 1965 mandating that public hearings had to be held on rivers prior to their classification. The Cleanup Committee then got the state to agree to hold a hearing in Fitchburg just on the Nashua, and the committee doggedly spent a year preparing for that confrontation. "We identified every organization in every community in the watershed and asked them [to prepare] a statement for the hearing," said Stoddart.

At the committee's urging, hundreds of people came to what state officials presumed would be a routine hearing. Instead, it lasted all day and well into the night. Citizens almost without exception asked for a "B" classification. Industry, joined by the state's public health department and the city of Fitchburg, asked for a "D." State and federal officials eventually compromised by giving the river a modified "C" rating, amended by the requirement that the water must meet "B"-level bacterial standards. These gains encouraged the Cleanup Committee, and it set out to ensure that federal and state funds would be available for river cleanup work. (The towns and industries along the Nashua did not have the funds to meet the new water standards alone.)

Fortunately, the local planning efforts and the completion of the federal classification process made the communities along the river eligible for federal matching funds to aid in wastewater treatment plant construction. But there was no guarantee that towns would actually procure the funds or ever use them to build effective facilities.

The Cleanup Committee first had to persuade Fitchburg's polluting paper companies to join with the city in trying to meet the new water quality standards. Stoddart and the committee therefore contacted all thirty-four Nashua communities to convince them to work cooperatively for an effective sewage treatment program. Six major industries helped the city fund a study of a joint industry-municipal wastewater treatment facility.

Weyerhauser Corporation had already started to build its own pollution abatement system before the hearings but had halted work, uncertain about what treatment standards the government would impose after the hearings. Stoddart took advantage of Weyerhauser's hesitation to solicit its cooperation. The city of Fitchburg's cooperation was also critical. William Flynn played a crucial role. He had become mayor in 1967 after election to the Fitchburg City Council in 1966 at 23—one of the youngest elected officials in the state. "Slim and boyish-looking, but with a firm outward-jutting chin, he brought to the office the enthusiasm of youth," said a local history book. And he made a cause célèbre of the river cleanup, canoeing the polluted river with Stoddart one afternoon to dramatize the river's recreational potential.

Flynn's administration had to face the difficult decision of appropriating money for building the treatment plants. The proposed $17.5-million bond issue which the city council passed in 1969 was the largest in the city's history—more than double its existing debt. From then on, Flynn's political career in Fitchburg was hitched to the successful operation of these plants.

Getting Weyerhauser's participation in a joint water treatment venture proved to be a crucial step for Stoddart. The smaller paper companies had been leery of getting involved with municipal and government bureaucracies. Now, after several discussions with Stoddart and others, these firms, too, agreed to twenty-year contracts with the city.

Following that, two large treatment plants were designed and approved by all concerned, and construction was slated for 1973. But just five days before ground breaking, the locally owned Fitchburg Paper Company withdrew from the agreement following a takeover by Litton Industries, a multinational firm without local roots.

Flynn said later, "All that we needed was for word to get out that one of the major companies was backing out of the deal, and then there would have been a domino effect...." If Fitchburg Paper were permitted to withdraw, Stoddart knew that Weyerhauser and the city would have to redesign their facility, a very expensive process that would have delayed the river cleanup for years. Stoddart therefore contacted labor union leaders asking them to attend the Fitchburg City Council meeting to urge the council to approve the bond issue and to protest the Fitchburg Paper pullout. She knew that despite paper company pressure, labor unionists did not want to live in an unattractive town with a dirty river.

Rather than see years of work evaporate, she and some members of her group also prepared to do legal battle to hold Fitchburg Paper to its agreement. "Weyerhauser didn't want to initiate action against this fellow company, and the city didn't want to," Stoddart said. "We were the only people that really could." Faced with the legal challenge, Fitchburg Paper capitulated and reaffirmed its agreement.

To expedite the raising of nonprofit funds and to become eligible for model river demonstration funds under a new federal program, the Cleanup Committee reorganized itself in 1969 as the Nashua River Watershed Association, Inc. Stoddart persuaded Donald Crocker, manager of Weyerhauser Corporation in Fitchburg, to sit on the new association's board along with other corporate members. And Crocker solicited support from other industrialists.

Soon after the association's formation, the New England Regional Commission chose the Nashua for a five-year model river demonstration program, and the commission included a multi-million-dollar request for Nashua restoration planning and sewer construction in its budget request to Congress. This eventually produced an additional five million dollars in Department of Commerce funds for the cleanup effort.

Flynn contends that the Nashua cleanup work saved all of the jobs in the Fitchburg paper industry. Without the plants, he claims the companies wouldn't have been able to afford to build their own pollution control facilities and would have had to close.

"It would have had at least a quarter of a century's negative economic impact," he said, likening the situation to the decline of the textile industry in Massachusetts in the thirties and forties. Weyerhauser Corporation did leave Fitchburg but was able to sell its facilities instead of having to abandon them, according to Flynn, "because there was a treatment plant there to take care of the effluent." Since the mills were not abandoned, Flynn added, 1,500 jobs were saved, and paper mills worth sixty to a hundred million dollars were kept in production. If each of those jobs was worth $20,000 in income to workers, then the decision to build treatment plants was worth thirty million dollars per year in before-tax earnings to the Fitchburg area, plus secondary economic benefits.

In 1969 the cleanup effort received a tremendous boost from an unexpected quarter. Fort Devens, the largest military installation in New England, is not far from Fitchburg, and the fort contains more than eight winding miles of the Nashua. So bad was its condition there, however, that military personnel were warned to stay away from the river. Base Commander General

John H. Cushman had heard about the Cleanup Committee's work and offered Stoddart the use of a two-story barracks on the base as an office, plus the full-time services of professional military officers and men to launch a full-scale cleanup offensive. To her amazement, Stoddart soon found herself leading a highly skilled military task force that included civil engineers, landscape architects, and a lawyer; there was even an accountant to help set up the new watershed association's books. One of her first moves was to obtain a $5,000 grant for hiring a planner to work with her two military landscape architects and association volunteers.

A comprehensive plan for the whole watershed resulted, including river restoration, and when Stoddart needed to have it published, she convinced one of the polluting paper companies to donate paper for the printing. Then she found a local school to print the plan gratis, and a local banker loaned his employees to collate.

Building on the Farnsworth greenway plan, association volunteers at the Fort Devens office drew up a map of the river showing each piece of riverfront property and its ownership. Stoddart then negotiated an agreement with the Massachusetts Department of Natural Resources providing that if any town along the river wanted to buy some of the river frontage to include in the greenway, the state would put up half the money. The association also produced a floodplain study and sponsored a hydrology and water resources study that proved useful in preventing inappropriate development over aquifers or on wetlands. The latter study was then incorporated with the greenway plan into the larger comprehensive watershed plan.

"We sent copies of the plans to every town along the river and to their selectmen, planning boards, conservation commissions, parks and recreation commissions, and libraries," Stoddart said. "We kept all the newspapers well informed and [also] sent it to all the regional planning agencies as well as to state and federal agencies." Stoddart by now had become a prominent public figure in the Nashua watershed. Some people half-seriously referred to her as the Queen of the Nashua, the Clean River Lady, Mother Nashua, and even Mrs. Nashua River.

The association tried to get everyone concerned to approve the restoration plan and to agree to help implement it. Sometimes changes in the plan had to be made to win someone's approval, but more often the plan was adopted with little change. "We've never tried to work in competition, but rather in concert with groups," Stoddart said. Because of this advise-and-consent process, the river basin plan helped unify the watershed's diverse communities into a cohesive force for restoration and protection.

But as communities and towns endorsed the plan, the promised federal monies for treatment plants failed to arrive. To spur Congress, Stoddart started a petition drive and the association sent petitions with 13,000 signatures to President Nixon, urging the prompt release of federal funds. The association also sent a blizzard of letters to congressmen and other officials. Their message: 250,000 people in the Nashua River watershed want clean water; make the appropriations! While the new association was urging the release of funds, it also worked to establish a greenway along the riverbanks to keep development out of the river's floodplain and protect wetlands. Greenways serve as natural buffers, protecting rivers by filtering pollutants from runoff, by absorbing some of the runoff, and by preventing erosion. They protect groundwater, too, by restricting development over zones where surface waters percolate into underground reservoirs. Simultaneously, wildlife and scenic resources also are preserved. And greenways can create economic benefits. Land values tend to increase along the river, and flood damage is reduced. Water supplies are conserved, and agriculture, forestry, and outdoor recreation along the river all are enhanced.

Not content with achieving the river reclassification and having mobilized government and industry to fund treatment plant construction, the association also sought a physical cleanup of the river. The U.S. Department of Labor offered to provide cleanup funds if the association would use high school dropouts from economically disadvantaged homes to do the work. Stoddart activated the association's allies: Conservation commissions and parks departments in towns along the river submitted work plans to the association and agreed to supervise the work in their areas. The commanding officer at Fort Devens loaned the association trucks and Green Berets to supervise the youths. "A lot of them had been in trouble with the police," said Stoddart. "Police, parents, and teachers felt that this was sort of a last chance for these kids." Between 400 and 500 youths worked during a five-month period, hauling tons of trash off the riverbed and banks. It was the first successful work experience for many of the youths, who earned job references and regained community respect.

A major force for acquisition of greenway lands was Lois Murray, a smiling young woman with silky brown hair and a great enthusiasm for environmental work. Murray directed the watershed association for five years and helped it add nearly seventy miles of shoreline containing 6,000 acres of land to the greenway. Major additions include the Squannacook Wildlife Management Area, which protects one of the state's best trout streams; the Oxbow National Wildlife Refuge, which provides a wetland sanctuary for migratory wildfowl; the pine-covered hills of the Bolton Flats Wildlife Management Area, with 300 different wildlife species; and the 500-acre Rich Tree Farm, an exceptionally diverse ecosystem including hemlock and yellow birch groves, glades of brilliant wildflowers, and a profusion of animal life. This large intact riverfront parcel would eventually have been subdivided had it not been for the association.

Nashua greenway lands are now in use by cross-country skiers, hikers, cyclists, hunters, birders, and strollers. While the association refines the greenway master plan into urban and rural greenway plans, it provides free landscape architectural assistance to riverfront landowners to protect and enhance their frontage on the condition that they implement the plans at their own expense. The association persuades governmental agencies to purchase desirable lands or convinces property owners to make donations by showing them how simultaneously to reduce their tax liability, take a tax credit for a gift, and win community appreciation.

Still, the Nashua restoration has not all gone according to

plan. Of the two wastewater treatment plants built in Fitchburg, the East Fitchburg plant using activated sludge technology has worked well, but the West Fitchburg plant—based on a supposedly advanced design—proved to be an engineering disaster. "Anything that can go wrong with that plant has gone wrong," said the watershed association's Ralph Perkins. "Right now there's a seventy-five-million-dollar suit brought by the city against the treatment plant's designers [Camp Dresser & McKee, Inc.]." (Several paper companies have joined the suit on the city's side and the plant's designers have counter-sued.) When the start-up switch was first thrown at the plant's opening ceremonies, only an ominous bump and grind of machinery was heard instead of a reassuring whoosh of flowing water: A pump had inauspiciously jammed, rendering the whole facility inoperable.

The plant consists of a conventional primary treatment stage for removing suspended solids and a secondary stage that relies on a carbon filtration column for removing organics. However, the technology had never been used before to handle paper mill wastes on such a large scale. Within six weeks of start-up, the carbon column began emitting a sickening odor resembling rotten eggs due to bacteria in the carbon column. The foul smell soon permeated the community, causing a flood of complaints. When plant engineers modified the treatment process, they only succeeded in substituting the stench of rotting fish for the hydrogen sulfide. Some people must have wondered whether, after all their trouble to restore the Nashua, they had not merely swapped polluted water for polluted air. The plant also failed to remove enough biological oxygen demand (BOD) from the water to meet the plant's discharge permit requirements.

Peter D. Hughes, 44, has been the general manager of the Fitchburg wastewater treatment plants since their ill-fated 1975 start-up. "As far as I'm concerned," says Hughes, "the primary objective of what we set out to do in Fitchburg was accomplished." Even the West plant, which doesn't meet the standards set in its discharge permit, does nonetheless remove more than 99 percent of the suspended solids it receives and 80 percent of the BOD received. "We've achieved the objective that the people of the city really wanted," Hughes said. "Now we're arguing about technicalities. The odors [in the river] are gone, the sludge banks, the foam, and floating solids and color are gone. The water looks like water instead of dishwater. We have fish, waterfowl, and water animals." And the malfunctioning treatment stage has been redesigned.

The Nashua indeed now has bass, perch, pickerel, and German brown trout, and it is fished by mergansers, bald eagles, osprey, and great blue herons. One of the filthiest rivers in the country has been cleaned up. Hughes's regrets are not about his plants' performance but about a failure on the part of many people in Fitchburg to "get excited about cleaning up the river."

Association staffers such as Ralph Perkins and former director Lois Murray point out that despite the enormous progress, the Nashua's problems are still far from solved. Excessive coliform bacteria and high nutrient levels persist in much of the river, and large quantities of polluted sediments remain in the river bottom, especially behind dams. In addition, some heavy metals, such as lead and chromium, are found in Nashua fish. Victory against pollution on the Nashua thus remains incomplete, and class B standards have not yet been attained; no easy solution for removing the polluted sediments is now available. Dredging, a conventional remedy, would present additional problems and expense as would their underwater encapsulation. "The lead that was deposited by automobile exhaust fumes— which was later washed into the river—is now in the sediments. How can you get that out?" Perkins asked.

High nutrient levels in the river also will persist despite the treatment plants. Removing the nutrients would roughly quadruple the cost of operating the plants, Murray noted. Even if all the treatment plants proposed for the Nashua River were built and operated correctly, "which almost never happens," said Murray, enough nutrients (primarily phosphates) would remain just in treatment plant effluents alone to prevent the Nashua from reaching class B quality.

The persistence of intractable water quality problems in the

Nashua watershed is a source of frustration to many who worked for its restoration believing that once treatment plants were built, all the river's problems would be solved, and the river would be swimmable and fishable.

Perkins faults U.S. water pollution control policy, calling sewage treatment plant construction programs nationwide a "multibillion dollar mistake."

"Here we are building these millions of dollars of treatment plants, so far about seventy million dollars has been invested on the Nashua, and yet they're only treating conventional pollutants—turbidity and oxygen demand, et cetera. [Meanwhile] the unconventional pollutants, such as the various chemical dump spills, or the nutrients, or the heavy metals accumulating in sediments, or the urban and agricultural runoff, the combined sewage, all seem to be ignored." Certainly the goal of the federal Clean Water Act of 1970—that all U.S. surface waters be fishable and swimmable by 1983—was not, and has not yet been, achieved. "We're not even close," said Perkins.

Nonetheless Marion Stoddart today has many causes for satisfaction when she thinks about the improvements in Nashua water quality and the protective greenway. "A few years ago," Stoddart said, "there was a picture in the *Fitchburg Sentinel* of a trout in the river at Fitchburg. It was so astounding it hit the front pages!" People are now canoeing on the river for pleasure instead of for political reasons, and bass fishermen are coming from as far away as South Carolina to fish. The river has become once again an economic and aesthetic asset to the region. "I canoed on it in the fall and it was the cleanest I'd ever seen it," Marion Stoddart said. "I saw my vision for the river unfold and my major goals accomplished."

2

Lake Revival

Long ago before the nineteenth-century dam was built that enlarged the aboriginal shoreline of Maine's Lake Annabessacook, beaver and otter splashed in the lake and native Abnaki Indians grew corn by its shores in south-central Maine. The Abnaki may have used some of the lake's plentiful perch to fertilize their corn mounds. Scholars think that the Abnaki word *anna-bessacook* (*anna-bessa-cook*) meant "fish-water-place" or "place where small fish are caught."

Today, by roadsides in Winthrop, Maine, near the lake's north end, locals sell fresh corn and crisp Maine apples from the backs of their pickup trucks, but the Abnaki are nowhere to be seen. Yet the area in other respects seems suspended in time, transfixed decades behind faster-paced communities. In the way that the people of the Winthrop Lakes region manage their lakes, however, they are among the most advanced, for they use the entire watershed rather than each individual lake as the fundamental unit for ecological management purposes.

Winthrop did not always employ exemplary environmental management practices. A decade ago, lovely Lake Annabessacook was dying. All natural lakes eventually do. But it normally takes 10,000–150,000 years before they fill with sediment and become, in turn, a swamp, a meadow, and later, perhaps, a forest. By contrast, Annabessacook's impending demise was premature; experts said it had only 20–30 years to live instead of thousands.

Annabessacook, four miles long, shallow, and warm, is naturally vulnerable to excessive algal growth. But the algae not only bloomed on Annabessacook, they grew three inches thick on the surface in the summer and washed ashore by the ton. Homeowners had to use backhoes to clean their beaches. The lakeshore stank and rotting algae in the water consumed dissolved oxygen and caused fish kills. In the 1970s, Annabessacook was one of Maine's three worst-polluted lakes. You could put your arm up to the elbow in its pea soup and not see your fingertips. From the air, the lake was a rotting lime green, splotched with iridescent purple. Its fish had a vegetable smell and taste—a cook could make bass Florentine without even adding the spinach.

Because of the lake's condition, nearby property values had plummeted, local businesses were crippled, and—despite the lake's forested beauty and prize-winning ten-pound bass—tourists shunned it. Through a connecting stream, its pollution even fouled majestic Cobbossee Lake, the secondary water supply for the state's capital city, Augusta.

Cobbossee resembles a Scottish loch and contained a valuable "two-storied" fishery: perch and bass in the surface waters; trout and salmon in the cooler depths. But before anyone quite realized it, Cobbossee's valuable cold-water fishery was dead.

Lake Annabessacook is actually a 1,420-acre catchbasin for seven lakes and ponds. They belong to the twenty-four-lake Cobbossee Watershed, a 240-square-mile region of forests, farms, and small towns in southern Maine west of Augusta. These towns are permanent homes to 25,000 people. Winthrop's only major industry apart from dairy farming is the Carleton Woolen Mills, so the loss of tourism was a major economic blow. Each summer, the area's population swells by 60 percent, and nearly 50,000 people in the region depend on the lakes for recreation.

Annabessacook's longtime neighbors have been deeply upset by the gradual changes they saw in it. Biology teacher Bob Millen, 58, who has lived on the lake all his life, loves Annabessacook and had hoped that his children would be able to enjoy it, too. He watched sadly as its freshwater sponges and clams died. Next he noticed the otters that fed on the clams disappearing. Millen's neighbor, William Carrigan, 61, another lifetime Winthrop resident, remembers the time his French poodle fell into the lake and turned bright green. It became, said Carrigan, "an Irish poodle." Larry Malmsten owns the Augusta West Lakeside Resort Kampground on the lake's southern shore, where he offers trailer sites and hot showers to summer visitors. As a teenager, Malmsten brought jugs of opaque lake water to water officials in the hopes of remedial action, but no action resulted. Yet people like Malmsten, Millen, and Carrigan who love the lake and live beside it kept alive a will to save Annabessacook when there were few signs that the lake could ever regain its clarity and normal life span.

During the 1950s, both the Albany Felt Company of nearby Monmouth, Maine, and the Carleton Woolen Mills of Winthrop were piping vegetable dyes into the lake. Leaking septic systems also contributed organic matter. Advocates of a new sewage plant claimed that it would improve the lake's water quality. A small sewer system was therefore built in the sixties for the towns of Winthrop and Monmouth at Annabessacook's north end. Sewage from the entire lake vicinity was collected at a new primary treatment plant. Its concentrated effluent—rich in phosphorus and other nutrients—was piped into Mill Stream, just above Annabessacook.

The effluent quickly created a flare-up of algal growth in violation of state water quality standards. The lake's waters soon contained enough phosphorus to grow 1.7 million pounds of algae. Rather than build an expensive tertiary treatment plant, the Augusta Sanitary District decided to divert the concentrated sewage to a more advanced treatment plant in Augusta. But the cement asbestos pipe that carried the sewage soon corroded, spilling its contents into the lake during the mid-seventies. By then, however, it was only adding to a huge mass of nutrient-enriched sediment on the lake bottom. From the sediments, which trapped the nutrients, phosphorus was regularly recycled to refertilize the waters. The phosphorus helped to nourish a tremendous growth of blue-green algae in the lake. The algae had become, in effect, a green cancer. And it was no easier to remove from the lake than a cancer pervading an entire organism.

"We were just living from one algae bloom to the next," said Larry Malmsten. "Each one got progressively worse throughout the summer as the water warmed up."

Local citizens had tried for thirty years in every imaginable way to cure Annabessacook by aeration (to oxygenate the waters), and by copper sulfate and even arsenic, to poison the algae. Conditions had so deteriorated that the property owners were pouring $4,000 worth of algicides into the lake every two weeks in the summer in a drastic effort to control a problem whose causes no one precisely understood. Local residents sensed they were just dumping their money down a drain, and they were intensely frustrated, but they did not give up.

In the late sixties, Maine had a few relatively dry years during which the city of Augusta was obliged to draw water from Cobbossee Lake, into which Annabessacook's pollution was oozing. "That [Cobbossee] water was putrid," said Larry Malmsten. "There was an uproar." The pollution of Annabessacook had not really bothered Augusta residents, said an observer, until they realized that they might soon be "cutting their drinking water with a steak knife." The decline in Annabessacook's water quality now finally began affecting the state's power brokers. People on Annabessacook tended to be of a lower income bracket than the people of Cobbossee, where many wealthy businesspeople and state politicians have summer homes. These politically powerful residents drafted a plan to establish a watershed district to tackle the lake pollution problem. Soon the legislature passed a law authorizing the district's creation. But the district had to be approved in an election by at least six of ten potential member towns in the watershed.

As a planner-administrator in 1971 with the Southern Ken-

nebec Valley Regional Planning Commission (SKVRPC), John
Forster played a major role in the campaign to get the district
ratified. Forster, a large, affable man with a silver-streaked beard,
tried to show people in the watershed's diverse lake and river
towns that they had common interests. "If you're upstream," he
said, "you've got a responsibility. If you're downstream, you've
got a problem." Without cooperation between towns, he pre-
dicted, even more expensive regional water problems would
ensue. Campaigning was difficult, because Forster couldn't predict exactly what the new district would cost. He was in essence
asking people in the small towns to sign a blank check. Nonetheless, Forster and residents of the Annabessacook vicinity fanned
out into surrounding communities to muster the necessary public support to create and fund the district. Eight of ten towns
voting—two more than necessary—agreed to establish the new
district. The people cared for the lakes, said Forster, and were
willing to take a financial risk that they otherwise wouldn't have
taken. "[People here] feel very bad about themselves when they
or someone else have abused a resource."

A new regional lake management authority, the Cobbossee
Watershed District, emerged from the elections in 1972 with the
power to prevent lake abuse. It was a unique governmental unit
empowered to do virtually whatever was necessary to improve
and protect the lakes, ponds, and streams within the entire watershed. Through its powers to tax, exercise eminent domain,
make regulations, and manage dams, the district had comprehensive watershed management authority in an area of sixteen
municipalities and two counties, including assorted water and
sewer districts.

The new district's first priority was to procure talented and
extraordinarily competent leadership. Its director would have to
research, plan, innovate, manage, budget, fund-raise, testify,
handle delicate public relations, monitor lakes, and survey septic
systems. Forty people, including engineers and attorneys, applied for the job. So did a lean, red-haired environmental activist
fresh from Colby College in Maine, with no specialized knowledge about lakes.

Thomas U. Gordon was only twenty-two years old. He had had an accidental encounter in a canoe with one of the nation's last log drives on the Kennebec River when he was in his teens. The river was completely blocked with floating logs to be pulped. After spending most of a day picking his way through floating debris and sticky sap, he emerged an environmentalist. By his college years, he was far more interested in practical environmental work than in his studies. At the time of his application to the district, he had already worked with the Environmental Protection Agency (EPA) for a year, had been a director of two environmental organizations, and had served for several years on President Nixon's Student Council on Pollution and Environment. Unlike most other applicants, who were specialized, Gordon seemed to have the broad background needed for taming Annabessacook's wild algae, and he saw the job as "an opportunity to give something of myself back to the people of the state."

Little was known in 1973 about saving lakes. Tom and one other staffer sat alone in the new district's office pondering the problem. "We thought about dragging parachutes behind boats to filter algae," Gordon recalls. Then he learned that parachutes were so hard to tow that the navy had allegedly used them to anchor aircraft carriers. Next, a local doctor suggested draining the lake and firing it with gasoline to burn the algae. Of course, that would have killed and polluted the lake. Then they thought of micro-straining (filtering with a very fine screen), but Annabessacook contains billions of gallons of water. "All known micro-straining systems would have burned out within twenty-four hours."

While Gordon considered these schemes in a mood of increasing tension, he began intensively studying the area's water quality problems to prepare a credible restoration plan that could win public support and funding. Local citizens were frustrated, however, and wanted immediate action.

"At the time, we thought [Tom Gordon] was kind of slow and too methodical," said Annabessacook campground-owner Larry Malmsten. "Annabessacook had had years of studies."

"There was tremendous pressure to do something," Gordon remembers, but he resisted all pressure and, in the process, even squelched a popular plan to build an artificial freshwater marsh in the lake to filter out pollutants. "Sounded good," said Gordon, but he held back, unsure that it would be worth the hundreds of thousands of dollars it would cost. He subsequently learned that the marsh would have been of little help. No matter how long it would take to find the right solution for Annabessacook, Gordon was determined to avoid any misstep that would exhaust the district's slender financial resources, destroy its credibility, and thus squander its chance to save the lake.

"The old joke was, well, let's just pave the lake," Gordon said. Something like that almost happened when some residents' sought to fill the lake's north end—where the sewage plant effluent had been discharged—and turn it into a park. Gordon resisted vigorously, and subsequent research showed that this destructive plan would have had little or no redeeming effect on the lake's water quality.

His first major coup came in 1975 when, together with Forster's regional planning commission, Gordon obtained a water quality management planning grant from EPA to scientifically monitor water inflows to Annabessacook and ten other lakes, to study their nutrient balance. Nutrients are used by plants in definite proportions; when one nutrient is in short supply, plant growth is limited. Algal and higher plant growth requires relatively large amounts of carbon, hydrogen, nitrogen, and oxygen, as well as small amounts of about twenty-five other elements. In North American lakes, and especially in warm, shallow lakes like Annabessacook, the "limiting nutrient" that is typically in shortest supply is phosphorus. Without enough phosphorus, much of the other available dissolved plant nutrients cannot be used: All other ingredients for a massive bloom may thus be present, yet the waters may remain clear until a threshold concentration of about fifteen micrograms per liter of phosphorus is exceeded. The phosphorus influx then can trigger explosive plant growth by allowing plants to use the other abundant nutrients.

Gordon's nutrient studies were designed to determine how

much phosphorus was getting into the lake, from which sources, and by what pathways. To his surprise, the studies revealed that large quantities of phosphorus were pouring into the lake in agricultural runoff, and that vast amounts of phosphorus now were emerging from the lake sediments to contaminate the waters. More than 9,000 pounds of phosphorus a year was entering Annabessacook's water, and the largest dose was coming from the lake sediments themselves. The studies showed that the primary source of the destructive agricultural runoff was local dairy farmers' practice of spreading manure on snow-covered or frozen ground in winter. When thaws came, phosphorus-rich manure would pour into the lake.

On superficial examination, the solution of Annabessacook's agricultural pollution problems may have seemed easy enough: just compel or convince the farmers to manure their fields only in the summer. But the dairies had no satisfactory place for their large manure accumulations during the harsh six-month-long Maine winter. When the manure pile beside a farmer's barn became too large, he simply had to haul it away and dump it somewhere. It was possible to build special facilities for this purpose, but for an individual farm this was a major and costly investment. Typical seasonal manure-storage facilities for a medium-sized dairy herd might be a concrete vault the size of a large barn, or a similar structure made of asphalt or concrete with earthen berm walls. It would be no easy task to persuade the area's individualistic and frugal dairymen to spend up to $70,000 each for such structures—especially considering their often precarious economic situation, and their general aversion to government interference in their affairs.

In consultation with the Maine Department of Environmental Protection and with Forster's regional organization, Gordon and his staff meticulously evaluated possible treatment methods for Annabessacook and finally prepared a careful lake restoration plan on the assumption that he could obtain farmers' voluntary participation in the lake cleanup program. The U.S. EPA was impressed by the plans and made the district a $500,000 matching grant through the EPA's Clean Lakes Program for 1977–

1981 to restore Annabessacook and build agricultural pollution control facilities.

This match was far more money than the district had ever raised and was many times its annual budget. Gordon, however, immediately began looking for in-kind contributions of goods and personnel to help him release the promised EPA funds. The district, for example, eventually bought about $65,000 worth of chemicals and equipment, with EPA funds matched by volunteers who contributed their time at various hourly rates. Local soil and water conservation districts provided technicians.

Not only would the Clean Lakes Program funds cover 50 percent of the lake restoration work, they would also cover 50 percent of the agricultural control facilities needed. Another $2,500 per farm could be made available from the federal Agricultural Stabilization and Conservation Service and other organizations, including the Farmers Home Administration.

The job of winning farmers' cooperation in the restoration effort fell to Kathy Sage, today a planning and research associate with the Maine Department of Agriculture, but in the early seventies a thin, shy district staffer. Sage first appealed to the farmers' enlightened self-interest by talking of the economic value of the farm improvements. She also tried to arouse the farmers' altruism. If all else failed, she would rattle the sword of environmental regulation and pollution abatement fines.

In her effort to persuade the farmers, Sage had to become a design engineer, surveyor, general contractor, and business manager for them. After a great deal of work with few results, Sage succeeded in getting Clement Smith, a respected local dairyman from Monmouth, Maine, to join her program and share the costs for a storage facility on his farm. Smith was tired of having to spread manure under sloppy, freezing conditions, he valued stored aged manure as a fertilizer, and, as he said, he didn't "want to do any more polluting than we could help."

"They built tremendous facilities that cost them a lot of money and that broke the ice," said Sage. Eventually, by dint of a patient four-year effort, a "do or die" attitude, and up to twenty visits to each of forty-one farms, Sage finally succeeded in winning nearly all the farmers' cooperation.

Large temperate lakes such as Annabessacook and Cobbossee experience regular seasonal cycles that alter their chemical composition and temperature. Water density naturally varies with its temperature, and water of different densities forms layers that resist mixing. Close to a lake's surface, the waters are well oxygenated; deep in the lake, far from the surface, dissolved oxygen levels are usually much lower, particularly if substantial decomposition of organic matter is occurring there.

During winter, when a layer of ice often forms on the surface in contact with cold air, the coldest water in the lake is found just beneath the ice. In the summer, sun-warmed surface water floats on the denser colder waters below. With autumn's arrival, the lake surface recools and densifies. Chilled surface waters therefore sink toward the lake bottom and the warmer waters rise from below, causing a fall lake overturn. In the absence of abrupt water density variations, the action of stiff autumn winds on the lake's surface brings about vertical mixing of the entire lake and water temperatures equalize vertically. The mixing process oxygenates the oxygen-deficient deeper waters and circulates nutrients released there during the winter to the rest of the lake. Essentially the same processes occur in spring overturn, driven by the sinking of cold surface waters liberated by melting of the surface ice. With overturn, the thermal strata of the lake are mixed once again until the lake restratifies later in the spring or summer.

The nutrient cycling that occurs during the stratification and seasonal overturn of Lake Annabessacook profoundly affects its biological condition and the viability of any algae control strategy.

When Annabessacook was still a healthy, unpolluted lake, small amounts of phosphorus from runoff, rain, and lake tributaries circulated along with other nutrients through the lake's ecosystem. Solar radiation supplied the energy for the aquatic food chain, and, when plants and other organisms in the lake died, they decomposed, releasing nutrients back into the water or muck on the lake bottom. Algae used the phosphorus in those nutrients. But if the phosphorus is not flushed out of the lake system through the lake's outflow after use, it will eventually find its way into the lake water again or back into the lake sediments through the excretion or death of phosphorus-containing organisms.

A sensitive balance exists between the phosphorus concentration in lake water and in the lake sediments. When the oxygen content is high, phosphorus has a greater tendency to remain bound to sediment soil particles. But when the oxygen concentration of the water is low, phosphorus dissolves from the muck and becomes available to support plant nutrition. Thus factors that influence plant growth and death and, hence, oxygenation of lake water, affect phosphorus cycling. (Some mediating factors are sunlight, the physical form of the lake, water temperature, chemical composition, and the residence time of water in the lake.) Once excessive amounts of phosphorus enter the lake, trouble begins. The phosphorus itself triggers conditions that release increasing amounts of phosphorus into the lake.

Most phosphorus in lake water is combined with iron as ferric phosphate. In a well-oxygenated lake, the ferric phosphate precipitates and is eventually incorporated into the lake sediments: That's one of Nature's ways of controlling excess phosphorus. But once the phosphorus loading of a lake is substantially increased, as in a eutrophic (well-nourished) lake, algae and other plants can utilize large, previously untapped reservoirs of nutrients, so they begin multiplying at geometric rates. Given sufficient sunlight and warmth, the algae will create "pea soup" water and surface scums, as at Annabessacook. Moreover, when this crop of supernourished vegetation dies—as it must when winter comes or when its nutrients are exhausted—dead vegetation drifts to the bottom of the lake. There bacteria and other decomposers begin consuming it, often using up all the available oxygen in the poorly aerated deeper zones of the lake. If the deoxygenated zone encompasses the habitat of a particular fish species, fish kills result, and an entire fishery can be wiped out, as in the case of Cobbossee's cold-water fishery. As explained above, in addition to killing aquatic life, oxygen depletion causes phosphorus from the sediments to go back into solution. Thus when lake overturn occurs, even more phosphorus is available for plant growth and a new intensified cycle of eutrophication may begin.

Dave Dominie is an athletic-looking Environmental Specialist III in the Maine Department of Environmental Protection who joined the watershed district staff in the late seventies. As Tom Gordon was completing the diagnostic studies on Annabessacook, Dominie was groping for a way to lock the high concentrations of dissolved phosphorus back into the lake sediments and to prevent phosphorus from leaking out of the sediments, rising in the water column, and fertilizing algae in the sunlit surface waters. If algal growth could be restricted there, algal dieoff would be limited, and oxygen demand would be proportionately reduced.

Dominie plunged into the literature on lake restoration to find a treatment method. He discovered that a still experimental process involving the addition of aluminum in the form of alum (aluminum sulfate) to eutrophic waters had been used with apparent success on a few small lakes in the early seventies, but the largest of these were only a tenth the size of Annabessacook. Restoration of a 1,400-acre lake was "beyond the scope of existing technology," as one district staffer put it. Not only were those lakes small, but they were highly alkaline Midwestern lakes, unlike Annabessacook. Alum tends to acidify water. This was not a problem in the alkaline lakes, but it could be a serious problem in the waters of Lake Annabessacook.

If the lake were suddenly to become too acid, aquatic life would suffer pH shock and die. If the change took place gradually, aluminum, which is a toxic metal, would eventually dissolve in the acidic environment. If all went well, however, aluminum when dumped into the lake would form aluminum hydroxide, a sticky white floc to which phosphorus adheres and with which it sinks to the lake bottom, thus removing the phosphorus from the water column. "It's more adsorption [surface adhesion] rather than direct chemical bonding," said Dominie. "The bond is not as good, but is still thought to be sufficiently strong to keep [the phosphorus] there." How long that bond would last, Dominie did not know, nor whether the treatment's cost would be prohibitive. No chemical treatment would last forever, so a key issue was whether Annabessacook could regain a semblance of a natural phosphorus cycle before the treatment effects wore off. The long-term toxicity of the aluminum was also in question. "How can we put this stuff in the lake and not harm the organisms?" Dominie wondered. He decided to seek answers by first studying the effects of combining alum with sodium aluminate, a base, for addition to the lake. The basic compound would neutralize the alum's acidity and would increase the aluminum input to the lake.

When Dominie proposed the idea of aluminizing Lake Annabessacook, Gordon viewed the idea with his customary caution. If the district accidentally killed Annabessacook's aquatic life, public confidence would evaporate; the district might never get another chance to save the lake. But Dominie argued persuasively for the new technology, and Gordon was tempted. Five years had passed since he had become executive director, and the lake's condition was worse than ever. He reviewed the results of alum dose studies by Dominie and the results were encouraging: Virtually no aluminum went into solution, and fish seemed unaffected during thirty-day toxicity tests. The lake was so badly out of balance, Gordon reasoned, it was like a terminal patient. Perhaps only heroic measures—a "shock to the heart"—would save it.

With district approval, Gordon decided on the gamble in the summer of 1978, knowing that it would be a complex and difficult job. Tons of expensive chemicals would be needed to treat the big lake. But how and where to store, transport, and apply them? Experts advised using a barge from which to inject the chemicals directly into the deepest and least oxygenated part of the lake, where they would have most effect. Easier said than done.

Dominie and Gordon finally found a sixty-ton oceangoing barge capable of supporting a heavy load of chemicals, but it was on the coast of Maine, fifty miles away. Eight tractor trailers would be needed to truck the vessel in sections to the lake, and that put it out of reach financially. Then Dominie thought of calling the National Guard for assistance. Soon, a military convoy was rolling toward Annabessacook carrying the barge and a crane, at no cost to the district.

Once at the lake, it took two cold and rainy days just to unload and assemble the forty-foot-wide barge. A work crew then placed an eighteen-wheel tanker truck body for holding treatment chemicals atop the barge. Now the idea was to float this odd-looking vessel through a shallow, narrow channel into the lake, but the barge promptly got stuck on a sand bar and proved almost impossible to dislodge. Dominie and Gordon were already beginning to think about dismantling the barge, which would have meant dumping the tanker into the lake, when the whole contraption was finally poled and tugged free with small power boats. Out in the open water, Dominie then rigged an 800-pound iron diffuser of perforated pipe to inject the alum and the sodium aluminate buffer. Both were caustic and had to be kept separate while applied simultaneously.

Many lakeshore property owners donated the use of their boats and volunteered as pilots to assist in marking the horseshoe-shaped treatment area, operating the barge, and transferring treatment chemicals. But no one had spare storage tanks. To save money, the district decided to receive its chemicals at the lake in two 4,000-gallon plastic swimming pool liners, instead of in standard metal tanks. To everyone's dismay, thousands of gallons of premixed chemicals, fuming and reacting at $140°$ F, arrived in trucks at the lake. There was nowhere to put them except into the plastic pools. Each day as new batches of chemicals arrived, Gordon crossed his fingers that the liners wouldn't melt, releasing a costly and potent chemical deluge.

Once the chemicals were pumped into the tanker, treatment of the lake got under way. With the diffuser extending from the tanker into the water, a lead boat equipped with a depth finder preceded the barge on a predetermined route around the deep parts of the lake. Often the boat would fail to detect a small rise on the lake bottom, the diffuser would strike the lake bed, and its welded joints would snap. Work would stop abruptly until a local welder could be summoned from town to reweld the pipes.

Caustic sodium aluminate was soon eating away the valves and walls of the old tanker, causing Gordon and Dominie to worry about losing its chemical load. There was no money left to replace it or the valves. Because of leakage the men at one point had to empty out the tanker and crawl inside its hot, dark, fume-filled hold to fiberglass it. Outside on the barge, slippery viscous material covered the deck; neither it nor the tanker top had any railings. "If a person wasn't very careful," said Dominie, "their feet shot right out from under them, and they flew into the lake."

Crews kept the pumps running from 6 A.M. to 7 P.M., seven days a week, hoping to complete the treatment before brisk autumn winds and the lake's fall overturn complicated matters. Finally, after three weeks of toil, the chemicals had indeed eaten through the tanker's walls. But the job was done.

A diver went down to the lake bottom to examine the results: It looked just like a new snow had fallen all over the lake. In settling through the water, the alum had formed the expected floc. In turn, the floc had removed phosphorus from the water by adsorption and then had formed a chemical barrier on the lake bed to keep phosphorus in the sediments from redissolving. But despite some increased water clarity, the lake failed to show a dramatic improvement. Dominie and Gordon were disappointed but did not lose hope. Dominie even managed to remain confident and that fall, as the biennial overturn mixed the alum even more thoroughly into the lake, bringing more phosphorus into contact with the aluminum, the water gradually cleared. Fishing guide Frank Smimmo was heard to comment on "a remarkable difference in the lake." By 1982 the water had become clear enough for a white disc to be seen from the water surface at a depth of nine and a half feet.

Although summer algal blooms still occur on the lake, they are coming later every year. In 1983, Annabessacook did not have any sign of a bloom until August 15. "Usually it had some bloom in July," said Gordon. "The lake is getting better year to year. And on Cobbossee in 1983, we did not have any algae bloom at all."

"I think it's just a fantastic improvement," confirms Matthew Scott, state fisheries biologist. "The water quality in Annabessacook should improve over time." Gordon is still cautious, believing that it's still too soon to predict what the long-term trend in the lake will be. But he is clearly pleased by current developments.

The district had systematically first limited or controlled point source, then nonpoint source pollution, and, finally, in-lake sources of water pollution. It had eliminated 90–95 percent of the phosphorus influx from agriculture and almost the entire input from the lake sediments as a net phosphorus source. All but about 3 percent of the lake's initial phosphorus loading was curtailed.

"Most people around the lakes feel pretty satisfied with the progress we've made," Gordon says. "Without the alum treatment the lake might have done this, but it might have taken twenty to forty years. The lake is going to be sensitive for a long time, and we could lose it again, very easily, if we don't protect it. The agonizing thing is that you can never stop protecting the lake."

True to these words, during more than twelve years of work as director of the watershed district, Gordon had never taken a formal vacation. "This *is* my recreation," he said. "It's a hobby, a passion. I wonder what I'd *do* on a vacation."

The in-lake work had cost only $200,000 and the district in 1980 received an additional $300,000 to support another four years of watershed work. Although the EPA's Clean Lakes Program that made the Annabessacook restoration possible also improved numerous other U.S. lakes, elicited voluntary participation in forty-seven states, and returned eight dollars in economic benefits for each dollar invested (according to the EPA itself), the program was virtually abandoned by the Reagan administration during its first term: The EPA requested no Clean Lakes Program appropriation from Congress for fiscal year 1984. (Congress provided five million dollars in spite of the administration's disinterest in the program.) Yet while the federal government was attempting to terminate the Clean Lakes Program, state water quality officials were reiterating their need for assistance—California alone had identified 186 lakes needing restoration. A Massachusetts official projected that excessive algal growth in the state's lakes would accelerate rapidly. And a Florida official forecast that water quality problems would increase in severity as Florida's population grew. There are cuts in so many other government programs right now, says Gordon, that the states cannot afford to continue their lake restoration programs when a broad array of social and environmental programs are also being scaled back by the federal government.

Of course Annabessacook's problems are not unique. More than 10,000 of the nation's 40,000 publicly owned lakes larger than one hundred acres are polluted by toxic substances, silt, weeds, and algae, according to the President's Council on Environmental Quality. About 80 percent of the 3,700 urban lakes have significant water quality problems. Thus a national need for lake restoration exists, and many people might benefit: More than 99 percent of the U.S. population lives within an hour's drive of a publicly owned lake.

How can more lakes be restored and protected? Each troubled lake needs to be individually assessed, and solutions have to be designed for each situation. Without the necessary funds, this is, of course, unlikely to happen. Controlling nonpoint source pollution is usually the most difficult lake problem to solve. To have a good chance of success, all activities in a watershed affecting its lakes and other natural resources need to be evaluated and vigilantly monitored. The activities to be watched are agriculture, forestry, and industrial land uses. This monitoring and prompt action against polluters will protect clean lakes and make spending years of work and millions of dollars on their restoration unnecessary. Similar monitoring is necessary to protect rivers and streams.

3

Sea-Run Brookies

During the 1700s before Cape Cod was heavily settled, the Quashnet River was one of the Cape's three best trout streams. Later the river was virtually destroyed by the local cranberry-growing industry. Until recently, most people who knew anything about the Quashnet believed its valuable fishery had perished forever. But strange things have been done to the Quashnet—and an unusual transformation has occurred.

Actually only a glorified stream, ten to fifteen feet at its broadest, the Quashnet flows near Falmouth, an old fishing village on the southwestern end of the Cape. The colonists who settled this area in the early 1600s cleared small farms, raised sheep, fished for blueback herring, built ships, and went whaling. Now Falmouth is a vacation and retirement community adjoining Woods Hole, the marine biology center, and the town of Mashpee. Within that township the Quashnet first shows its silvery, bubbling headwaters in a cedar swamp just east of John's Pond. Although small, the Quashnet even today harbors an abundance of wildlife.

When the first Europeans settled this area, the Quashnet,

known then as the Quash*nut*, flowed beneath the leafy canopy of a climax forest filled with huge oaks and cedars, immense hemlocks, giant beeches, and white pines twelve and a half feet in girth. Silvery sea-run eastern brook trout darted through the clear waters, numerous as the schools of greenish herring that also migrated through the stream. A hundred or more red-finned native brook trout, locally known as brookies—which often can reach two to three pounds—could be caught in a day of fishing. Orator Daniel Webster filled his creel with brookies in the Quashnet and also fished the nearby Mashpee River.

In Webster's day, the Quashnet was a meandering stream surrounded by shady thickets and fed by hundreds of small springs all along its gentle descent to the Atlantic. Watercress grew in profusion and, where sunlight pierced the forest, grasses and wildflowers carpeted the stream banks. The water surface trembled with aquatic insects.

But men with axes soon attacked the woods. Forest fires swept through the surrounding watershed; soil erosion followed. Then, beginning about 1860, a gristmill and dam were built on the Quashnet, and much of the stream became a millpond. No fish ladder was built around the dam, so the trout and herring were cut off from their headwaters' spawning grounds and became scarce. Finally, in 1895, the cranberry industry came and the river basin was turned into cranberry bogs. To water the berries, numerous little dams and dikes were built, and the river was channeled to go where the cranberry growers could best use it. During the summer, they poured sand into the bogs to prevent weeds from growing, and in the winter, they flooded the cranberries to protect their roots from freezing.

The channeling destroyed the river's meanders and the overhanging banks where trout once hid. Deforestation left the stream exposed to the sun's heat, and, of course, trout like cool water. Sand from the cranberry boggers' weed-control work covered the stream's clean gravel bottom that the wild brook trout needed for spawning. The Quashnet, in effect, became part of a swampy, pesticide-ridden cranberry plantation instead of a fishery.

In the mid-1950s, many of the bogs were abandoned and soon were overgrown with wild blueberry bushes, sweet gale, and young trees. The newly shaded waters once again provided ideal trout habitat, and the Massachusetts Division of Fisheries and Game (now the Division of Fisheries and Wildlife) stocked them with hatchery brook trout. Fishing was good, and so the division bought some of the stream's lower reaches in 1965 to protect the fishery.

They also stocked European sea-run brown trout—with extremely gratifying results. These fish, *Salmo trutta*, range from ten to eighteen inches; a world record specimen weighing thirty-nine and a half pounds was once caught in Scotland. Released in the Quashnet as wispy little immature smolts, the baby browns eventually rode the brook down to the ocean, where they matured before returning in schools to spawn. Local fishermen soon found browns as large as twelve pounds cavorting in the little stream. This drew so much attention to the stream's potential as a fishery that a program was set up to study the European brown trout.

Conditions on the river meanwhile had once again begun to deteriorate. The tangled brush that had replaced the cranberries and had at first provided welcome shade began to thicken and fill the stream. Like webbing, it trapped silt and debris in the channel, forming countless tiny dams. This blocked the Quashnet's flow and caused the banks to collapse, forcing the stream to become broad and shallow. Soon the riparian zone became a jungle so overgrown that fishermen could scarcely find the river anymore, much less fish it.

A biologist, Joseph Bergin, who headed the state's brown trout study, was dismayed by this setback; he had hoped the Quashnet with his help would once again become a renowned fishery. But the river itself was now literally disappearing, and Bergin was searching for a remedy. About this time, in 1975, Bergin was invited to give a talk at a meeting of the Southeastern Massachusetts Chapter of Trout Unlimited, a group dedicated to restoring, protecting, and enhancing North America's fisheries.

Bergin used the occasion to propose that the group attempt the Quashnet's restoration.

This idea strongly appealed to member Francis Smith, a sturdy New England plumber of 37 with an aquiline nose and work-hardened palms, whose interests were not limited to washers, pipes, and faucets. His reading was apt to include symposium proceedings on wild trout and *The Wall Street Journal.*

Smith had grown up in western Massachusetts near the badly polluted Westfield River, just below the Strathmore Paper Company plant and its hydroelectric facility. As a boy he had once fished on the river using a fly he made from the hair of his springer spaniel's tail. When a shad took the fly, Smith was hooked on fly fishing. Unfortunately, the fish reeked from the polluted water and was inedible. "I used to wonder what the river would really be like if it were clean, and what I could then do to enjoy it," Smith recalled. Although he had had the impulse to clean it up, he never attempted the task.

His first experience with restoration came when his Trout Unlimited chapter undertook two stream restorations in 1974. The first stream they were working on dried up, and summer water temperatures in the other proved too warm for native brook trout. Chapter members refused to be discouraged and were eager to try again.

Bergin spoke persuasively to the chapter about the results they could accomplish on the Quashnet and he even led an electrofishing survey of the stream, stunning its fish so they could be counted without killing them. The surveyors found an average of only one trout in each hundred lineal feet of the Quashnet, for the stream was full of white suckers—large, undesirable scavengers. But Bergin drew the group's attention to the stream's still excellent spring water. Despite the ecological damage the stream had suffered, the water had remained clean and cold, the way trout like it. Bergin captured the group's imagination by predicting that a restored stream would support twenty trout per hundred lineal feet. Francis Smith was excited to learn that. He had fished the Quashnet for years and had enjoyed it even in its degraded condition, before the fishery had been entirely ruined. Restoration of the Quashnet was a challenge to him and he wanted to see if he could do it.

As a youth of 15, Francis had won a school essay contest with a forty-plus-page essay on the effects of water pollution on his community, Westfield, Massachusetts. The prize was a trip to a Massachusetts Junior Conservation Camp, cosponsored by the Massachusetts Division of Fisheries and Wildlife. At the camp, Francis was taught about trout stream habitat improvement and was impressed by stream improvement work he was shown on a camp trout stream. Since then, as he grew older and fonder of trout streams, Francis had on occasion rolled rocks around to make similar modifications on streams he fished. Now his impulse to repair streams was heightened by mounds of reference material Bergin produced for Trout Unlimited showing in vivid terms how beautiful and productive the Quashnet's fishery once had been. Smith saw his goal as restoring the Quashnet to "a semblance of its former self," as a recreational fishery.

His group at first did not know how to fund the restoration work, so Smith searched in vain through library reference books on grants. "None of us could quite see how we could ever raise money to restore a trout stream," he recalled. Finally their chapter received a $2,000 grant from Trout Unlimited's national office. Each dollar and a half donated had to be matched by an hour of labor donated by local chapter members. The members also donated about $800 of their own money to the project.

With its small grant, the local chapter set out to restore a mile of the Quashnet's lower reaches. The first job was to clear the brush back twenty to thirty feet away from the stream on both stream banks. This would unclog the stream and enable it to continue clearing itself. The group also planned to install deflectors in the banks, to help the river scour out its channel, and to install bank overhangs to protect the trout. As many as a million herring and alewives then would be able to migrate up the Quashnet to spawn. Their young, descending the stream, would be food for newly established trout.

Once Smith turned his attention to the Quashnet project, he

knew he had found his calling. He immediately began studying materials Bergin had provided on stream restoration techniques and on what the Quashnet was like before disturbance. He also read about trout biology and about how streams function as biological systems. Simultaneously, he began making preparations for the restoration work.

Although actual brush clearing of the stream would not begin until the summer of 1976, Smith knew by the previous winter that great quantities of costly lumber would be needed for the in-stream work. Luckily, he heard about a large property with hundreds of cedars that was about to be subdivided, and he got the developer's permission to remove them. Dump truck driver Grafton Briggs, hearing of the planned restoration work, said, "If you're crazy enough to do something like that, I'll haul all the logs you cut for nothing." The club gained 500 valuable cedar logs. Next they needed a storage area, and when Smith explained his project to people at the Falmouth Rod and Gun Club, they gave them their land to use.

By July 1976, a project area more than a mile long owned by the Massachusetts Division of Fisheries and Wildlife had been selected, surveyed, and divided into eight sections. The chapter secured proper permits and then proceeded to gather tools and equipment for clearing the first 800-foot-long section.

Bergin and a group of volunteers began by removing brush using chain saws, machetes, axes, hoes, shovels, and a gas-driven circular saw called a Brush King. During an early work session, a volunteer using the Brush King hit a nest of yellow jackets. "They seemed to attack everybody," Smith remembers. "There were people leaping in the river to try and get away. It was awful. . . . The whole crew took off.

"After that particular session, we stopped cutting brush on the banks, and we got into the channel of the river, and we started opening the channel up, to try and make the river flow. It was very, very deep, and in some cases we were cutting brush in water up to our necks." Even in summer, the spring-fed Quashnet waters are very cold.

Initially, it took the group six months and 760 person-hours to clear only 800 feet of the Quashnet. With the benefit of experience, they can now clear 600–800 feet of stream in a day. The group also managed to install a single in-stream wing deflector to narrow the stream and speed up the water flow to scour out the stream bottom. A deflector is a V-shaped structure attached at two points to one bank of the stream. It makes water ricochet from bank to bank, intensifying the river's scouring action by increasing the turbulence. Electrician Mike Arritt, 36, a heavyset, boisterous man with anarchic brown hair and an irreverent tongue, has put more than 700 hours of his own labor into repairing the Quashnet, and has become adept at building wing deflectors. "We've [each] chewed up five pairs of waders working down here, and it's tough work, but now when you see what's happening, it's a rewarding thing. . . ."

Trout Unlimited also built bank overhangs in the Quashnet to protect the trout from predators—"condominiums for trout," as Arritt likes to call them. The supporting structures must be completely submerged in the stream for they will rot in two to three years if wet and then exposed to air. So well does the vegetation on top of the overhang blend into the rest of the riparian-zone vegetation that if you stand on an overhang jutting three feet out over the water, it resembles a solid riverbank. Here again, posts had been driven deep into the stable river bottom. "They're cut off about three inches below the water level, and stringers are driven into the stable bank out to these posts all along the entire eighty-foot length of the device," Arritt explained. "On top of that we lay a double layer of two-inch-thick oak planking." The planks are covered with earth and planted with reed canary grass. TU then builds a log border along the edge to keep the newly added soil from washing away.

Sometimes Smith would load a truck full of big logs, heavy tools, and food for twenty people and drive everything to the Quashnet for a scheduled work session to find that only one or two other people had shown up. "You'd stand there and scratch your head and wonder why you went to all that trouble to put it together." But sometimes, to Smith's amazement, when the weather was at its worst, volunteer crews would turn out willing to get soaking wet and covered with mud.

At first not all of Trout Unlimited's structures worked exactly as designed. Often in electrofishing stream surveys, biologists had found badly scarred trout which had narrowly escaped the bills of hungry great blue herons. TU therefore built a particularly large bank overhang which members affectionately called the Quashnet Hilton to shelter fish. But after the Hilton's construction, Arritt and others went downstream and removed brush from the river, only to discover that this had dropped the water level several inches upstream and left the new Hilton overhang high and dry. To avert these problems, they built a rock dam to raise the river again. "Then one Saturday," Arritt said, "some Boy Scouts came down and completely redid the rock dam ... to help us." The stream now swept completely around the dam and washed the whole bank away. This time, to raise the water level, Smith and others decided to build a log barrier known as a K-dam perpendicular to the river's flow—not realizing how laborious its construction would be. It took 240 person-hours to build. That dam, incidentally, is now working well. "The river is coming up, going over the log barrier here, and plunging straight down and making a plunge pool," said Arritt. To cope with the problem of stranded in-stream structures, member Reggie Washburn, a professional surveyor with an airplane pilot's license, did an aerial survey of the Quashnet from its source to its mouth. This enabled the group to project future changes in water level and thus to determine where to cut brush.

The restoration work also required the building of silt control devices to protect restored areas downstream. The principal silt control device on the Quashnet is a large pit ten feet deep and twenty feet in diameter that the group dug in the streambed with a rented backhoe. Silt from eroding lands in the watershed settles in the hole and is periodically scooped out instead of washing downstream to blanket spawning gravels and initiate a new cycle of sedimentation and stream blockage.

Sometimes progress on the Quashnet was set back by vandalism. A fish ladder built by the state's Division of Marine Fisheries around a concrete dam has been a frequent target. But the TU chapter kept repairing the damage. "You've spent so much time working," Arritt said, "and the camaraderie down here with the people is just amazing. Everybody busts their butts, and they're a great bunch of guys and girls, and you just have a good time, believe it or not."

To make the restoration happen, Smith has had to shoulder many responsibilities. He rounds up everything needed for the work crews—logs, lumber, spikes, mauls, and meals—and he keeps all the group's records, raises funds, schedules work parties, and handles public relations. "Logistically it's been a nightmare and has cost me a tremendous amount of time," Smith said. He has sacrificed family time, not to mention the fishing he loves, and has missed business opportunities and tens of thousands of dollars in forgone income over eight years. He has also donated funds to the project.

Given all the work, time, and money it takes, why bother restoring the Quashnet? someone once asked Arritt and Phil Stewart, who is a phone company line splicer and a Quashnet volunteer. "I fished this stream when I was a kid," answered Stewart. "I'd just like to see it like what it was thirty years ago."

Arritt replied: "I've been a fisherman for a good portion of my life and I've seen so much of the good fishing areas we've had destroyed because of developers. This is one of the few places we have left in this area that's worth fishing. . . . If you want to have a nice place to bring your kids down and look at birds and flowers, you're gonna have to put some work into it and restore it yourself. Nobody's going to do it for you."

Restoring the Quashnet required more than just brush-clearing, wing deflectors, and overhang construction. Trees were needed along the Quashnet to stabilize and shade the banks so the cut brush will not regrow. The group's aim is gradually to exchange brush for trees and grass—tall, thick reed canary grass (unfortunately a nonnative). They have already planted about a hundred trees, including swamp maples, cedars, and hemlocks. By contrast, Francis Smith some years ago was in the defoliation

business. He enlisted in the Air Force at the age of 19 and was
sent to Vietnam. There he maintained aircraft as part of the
Twelfth Air Commandos, the outfit responsible for the aerial
spraying of Agent Orange on millions of acres in Vietnam. "I
plant a lot of trees nowadays," he said.

Because the members' goal is to rebuild a complete functional ecosystem, they are also restocking the stream with
aquatic insects that serve as trout food. At the start of the project,
the streambed was virtually devoid of insects. So Arritt and
others went to the Mashpee, a neighboring stream not destroyed
by the cranberry boggers. "We brought back insects from it:
stoneflies, mayflies, freshwater scuds, damselflies, dragonfly
nymphs, crayfish, and caddis flies," Arritt said. "What we did,"
he admitted, "wasn't very scientific—it was a couple of us going
down with some buckets and a few beers and digging up what
we could get." By the spring of 1983, however, mayflies were
once again hatching by the thousands in the stream. Brush removal increased the speed of the water and allowed sunlight to
enter. The Quashnet's dissolved oxygen content increased and
the streambed became a more hospitable place for insects.

To date, the Quashnet restoration has cost the local Trout
Unlimited group about $6,000 and nearly 10,000 hours of do-
nated labor. In addition to the group's initial $2,000 grant from
the national office, TU got $3,500 from the Federation of Fly
Fishers; public agencies were also helpful.

After what seemed like eons of slogging through the muddy
stream yanking out mountains of brush, and an eternity of Sat-
urdays devoted to stream repair, group members wondered
whether the work ever would pay off. Then, shortly after the
group installed its first deflector in 1977, Smith and others felt a
keen rush of excitement as they observed a pair of native eastern
brookies spawning in the gravel exposed by water ricocheting off
a deflector. As the work progressed downstream and more gravel
streambed was exposed, more trout spawned successfully and
the upstream trout population burgeoned.

Smith enjoys savoring the group's accomplishments by occasionally fishing the Quashnet on summer evenings. Slowly he

works his way upstream with fly rod and barbless hook doing a section or half-section of stream an evening. "I just look it over, and see what it's doing and how it's faring, see what the fish are like, and let 'em all go. . . ." Most people who work on the restoration likewise do not keep their fish.

What would ultimate victory in the Quashnet campaign mean to Francis Smith? "If we finish the habitat restoration and don't reintroduce the original sea-run brook trout, then we haven't really accomplished anything," he said. Stocking is planned for 1985.

The results of the Quashnet restoration are by now quite apparent. Before repair began, the stream was straight, slow, and shallow—almost invisible in a tangle of brush. Now the stream has reemerged. It flows along gracefully curved lines. The banks are firm and well defined. Shores are covered by three-foot-high canary grass. The channel is filled with swiftly flowing deep water, its surface dappled with undulating water starwort. The silt and organic debris have been washed off the bottom. The original pea-sized gravel is once again visible through the clear, cold flow.

Smith, however, is hooked on a vision of even better things to come. "It has been over 150 years since true sea-run eastern brookies ran the river. It's about time they were back again."

4

The Marsh Builder

Most people today still regard marshes merely as muddy, uninhabitable places to be avoided, drained, or filled. Yet the nation's vanishing saltwater wetlands are a valuable natural resource and a living reminder of the abundant aboriginal wildlife once found on our coasts.

When salt marshes disappear, shorelines erode at accelerated rates, fisheries collapse, bird populations vanish, wildlife retreats and some of Nature's most remarkable plant communities are destroyed. Yet approximately half of this country's salt marshes have already been eradicated.

A marsh can die in many ways. Some marshes have simply been filled for housing tracts, industrial parks, airports, and garbage dumps. Others have been buried alive by erosion from clear-cutting and harmful agricultural practices that send millions of tons of silt into once clear rivers that pour into coastal wetlands. Still other marshes are routinely killed by spilled oil and other waterborne pollutants, or by heated water discharged from power plants.

Edward W. Garbisch, Jr., 51, has responded to this ecological carnage by becoming a marsh builder, pioneering the technology he needed and transforming marsh restoration, through a decade's work, from the experimental stage to a proven process. Garbisch's appreciation for marshes and their biological importance is easily understood. When Ed Garbisch, a former chemist, looks at a marsh, he sees the world's most productive ecosystem, generating more than ten tons of useful organic matter per acre—more than twice the yield of a cornfield, ten times as much as coastal waters, and thirty times as much as the open ocean.

In essence, salt marshes function as vast, solar-powered, organic factories that trap silt washed off the continents. From this runoff, marshes extract otherwise inaccessible nutrients, converting them to plant life. These plants then form the base of an entire food pyramid, supporting bacteria, algae, and plankton, on up to simple invertebrates, mollusks, insects, fish, shore birds, mammals, and, finally, humans. Even remote ocean fisheries are at stake when a marsh is destroyed. More than half of all commercially useful fish live in coastal waters or use the coastal marshes as spawning beds, hatcheries, nurseries, or feeding grounds.

Marshes also help purify water by filtering out suspended solids, phosphates, and nitrates. Scientists are now searching for ways to use marshes in removing toxic heavy metals and other poisons from water. Apart from improving water quality, sustaining fisheries, and supporting marine food webs, marshes are also important as wildlife habitat and to protect shorefront property.

As a boy, Ed Garbisch spent his summers in the tidewater country of Chesapeake Bay. As a young doctoral candidate, he was already planning on retiring near the bay someday. After receiving his degree, he acquired a home, a worn colonial farmhouse on ten grassy acres overlooking a Chesapeake tidal lagoon at St. Michaels, Maryland.

While on a sabbatical there in 1970, Garbisch chanced to read a quaintly titled book, *The Life and Death of the Salt Marsh*, by John and Mildred Teal. "Until I started reading,"

Garbisch said, "I had never thought one way or the other about marshes." The book showed that marshes are valuable renewable resources, and that they were vanishing rapidly. Forty percent of Connecticut's salt marshes had been destroyed since 1914, and in New York State, 30 percent of the magnificent Long Island salt marshes had disappeared in just ten years (between 1954 and 1964). Garbisch was fascinated and concluded that restoring a natural resource would be worthwhile.

The year was 1970, and Garbisch at 37 was in the midst of a dazzling research career in organic chemistry and a newly earned professorship at the University of Minnesota. Few people would have given it all up for the saltwater marshlands of Chesapeake Bay. But Ed Garbisch is anything but conventional. He is a big rugged man with work-toughened hands and reserved blue eyes. He walks with a steady, purposeful step, his hair seems tangled like marsh grass on a blustery day, and he looks more like a construction worker than a former professor. On his face, clean-shaven around muttonchop sideburns, there is an air of determination and conviction. "At the time," he said, "I was looking for a way to get out of pure research and into an applied field." Thus he decided to test the virtually untried concept of marsh restoration, and the method he chose was similarly straightforward. First, he gathered some cordgrass (*Spartina alterniflora*) seedlings from a nearby wild marsh; then he transplanted them into the intertidal beach flats in front of his house. The experiment took several months, and the outcome changed Garbisch's life.

Within months, he saw that, instead of wilting or washing away, the plants were slowly taking root and collecting sediment. As more and more silt was trapped, the plants began to elevate themselves out of the water, adding new land to the shores and fighting erosion. Greatly encouraged, he began reading everything he could find about salt marsh ecology and botany. He knew that before he could become a serious builder of marshes, he would have to understand the principal marsh plants better than most botanists did. He scarcely suspected, however, that he would also have to act as a civil engineer, construction worker, contractor, entrepreneur, and skipper as well. To test his proposed technique for large-scale marsh restoration, Garbisch prepared a formal research proposal. The Nature Conservancy, dedicated to conserving land and protecting ecosystems, liked the proposal and created a new Center for Applied Research in Environmental Science for him to direct. Soon, with four center employees, he was slogging through the natural salt marshes of Assateague Island National Seashore in Maryland, stripping seeds from the marsh grasses by hand until they had about a million and a half seeds, which they germinated and raised in greenhouses.

Within a year, Garbisch was ready for a full-scale experiment on his own. Using personal savings and family loans, he founded Environmental Concern, Inc. (ECI), a nonprofit group, and became both president and director in 1972. The organization's first major challenge was the restoration of Hambleton Island, a small, naturally eroding Chesapeake Bay strand about a mile from Dr. Garbisch's home. By studying historical land survey records, Garbisch found that Hambleton Island had been fifty-five acres in the mid-nineteenth century, but it had since eroded to approximately half that size. In addition, the island was missing a chunk in the middle. Garbisch's plan was to prevent the island from disappearing entirely into the waves by planting a new marsh directly in the channel cut by the bay through the island. The channel, however, already was too deep to be planted, and unless it could be filled, bay currents would remove seedlings before a marsh could root.

Even if waves did not wash away the new fill and destroy the plants, Garbisch's experiment faced other serious obstacles: Drifting sediment could damage the new shoots; organic "litter" from nearby marshes could choke them; and the transplants might not grow. For this experiment, Garbisch bought the cheapest available marsh material—3,000 cubic yards of fine quarry sand—and loaded the sand himself by crane onto a flat barge. "The whole operation was based on what was most economical," he later explained.

Working twelve hours a day for several weeks in March 1972,

the Environmental Concern crew brought 300 bargeloads of sand to the island and built a sand flat several hundred feet wide over the eroding channel. Then Garbisch, his crew, their spouses, and all the friends they could muster transplanted a quarter-million seedlings of cordgrass, salt hat (*Spartina patens*), and rushes *by hand* into the lifeless sand flats. The job that today would take a small, mechanized Environmental Concern crew only five days took the experimenters five months, until August. Gradually, however, the marsh plants took root and grew in height, and the restoration effort began to seem rewarding. Then, in midsummer, just when the work crews were beginning to congratulate themselves, their carefully planted marsh was suddenly flattened by the high winds and waves of Hurricane Agnes.

Garbisch did not betray any emotion at the setback, but calmly began laying plans to replant. "If things didn't go well," he said wryly later, "we didn't sit down and cry." Fortunately, within several weeks, the grasses straightened up on their own again, and the marsh builders rejoiced.

Although other researchers had occasionally planted a single species of marsh grass on dredged mud, the Hambleton Island experiment was a complete large-scale artificial marsh. And Garbisch the scientist was determined to document every phase of the experiment in minute scientific detail. If the project ultimately succeeded, he would then have a reliable documented formula for marsh restoration.

Thus Garbisch and company often observed what went on at Hambleton Island twenty-four hours a day. He or another center scientist camped out in a small tent in the marsh, and Garbisch awakened himself every two hours with an alarm clock to sleepily observe raccoons and other nocturnal visitors. He wanted to know how wildlife would relate to his handiwork and what effect they would have on it. He soon found out.

One morning in December 1972, new arrivals brought catastrophe: A large flock of Canada geese had seen the marsh from the air and had irreverently uprooted and eaten half to three-quarters of the world's most extensive artificial marsh. "Our researches had indicated that our plants were not the principal favorite food of geese," Garbisch said ruefully. "We were obviously surprised and dejected by the devastation. We had rounded up considerable money to do the research, and it was basically a scientific project. We had spent a lot of time statistically laying out the plots and replicating the planting, and then all our data were eaten! The scientific aspect of the project essentially terminated."

Scarecrows, aluminum mobiles, and balloons all failed to deter the geese. Still, Garbisch was not ready to quit. He unsuccessfully tried covering the new marsh with protective netting. Finally, he noticed that the geese always seemed to begin their meals by eating inland from the marsh's seaward edge, and this observation led him to a simple solution: to replant the grasses densely enough there to block the geese's entry. It worked.

The new Hambleton Island marsh now grew thick and tall—living proof that marshes could be reestablished. Later tests showed that, through colonization from neighboring wetlands, wildlife on the island was similar to that of nearby natural marshes. Exhilarated, Garbisch immediately began planning eight other restoration projects for the next year.

If ECI was in a hurry to begin work after its first success, it was not because Dr. Garbisch possessed any messianic zeal to stop the rapid destruction of U.S. marshes. "I'm not a conservationist or an environmentalist who wants to get back the system that's been destroyed over the years," Garbisch vows. "It doesn't disappoint me that many thousands of acres have been lost for every one or two that have been reclaimed. I'm just not interested in going back in history and replacing wetlands that were in existence five hundred years ago. These wetlands now are New York City, Brooklyn, San Francisco. Yet if an oil company currently is destroying a thousand acres of wetlands to put in a pipeline from a drilling platform to shore, I would certainly want to restore the marsh." In fact, 60 percent of Garbisch's contracts are for damage mitigation, in which, for example, five acres of marsh destroyed by a utility in one area might be replaced by six new acres of marsh elsewhere, with the extra acre a bonus to compensate for any differential in the quality of the new marsh.

Because Garbisch plants only the principal native plants, his marshes at first may be ecologically simpler than some natural marshes. Garbisch relies on other plants to invade his sites naturally and add diversity to his marshes if conditions are suitable for those species.

Within the twelve years after the Hambleton Island job, ECI has conducted about two hundred marsh creation projects. Only a few of the restored marshes were unsuccessful, and those setbacks occurred during the organization's early years. All work is now guaranteed and projects invariably succeed.

Much of Garbisch's time during the marsh planting season is occupied with wide-ranging travels to advise on, or to implement, marsh-creation projects all along the East Coast and, occasionally, on the West Coast. Some of ECI's marshes are twenty acres or more in size and lie like green ribbons along the shores from Maine and New York south to New Jersey, Virginia, and Maryland. Garbisch has also done extensive consulting on countless marsh restorations performed by governmental or academic institutions, and he publishes on subjects such as "salt marsh development for erosion control," "salt marsh establishment on intertidal dredged materials," and "the propagation of vascular plants."

There are economic as well as aesthetic reasons for Garbisch's success: Stone revetments to protect an eroding shore can cost $150 per lineal foot; Garbisch can build a twenty-foot-wide protective strip of salt marsh for $15–$25 a foot (1982 dollars). This can result in savings of $100,000 or more to owners of large shoreline property who may thereby be safeguarding a large residential or commercial investment. In addition, Garbisch has made barren, desolate, excavated beachfronts into dense, lush, emerald marshes extending as far as the eye can see.

Marsh establishment on a large scale requires a substantial amount of precise grading and filling. A new marsh-in-the-making looks like a large construction project, with things definitely made worse before they are improved. Sometimes, civil engi-

neering know-how is needed. Serious problems can arise if the
graded and gently sloping elevations are slightly too high or too
low. In one ECI project in New Jersey, the marsh was too high
and was consequently exposed to too much sun between high
tides. Salt in the drying soil percolated upward, crystallized, and
killed the plants. At considerable expense and inconvenience,
ECI returned to the site, furrowed the mud flat, and planted new
marsh grass deep beneath the flat's salty upper crust. This time,
the transplants survived.

Twenty percent of Garbisch's work is in the stabilization of
dredged spoils. The U.S. Army Corps of Engineers often
dredges shipping channels to keep them open, and disposal of
the resulting muck is often a problem. When dumped in nearby
estuaries or along the coast, it smothers bottom dwellers, and the
spoils also tend to drift back in the water to the place from which
they were dredged. Consequently, the corps often disposes of
the spoils on land at great cost. Garbisch, however, found a solution that saves the corps money, earns revenue for Environmental Concern, aids wildlife, and creates new marsh. After the
corps dredged a channel near Barren Island in Chesapeake Bay
in 1981, Garbisch had them deposit the spoils as a giant twenty-
five acre mudpie in the bay. Because the corps wanted to provide
nesting areas for least terns as a fringe benefit, the spoils were
raised two to three feet above the mean high tide—just the way
least terns like it. Next Garbisch and his crews planted 60,000
young cordgrass and salt hay plants from among the half-million
or so plants he raises each year in his nursery. He also seeded a
portion of the new island.

Within a year, the plants were well enough established to attract the country's largest tern colony. Two years later, the
cordgrass stood over three feet tall and the salt hay reached eighteen inches in height. Three years after planting, Garbisch expects that the marsh will look the same as a 1,000-year-old
natural marsh, although it will lack the accumulated marsh peat.
But given five additional years, the marsh will have created a
six-inch-thick peat base.

The new marshes have proved popular with a wide range of

users: government agencies, educational organizations, environmental groups, public utilities, and private citizens. "[Public utilities] are obliged to agree to restoration," Garbisch explained, "because otherwise they can't get state and federal permits to do construction in wetlands. Rerouting a pipeline fifty miles around a wetland could cost millions of dollars."

Because his environmental tampering sometimes makes life easier for large corporations, Garbisch's work has aroused some controversy. "I began as an advocate of what he was doing," remarked John Clark, director of Coastal Resources Projects for the Conservation Foundation, "but I'm troubled now by the fact that it seems like an easy technical fix to a very difficult problem. I'm afraid the wrong forces may utilize his methods in ways that would violate the public interest.

"If someone comes into the middle of a contested-permit situation and says, 'Don't worry, Garbisch can fix any ecological damage that occurs,' it has the effect of limiting the review and eliminating the kind of thoughtful consideration that should go on."

Newly created resources indeed may not be biologically identical to what has been destroyed, even if they appear similar on superficial inspection. "I hate to see it done as a trade-off," said Bob Boyle, a writer for *Sports Illustrated*. "My intuition as a fisherman tells me the new marsh may not be biologically equivalent to the old one. If salinity values at the new location differ, the marsh may be much less useful to certain fish. Although in general I applaud what he's doing, it does give the corporations the power to play God—and that can be abused." Nevertheless, even Garbisch's critics recognize that, once wetlands have been obliterated, marsh restoration is the way to transform wasting shorelines into useful resources again.

Today, using marsh restoration guidelines developed by Garbisch and others, virtually anyone with the necessary resources can turn the right seashore frontage green with a small-scale restoration project. Cultivation on tidal land may be simpler than farming, in fact, because fertilizer is already available in the water in the form of dissolved nutrients.

The essence of Garbisch's restoration method is to plan all aspects of a marsh project at once, considering which plants to use, their correct elevations, and the on-site stresses. Success depends on the right plant materials, enough understanding of the aquatic environment to plant at the right times, and tidal elevations. For reasons of speed and economy in planting, Garbisch prefers to start new marshes from seed rather than with seedlings or grown plants. He simply waits for high tide and drops seed into the wake of his airboat over the properly graded site. The seed sinks, and he then drags the area to cover the seed. The cost is less than $1,200 an acre. The elevation of the seedbed is critical for a new marsh, so if Garbisch is repairing a damaged marsh he removes all the old peat, which would be impossible for him to grade accurately. When necessary, Garbisch protects his new plantings from erosion with specially designed temporary baffles that he places offshore, or sometimes with low stone revetments.

Through Environmental Concern, clients get needed technical advice as well as custom-developed seed, sprigs, bare-root seedlings, and peat-potted plants of many different marsh grasses. Costs of marsh creation ranged from about $2,000 to $10,000 per acre in 1983, depending on the particular marsh design. That is far less than the worth of the marsh as a resource. (Although a marsh's value cannot actually be reduced to dollars and cents, biologists in Louisiana estimated some years ago that an acre of salt marsh was worth $82,000.)

At these prices, large-scale restoration is not cheap, but it is not beyond the financial reach of government agencies. For example, a one-hundred-foot-wide band of coastal marsh more than fifty miles long could be built for about six million dollars. Lakes, swamps, ponds, and tidal freshwater areas also can be restored, although they are technically more complex. Currently, Garbisch is experimenting with freshwater restoration technology for lakes, ponds, and estuaries.

Aquatic plants have been used with varying degrees of success by some sewage treatment facilities to remove nutrients from wastewater. Garbisch is consulting with the town of Easton, Maryland, on the use of two freshwater wetland species to purify the town's sewage. If his experiment succeeds, he expects that the well-fertilized plants will be a source of new marsh seed for him.

What began as a small experiment with a few marsh grasses in the mud of Chesapeake Bay is now a thriving business that takes in well over half a million dollars a year and has $1.3 million in capital investments, including a fifty-foot landing craft, a barge, and much heavy excavating and trucking equipment. While the nation has yet to make a major commitment to marsh restoration, Ed Garbisch's private armada is creating flourishing artificial marshes and is earning good money doing it.

II

NEW LANDS

Worldwide, some 23 million acres of forests—an area
the size of Indiana—disappear every year. . . .
—Maryla Webb and Judith Jacobsen,
U.S. Carrying Capacity, An Introduction

5

Redwoods Rising

Established in 1902, Big Basin Redwoods is California's oldest state park. Its rugged hillsides cradle flowering meadows and offer unsurpassed views of clear mountain brooks that cascade over polished sandstone escarpments toward the Pacific. The park's 15,000 acres are crisscrossed by trails with names like Opal, Meteor, and Skyline, and its vaulted canopy of mature redwoods shelters visitors from summer heat and winter downpours. Big Basin is also home to the madrone, the Douglas iris, the tan oak, the Columbia blacktail deer, and once was part of the North American grizzly bear's extensive range.

But in recent years, some of Big Basin's finest haunts have changed. On many heavily used trails and eroded stream banks, thousands of footsteps have trampled vegetation and compacted the earth so that new trees cannot set seed. Without protective vegetation, humus and leaf litter are washed away by rains, leaving only hard, barren soil. The trees cannot regenerate; as the old ones die, so does the forest. The scars of earlier logging operations—haul roads, staging areas, and sawn tree stumps—also mar parts of the park.

As recently as the 1950s and 1960s, sawmills were ripping up trees in the Santa Cruz Mountains at a ferocious rate and local timber companies were preparing a rich harvest: Big Basin's virgin timber. One man, Tony Look, perhaps more than anyone, opposed them. He knew that where once there were 200,000 acres of old-growth redwoods in the state, only 18,000 remained, and each was precious to him. His interest in nature dated back to early childhood.

Tony was six, in 1924, when his family moved to the little town of Garberville, snug in the redwoods of northern California's Humboldt County. There his father operated a restaurant and lovingly cultivated irises. Tony may have inherited the green thumb, for soon he was bringing young redwood seedlings home from the forest to plant on the family homestead. In those days, much of the county was covered with virgin redwoods, and its creeks and rivers teemed with fish. Tony particularly liked to fish for salmon, steelhead, and trout in the wild Eel River and to hike along Sproul Creek.

Just half a century before Tony's jaunts through the woods, peaceful Native American tribes still lived there. By the 1920s and 1930s, however, white settlers had virtually eliminated the Indians. And once the native people were destroyed or driven out, their former lands were next to feel the scourge. The new round of destruction was so thorough, it radically changed the entire ecosystem and drove the white settlers in turn from the land. Although the calamity appeared as a natural disaster, it had human origins.

During the Roaring Twenties, lumber companies were virtually unregulated and felt perfectly entitled to destroy land for profit. A landowner in Humboldt who wanted to sell his trees would call in a "jackrabbit" lumber company, so named because the operator would "pop in and pop out" when the trees were cut. Also known as a gyppo outfit (from *gypsy*), the loggers would clear-cut all the marketable lumber and would saw it on the spot using a portable sawmill. Then they would burn the land to strip the vegetation. This prepared the ruined forest for conversion to range grassland. Sometimes the burning was used to assure the lumbermen easy access to the property if they planned to come back years later for a second cut. Large areas of climax forest suddenly became charred, treeless wastelands.

Many of the canyons familiar to Tony during childhood on the Eel River's tributaries suffered this fate, including the Bull Creek basin, a 25,000-acre region similar in appearance and vegetation to Big Basin Redwoods. When most of the trees that were worth taking and not protected by law were cut, the jackrabbit loggers folded up their sawmills and went off in search of virgin timber elsewhere. The awful consequences of their logging in Humboldt County, however, were not to be felt for a generation.

While the logging was taking place, Tony Look was growing up in the timber country. In 1936, when he left the north woods for a college education, he was still fond of trees, and so he naturally applied to the University of California at Berkeley in forestry. The forestry department was small and was regarded as an academic backwater by "sophisticated" faculty and administrators, who were oblivious to the state's critical needs for sound forest management. Instead of expanding the department, they restricted its forestry admissions and discouraged students about forestry job prospects. Look therefore took a degree in pharmacy and, later, an advanced degree in pharmaceutical chemistry.

While he pursued his new career, the wounds made by the jackrabbit companies in Humboldt County healed superficially. But no trees and vegetation with root systems comparable to the original redwood forest or its natural understory vegetation reestablished themselves. The long-delayed but inevitable consequences came in 1955.

That year, after a normally wet winter, a torrential storm suddenly dumped eleven inches of rain on Humboldt County in about twenty-four hours. Without sufficient vegetation to soak up the water and bind the soil, the wet land on the steep hillsides began to slip. It melted off the slopes of Bull Creek Basin and millions of tons of gravel slid into the streambeds and flowed downstream, filling Bull Creek. Heavily laden flood waters overflowed the channel and raced across the basin's alluvial flats, toppling large redwoods. The fallen trees then formed natural dams that blocked silt and gravel, causing the rushing waters to spread even further into the flats, felling still more redwoods.

Unfortunately, the town of Bull Creek, where Look's father had been born, lay directly in the flood waters' path. The deluge poured down the hillsides until the entire town was completely buried by silt and gravel. When the waters finally receded, *nothing* remained to be salvaged. Fortunately, all residents had been evacuated before the disaster, but the Look family experienced a particularly painful loss: Tony's family burial plot—for decades situated far above the waters of Bull Creek—was completely washed away, with all signs of his forebears.

The loss of the native Indian tribes, the cutting of the timber, the reduction in forest wildlife, the destruction of the basin's fisheries, and finally the loss of the town completed a cycle. An entire era of life was now over in a land that once had been a natural paradise.

But the destruction of the region did not stop there. In 1964, a second major flood followed the first and spread even more devastation. The erosion and flooding at Bull Creek generations after the land was first abused is but an especially violent example of what has happened more slowly and piecemeal to many of this country's virgin forests.

Tony Look emerged from the Bull Creek disaster resolved to prevent its repetition, if he could. He had joined the Sierra Club in 1940, while still a student at the university, and he had gradually become an active member. His commitment to conservation was strengthened in 1946, long before the flood, when he returned to visit Sproul Creek, his boyhood haunt, and found its banks stripped of trees and the fishery ruined. Soon, Look was tackling environmental problems on a regional basis as chairman of the Sierra Club's Conservation Committee, addressing issues such as coastal management, the proposed California aqueduct project, and public access to San Francisco Bay.

Due to the committee's efforts, the Sierra Club was able to prevent the damming of the Eel River in Round Valley, California, a project that would have flooded much of the Round Valley Indian Reservation. This kind of club work taught Look how to mobilize influential people, as well as the general public. "Let people know what the problem is, and then show them how their energies and money can help solve it," Look said, describing what he had learned. In later years, with maps and leaflets, he used these tactics to good effect at Big Basin.

During his quarter-century as a club volunteer, Look studied the natural sciences, taking courses for six years at San Jose State University. He also established his own pharmacy and helped raise his two children. There was never enough time for conservation, family, and study, so, inspired by Thomas Edison's example, Look trained himself to sleep less; he would get to bed at one or two in the morning and rise at seven to go to the pharmacy.

So that Tony could do conservation work, the Looks lived modestly and did little entertaining. The rewards of working in the woods, said Look, "were greater than those of sitting around at a party." The Looks made their clothes and cars last longer than their neighbors', and Tony Look worked seven-day weeks. Looking back on those years, he remarked, "I just felt I had to give more to life than making money out of it. People usually get greedy at some point, and I didn't like that."

Because of his Conservation Committee work, his Bull Creek experience, and his science background, the Sierra Club asked Look in 1965 to help enlarge Big Basin's boundary by a hundred yards to prevent logging of some beautiful trees within sight of a scenic park waterfall. Look quickly expanded that goal and began working for the incorporation of *all* private basin landholdings into the park, to protect the basin as a natural unit forever.

He first helped achieve the boundary extension through a vigorous Sierra Club campaign to raise funds and gain allies. He persuaded Save-the-Redwoods League, a well-endowed conservation organization, to renew its interest in acquiring the park margin. His intervention came none too soon: It was only on the very day when that coveted timber was already being cut that league president John DeWitt finally convinced Big Creek Timber Company to stop work, accept half-payment for the land,

and donate the rest of it to the park for a tax deduction. Then in 1968, the park's beautiful heartland and its tall trees were themselves threatened: Santa Cruz Lumber Company, which had been holding the land until the state could buy it, unexpectedly decided to close its old-growth redwood sawmill. If the state would not buy the land immediately, the company said it would have to log the land before the mill shut down. That would mean the end for Big Basin as a coherent relic of the aboriginal fir and redwood coastal mountain forest, a chain of being that had extended unbroken in that place since ancient times.

No TV cameras, however, were on hand to catch the drama for the six o'clock news, so the general public was unaware of the danger to Big Basin. And the few residents living in the remote mountain woods were hardly strong enough politically to oppose the timber interests. Nor was there any planning agency ready to intervene for the trees. The only people protecting the land were Tony Look and a small group of underfunded environmentalists. Look and allies needed millions of dollars in a hurry if they were to save the park. Although he did not know where the money would come from, Look knew that the land *had* to be bought: if the entire watershed were not protected, clear-cutting high in the basin could erode and disfigure parkland below, ultimately destroying many of the other trees. "We could have ended up with the same situation as in Humboldt," said Look. "The logging pressure was here, and there were 520 acres of virgin trees."

The Sierra Club did not have the money needed, so Look and five other club officials decided to try resurrecting a defunct organization, the Sempervirens Club, in an effort to raise the funds. Sempervirens had originally been founded by commercial photographer Andrew P. Hill in 1900, after Hill had tried to photograph a redwood in Felton, California, but had been told to leave by the property owner. Impressed by the trees' beauty, and believing that there should be a place where people could enjoy them, Hill formed his club, which he named after the coast redwood (*Sequoia sempervirens*); Hill later raised the money to buy Cowell Redwoods, now a state park in Felton. Revival of the club, renamed the Sempervirens Fund, proved to be a prudent step for Look; the Fund had a prestigious image and some of its original members were still active in conservation.

The battle for Big Basin was protracted. The state in 1969 formally defined the park's boundaries, identifying the lands that could be bought with state aid. Not long afterwards, Save-the-Redwoods succeeded in raising half the funds needed to buy the threatened lands, and the state later matched those funds, closing the deal. Funds were still needed by May 1 for purchase of another heartland tract in the part that was threatened with residential subdivision. The state had $120,000—eighty-five percent of the amount needed—but somehow was unable to find the remaining funds in its budget. Look formed an ad hoc group called the May Day Committee to raise the money needed. Working feverishly, this small group managed to raise $20,000, so the state could complete the land purchase, and another $8,000 toward Sempervirens' goal of purchasing all the remaining Big Basin inholdings within the park, as well as some adjacent land.

For these purposes, Sempervirens in 1974 managed to collect $80,000 in small contributions from direct mail and foundation grants. The $80,000, combined with matching state aid and with tax write-offs for the timber interests, made it possible for Sempervirens to add to the park Locatelli Lumber Company land worth seven times that sum.

The final crown jewel in the Big Basin setting was a 2,200-acre tract of virgin redwoods called Rancho del Oso. Again, millions of dollars was needed, but smart money rather than big money won the day. Look mounted a campaign to raise $15,000 to option the property so as to buy time. When he was midway to his goal, the state came to the rescue and appropriated $2,500,-000 to buy most of the land. The park's integrity was thus preserved, and one can now hike twenty miles on a diagonal across the land without ever leaving the park.

Once the land was protected, Look turned his attention to restoring the forest, which had suffered some overuse and included a few logged areas. Sempervirens' reforestation in Big Basin had its origin in a Sierra Club project that began about

1966. The Club had made money available from its conservation fund for tree purchases, and Look had supervised large plantings in Big Basin by the club's Loma Prieta chapter—sometimes 10,000 seedlings in a single day. About 1970, Look put the plantings under Sempervirens' auspices. Group members made donations for the trees they planted, and Sempervirens began spending the profits to help buy more forest land.

The combined results in Big Basin of Sempervirens Fund, Save-the-Redwoods, the Sierra Club, and other concerned conservationists are a pleasure to behold today. Sempervirens Fund volunteers have replanted between 250 and 300 acres of Big Basin by hand since reforestation began there. Old logging decks, asphalt parking lots, fire-damaged tracts, even run-down campgrounds and picnic areas have all given way to newly planted firs and redwoods. In the past year, Sempervirens has also begun planting ferns and huckleberries, enthusiastically provided by the state park service. The park's chief ranger-naturalist, Harry Batlin, likes Sempervirens' work so much that he is attempting to have the state put native-tree nurseries in every state park, so restoration can begin throughout the park system. The Sempervirens reforestation is now something of a showcase in California.

Much of the planting has been done in the alluvial flats of the valley most accessible to the public and therefore the most overused. Near park headquarters, a campground was fenced off, and Sempervirens volunteers enriched the soil by working redwood chips into it and then planted new ground cover. Between fallen tree limbs, new yard-high redwoods have begun taking over. Nearby, the asphalt paving of an old parking lot has been removed, and new redwood groves are sprouting there. In addition to reclaiming campgrounds, some of the valley once used for park maintenance vehicles and a wood yard have been transformed into young forest. "I do this," Look said, "so that if you came back in 1,000 years, you could see the natural succession here. That gives me a feeling that time, trees, bugs, and all things are connected. Eighteen thousand acres of redwoods is all there are now, and all there ever will be. We need to look at things that were here before we came. That's what those trees are."

Higher up in the park, Sempervirens has put in a 120-acre stand of Douglas fir. Elsewhere, new eight-foot-tall trees are sprouting from a former roadbed. A few steps away, young trees awaiting planting are stored in green nursery cans. All told, Sempervirens Fund has saved thousands of acres of forest and has planted some 10,000 trees (in addition to the seedlings) in Big Basin.

From afar on a sunny March morning, it looks as if tree worshippers have invaded a steep Big Basin glen. Half-a-dozen families are bustling among the huge trees, easing young redwood saplings out of nursery cans into the spongy earth. Children dash about, helping to nestle young firs and redwoods into the ground. Coordinating the work is a small, middle-aged man in a Tyrolean hat and baggy woolens. Tony Look seems almost elf-like in the enormous forest, except for his strong neck and powerful arms. The trees of the mature redwood forest around him are on so vast a scale that Big Basin seems a Notre Dame among forests.

The easiest thing to plant is the bare-root seedling, he says, but it has the worst chance of survival. To demonstrate how it's done, Look sticks the white, tubelike container of a seedling into the ground like a stake to make a hole. Then he gently removes the seedling from its plastic tube, and tamps in the tree, all in less than a minute. Planting larger trees from the nursery cans is also surprisingly easy. Before planting, the roots are soaked in water to improve their contact with the ground into which they will be put. A few turns of the earth with a spade in the rich soil of the climax forest generally makes a suitable hollow for the young tree's roots. The compact root mass is then loosened and placed in the hole; earth is shoveled on top, sealing air spaces. In dry terrain, leftover soil is piled in a ring about a foot from the tree to dam scarce rainfall. Where rainfall is heavy, trees are planted in a slight mound, to promote better drainage. The young trees are carefully watered twice during planting to prevent their roots from drying out and to minimize transplantation shock.

Sempervirens' techniques are constantly improving. "Between 1964 and 1968," Look explained, "the Sierra Club had only a 25 percent survival rate for its transplants." Sempervirens, which incidentally means everliving, has now achieved an 80–90 percent success rate mainly by planting trees that have grown beyond the bare-root stage, and by more careful follow-up. Most transplants that die do so during the first summer. Consequently, volunteers monitor the new trees like houseplants and return to water them every three weeks during summer for two successive years. Planting is done in winter, under the supervision of qualified volunteers.

Tree planting is not only an integral part of Sempervirens' activities, but is an essential source of funding: Sempervirens earns about $18,000 a year by assigning trees as gifts or as memorials to donors. Half the proceeds provide the group with operating funds, the rest is used for land acquisition. Sempervirens thus buys thirty to forty acres of redwoods each year for preservation as parkland. (Some of the land costs only $300–$400 an acre.) At this rate, hundreds of acres can be saved in a decade—in a lifetime, thousands. And Sempervirens does it with only two paid full-time staffers. After he worked as a volunteer at Sempervirens Fund for six years, the organization was finally able to pay Look a salary as its director in 1976.

Far from resting on their laurels, today Look and Sempervirens are also working in California's Castle Rock, Butano, and Cowell state parks, enlarging, completing, and reforesting them with redwoods, fir, or madrone—whatever is native to the site. Yet with lumber selling today at premium prices, conservationists in general face intense opposition from lumber companies that demand annual timber yields—particularly in the national forests—far beyond annual replacement rates. This means higher profits now for the timber companies at the expense of long-term forest productivity. It also means there is lots of U.S. forest land in need of restoration.

6

The Land Skinners

An irregular vertical crease parts Fred Ulishney's forehead when he talks intently. The seam is joined by thinner jagged tributaries like stream courses in the hilly western Pennsylvania coal country where he has worked for most of his fifty-five years. He knows as much about coal mining as anyone in the region and can look at an unmined hillside and predict where the coal outcrop can be found. Ulishney has been mining for forty-five years—since he first began helping his father when he was only ten. But unlike most miners, he is more interested in repairing land than in extracting minerals. Most of his life, Ulishney has been an independent coal miner in business for himself. Now he is a mine inspector for the state of Pennsylvania.

Fred Ulishney's early childhood coincided with the worst years of the Great Depression. Ulishney learned to labor willingly then, and in later years never regarded the effort he put into land reclamation as drudgery. Starting in the 1950s, he would often spend two or three months a year of his own time hauling and bulldozing to repair a site he had mined. "I didn't know what an eight-hour day was. And I enjoyed what I was doing. I would look forward to getting up tomorrow morning and go back to doing it." That was long before the states or the federal government required coal mine reclamation. "There was a time when a coal operator could go in one end of a field and out the other end, and never look back. I never did this. Never," he said. "I surface-mined and I deep-mined, but restoration was always my primary interest." By contrast, the marks of less conscientious miners are still evident in Pennsylvania.

Ulishney's clean-shaven face is often bronzed from hours spent on mine sites in the Pennsylvania summer sun, and the white hair on the sides of his head contrasts with still brown hair on top. His courteous and modest manner belies a quiet and unassuming firmness at which his thin, determined lips barely hint. Beneath this exterior is a deep love of land and an unflinching dedication to enforcing mine reclamation (and other) laws.

Ulishney and another Pennsylvania mine inspector, John Maryott, stood talking one day in the summer of 1982 on the site of a Morcoal Coal Company mining operation in Westmoreland County's Donegal Township. The Morcoal property is a harsh, gray wasteland which has been described as "a suitable landing strip for extraterrestrials." A mine road leads to a barren plateau that falls downhill to steep, unstable highwall cliffs above the mine's exposed coal seam. A deep mine pit is now filled with water, and telltale white stains on exposed rocks reveal acidic overburden—the rock and soil above the coal seam. Water that has flowed through this acid-bearing stratum has itself turned highly acid and now flows into a stream below the site. The highwall precipice and unfenced pit are an invitation to accidents. Illegally dumped garbage on the site is a serious fire hazard: Once ignited, open coal seams are very hard to extinguish—some may continue burning beneath the ground for years. On land that once was a pleasant woodland adjacent to wooded state game lands, a few hardy weeds are all that survive amid rocky outcrops. This derelict mining operation was initiated by two Pennsylvania lawyers, State Senator Jim Kelly and his partner, Robert Stefanon, who served as chief counsel for the state's Democratic Majority Committee. Topsoil was not saved during the mining. The two men disclaim responsibility, saying that they assigned the lease to someone else. Present and former state officials involved in litigating surface mine violations believe the two men are at fault.

This mine has been the subject of litigation for seven years (as of 1984) and the case is still in court in Philadelphia. "They [Kelly and Stefanon] have five other sites where there's been no reclamation," Ulishney said, speaking cautiously and deliberately. "They wanted a new license to continue. The department denied 'em a license. They said, 'Well, no license, no restoration.' " Robert P. Ging, Jr., Pennsylvania assistant attorney general and general counsel for the Bureau of Surface Mine Reclamation, filed suit on the state's behalf to force Kelly and Stefanon to reclaim. To date, the effort has not been successful. "They dug coal and ignored all their environmental responsibilities," Ging said.

Operations such as Morcoal unfortunately are not unique in the nation's coal-mining country, and their consequences are far-reaching: Acidic discharges to surface and groundwater from abandoned and from some active surface mines frequently kill stream life. The acid drainage is caused by the weathering of sulfides in the ground, which produces sulfuric acid. Sulfides in the eastern United States are generally compounded with iron as pyrites in the strata overlying coal seams. Air, water, and certain iron-oxidizing bacteria help convert the sulfides to acid. In eight Appalachian states alone, 5,700 miles of streams have thus been damaged by acid mine drainage, mostly from deep mines. The U.S. Bureau of Mines has put the cost of reclamation to correct 95 percent of the problem at $13.7 billion. Pennsylvania itself had 225,000 acres of abandoned surface-mined land in 1981, according to its Environmental Quality Board, as well as 2,000 miles of streams polluted by acid mine drainage. "There are streams that you can see in Pennsylvania," said attorney John Dernbach, "that look like orange Kool-Aid." Dernbach is assistant counsel to Pennsylvania's Bureau of Mining and Reclamation.

The task of coping with acid mine drainage falls to Inspector

Ulishney. He first tries to prevent it from occurring by recommending which mine permits should be issued and by giving expert advice to mine operators on how to mine and reclaim. If acid drainage occurs despite these precautions, he develops remedial strategies for treating it, and he enforces mine reclamation laws.

"When I go out to regulate," he said, with a deadpan expression, "... I can be very dumb, especially if the [operator] doesn't know what experience I've had. I used to just smile under my breath at some of the things people told me—a lot of them operators were doing a lot of wrong things. The ones that didn't know, you tried to educate them." In contrast to some inspectors, his goal is not to collect as much money in fines as possible, but to get miners to comply with the law "to maintain or better the environment." To this end, Ulishney spends hours of his own time on the phone at home in the evenings giving miners free technical advice. Looking back over the years, Ulishney said, "I tried to work with operators; they worked with me. But when the job was a little bit worse when you went back [to inspect], or they ignored your warnings, you brought the hammer down."

"This is a beautiful job," he said one day as he visited an active mine of Szerba and Grimm Coal Company in West Newton, Pennsylvania. The operator had large ditches to catch surface runoff from the mine site and sluice it into a spacious pond to treat any acid pit water with soda ash or lime. Soon after leaving that mine, he pulled his truck over to the side of the road beside some flat grassy fields. There were no signs of mining. "This happens to be a completed job," he said. "That whole flat area was totally stripped out to the depth of sixty feet."

Other reclaimed mine sites in varying stages of repair swept by the cab window of Ulishney's pickup truck. Some of the land had only a sparse cover crop poking up out of bare ground; some ground was already completely carpeted with healthy clover. At a site mined by Paul W. Kendi, Ulishney recalled how he had averted a water pollution discharge from Kendi's active mine. "He's on the Mahoning Coal Seam here," Ulishney explained.

"Now the Mahoning Coal Seam is normally very hot [acid-producing]." So Ulishney had the operator strategically place a layer of black calcareous shale—which had been removed with the overburden during mining—down at the bottom of the mine pit as the operator backfilled. The shale neutralized acidity in the mine drainage and, as a result, the groundwater near the site after mining emerged even less acid than before mining began.

Farther along the highway he gestured toward the flank of a large natural-looking mountainous area on the Lathrop anticline and he said, "From this knob up to the woods, that's all been surface mined. It wouldn't surprise me if twenty to thirty years from now someone'll come in here and drill this thing with the hopes of finding some coal."

At the end of a long day of visiting mines, he drove to a spring-fed four-acre lake surrounded by maples beside a hill on Route 30 in Westmoreland County, Unity Township. The banks were covered with grasses; geese and ducks were sporting about in the clean water which reaches a depth of fourteen feet and has a substantial bass population. When he bought the sixty-four-acre parcel of land on and around this site, the land had been devastated by coal mining and coking: Huge beehive coke ovens stood on the site and the land was smothered with ashes and refuse. "You name it, it was here. There wasn't a square inch of it—I mean a square inch—that was of any good use," said Ulishney. "It was worthless land."

But he worked on the land by himself in the 1950s, hauling away coal spoil banks, coke ovens, ashes, and debris of all kinds to a disposal area. His site was too unstable for heavy trucks, so he took 10,000 small truckloads to clear the land. Then he moved a large natural hill back about a hundred feet from what is now the lake. He used the material from the hill as fill and topsoil where needed. Afterwards, he terraced the new hill slope down to the lake and totally revegetated it. Now scarcely a trace of the land's previous association with surface and deep mining remains, save for some antique earth-moving equipment that has sentimental value to him. "I like to take something that's totally worthless and make something out of it," he said. "I like to build." A small but tidy woodland creek flows near the lake. The creek is on public land, but it was brush-choked, so Ulishney spent the winter of 1982 working without pay to clear it with his chain saw.

After inspecting many mines one hot summer's day, Ulishney stopped for a break at Brady's Diner, a small country cafe in Westmoreland County's coal-mining country. The clientele were mining people: inspectors, company officers, and foremen. Knitting his brow, Ulishney talked shop with them over his coffee while the cigarette between his lips smoked against his eyes.

Nile Lindgren, a young mine inspector with a large mining district to supervise, greeted Ulishney warmly yet respectfully. "Thousands of jobs" could be created in Pennsylvania by more active reclamation of abandoned sites, Lindgren declared in the conversation that followed. The jobs would not only be in the mining construction industry itself, he said, but in industries such as seed, fertilizer, limestone crushing and quarrying, equipment sales and repair, and trucking. The coal region of Pennsylvania can stand some economic revitalization.

Back in the late 1960s, Fred Ulishney served as a mine inspector under William E. Guckert. Pennsylvania was then providing national leadership on surface mine reclamation legislation, thanks in large part to Guckert, who led the grassroots fight that resulted in Pennsylvania's first surface mine reclamation law—over stiff coal industry resistance in 1964. That law made Pennsylvania the first state to require that strip-mined land be restored to its approximate contour.

The mining industry fought the passage of reclamation laws for years in the United States, arguing that reclamation would be too expensive. Fortunately, however, when performed during mining, land reclamation generally is easy and relatively inexpensive—on the order of 8 percent of the cost of mining. Furthermore, society has benefited enormously in economic and aesthetic respects from passage of the federal Surface Mine Control and Reclamation Act of 1977 and the state reclamation laws that preceded it. Mines that would have been left scarred, and some abandoned mines as well, have now been transformed into sites for homes, industry, commerce, offices, parks, and schools; some land has been restored as wildlife habitat or for agricultural uses. Many coal companies today are proud of their land restoration.

In addition to battling for the state's reclamation law, Bill Guckert also led the fight to pass Pennsylvania's Pure Streams Act of 1965, which required mining companies to treat their acid discharges. He ran both campaigns as a private citizen with nothing but grass-roots support, beating the industry on its home ground in the heart of the state's coal country. Eventually, in 1966, Governor Raymond P. Shafer appointed Guckert to head the state's Bureau of Surface Mine Reclamation, at which point he supervised reclamation inspectors like Ulishney and Lindgren.

Guckert is a decisive, heavyset man with keen blue eyes, extraordinary energy, unwavering determination, and intense curiosity about nature. Traveling through the back roads of the Pennsylvania countryside, which he knows intimately, he is liable to pull his truck off the road unexpectedly to go bounding across a stream through the woods in pursuit of a red-tailed hawk. At 76, he still wants to know what prey that hawk is clutching.

He seems to live in a perpetual state of righteous indignation. His normal tone of voice is a low conversational roar which sometimes ascends to a full bellow when he expresses his convictions. He employs a broad emotional range in speaking, and his voice in one sentence will go from a low growl to a whoop of exhilaration. When in good voice, he is about as easy to stop as a gale. For emphasis he will pound his table with a powerful fist or tap a listener insistently on the leg. He can declaim for hours about coal mining until the sweat drips from his face and sprays into the air as he shouts. Yet he loves a hearty laugh and chuckles often.

His talk is a blustering torrent of words in which homespun epithets and an occasional vulgarity are substituted for outright obscenity, which he almost never utters. So possessed is he by an impelling need to communicate that he often drops articles and conjunctions in his haste, speaking in unconnected phrases that fall like hammer blows.

He is old enough to remember the human consequences of strip mining before reclamation was mandatory. Passing a deserted house on Lisbon Road in Venango County, which has the remains of a water-filled mine pit next to it, Guckert said, "A lot of these elderly people leased out their coal rights [in the early forties]. The result [was] what the Hay, they didn't get anything. When they ended up, their house was gone, their property was shot. . . . Oh-ho Jesus I used to get mad. They were so cockeyed arrogant, these strip miners. They thought nobody's gonna bother 'em."

Much of their devastation is still evident throughout the coal-mining region. The only time Guckert sounded sad rather than combative during an extended visit to the mining areas was when he came to Bear Creek Valley and said, "Here's an area used to be a beautiful place. They destroyed it. Son of a bee! Come in and strip-mined the whole cockeyed thing—ruined the whole valley!"

As a citizen activist, Guckert's title used to be executive secretary of the Allegheny County Sportsmen's League, a post he held for thirty-five years—from 1932 to 1967. One of his most successful tactics was to take state legislators to mined sites. "We took the senators and representatives out and showed them, 'Here it is, and here's what they're doing.' The other side can't offset that. . . . When you see things firsthand, you ain't gonna let anybody b.s. you and say it ain't that way. You saw it. That's the way it is. . . . The miners couldn't get out [of hearings] without the legislators saying, 'What about this? What about that?' "

In the battle for a clean water bill, Guckert fought the Pennsylvania Railroad, the Baltimore and Ohio Railroad, and other big mine and mineral-owning corporations. "Even the union, the United Mine Workers, who should've been sticking up for the public, was against the cockeyed [program] of giving them clean water. . . . We got fish in our streams today we wouldn't have had if we hadn't made the big corporations treat their acid wastes."

Guckert's 1964 surface mine reclamation law required only that the land be returned to its approximate original contour and that trees had to be planted. Back then, unlike today, mine operators weren't obligated to save the topsoil or ensure that the trees survived. He paused at a site where stunted trees had been growing for thirty years out of coal mine spoil. No vegetation could be seen between the trees on the barren ground. "The land's no good," he said bluntly. "Who can use it? Who can live in it? A place like that's a biological desert."

Near the home he built in Clintonville, Pennsylvania, flows a stream. "In 1945," he said, pointing across a road, "they started to strip over there. In '45 I stopped them. I got so mad that they were ruining everything, polluting the streams." He fervently believes in the value of clean streams and good water and has built several lakes that are now loaded with bass and trout. Unfortunately, the Sanitary Water Board allowed Bill Harger's Sunbeam Coal Company to remine the land in Clintonville in 1955, and that finished Guckert's stream.

Guckert did not forget the plight of Pennsylvania streams when he was put in charge of surface mine reclamation for the state. He spent most of his days in the field insisting that the mining companies obey the law or have their permits revoked, and he frequently made surprise inspections.

On a tour of his old territory one day, Guckert parked his truck beside a large field off Highway 80 in Venango and Butler counties; the land was mined in 1976 by Pengrove Coal Company (now Adobe Mining Company). "Now that's a beautiful job!" he exclaimed. "They got the coal out. The people got the money out of it. Land's back. Land's useful. People can grow their cattle or harvest their crop of hay on it or whatever they want. If the [strip miners] do a good job, you give 'em credit for it. If they do a lousy job, you give 'em H for it!"

Guckert likes to show visitors Porter Fleming's farm in Butler County. It has some of the healthiest-looking cows and the lushest, greenest alfalfa fields in the state of Pennsylvania. But the buckwheat farmers who owned the land before Fleming apparently never limed the soil. It was in bad condition, and beneath that exhausted soil lay a fat black coal seam that grew more valuable every year. Fleming thought the matter over carefully and then, in 1972, he leased his land for stripping.

Fleming is a gaunt man well into middle age who, with his long, slender neck and wrinkled brow, looks vaguely like E.T. He moves slowly with his back bent slightly from the waist, as though painfully stiff. Though the frown between his eyes is deep, it is not unfriendly.

He said to the strip miner, "Save my soil over there, but over here it's junk; I don't want it." Sunbeam obligingly buried that topsoil and instead brought up the subsoil, which was richer in nutrients. Fleming had the soil analyzed and supplemented the mineral-rich layer with an appropriate fertilizer mix. Today the mined land on Fleming's property is better for agricultural purposes than before mining.

"The magnesium's what we lack in this country. That's the reason our cows were dying back ten, fifteen years ago. . . . Now we got it in our soil. . . ." So on balance he has never regretted his decision to let the land be stripped. But the effects of strip mining itself were not beneficial. "The worst thing that strip mining does," Fleming said, "is the hill won't take [absorb] the water after you're done. . . . I don't know if it'll ever come back to the way it was."

There is no love lost between Bill Guckert and H. Porter Duvall, Fish Warden of Jefferson County, Pennsylvania, and winner of an Outstanding Environmentalist of the Year Award from Trout Unlimited. Duvall was sent by the Pennsylvania Fish Commission to Jefferson County in 1970 to police the county's streams. "We don't really care what happens on a surface mine site," he said. "They can pile it to the moon . . . as long as it doesn't affect the waters. When it starts to affect them, then of course I get bent out of shape."

Duvall is deeply tanned and resembles a Hollywood version of a law enforcement officer. He believes that while some good reclamation is occurring, subsurface problems sometimes are not correctly handled by mining companies. "It's like a doctor went into a compound fracture, just knit the surface closed with a few stitches, and never set the bones."

Whereas the state's first strip mine reclamation law, which Guckert championed, required grading and filling of the land after mining, it did not require the saving of topsoil as did a subsequent law passed in 1972 while Guckert was in office in Harrisburg. "That was when Bill Guckert and I parted company," Duvall stated. "Miners would claim they were complying with the law but they weren't stabilizing the topsoil. Of course it was affecting the streams. The Fish Commission and [the Department of Environmental Resources'] Bureau of Mining and Reclamation had a difference of opinion."

Duvall claimed that Guckert in office didn't do enough to prevent erosion of mined land into streams, and failed to apply erosion and sedimentation regulations stringently enough to surface mining operations. "We lost five years of mud into these streams," he said.

Mining naturally brings hydrological changes. "Perch tables are destroyed," said Duvall. "Your capillary action, which you normally rely on to bring water up at this time of the year, will no longer exist; it's been broken. What you've done, in effect, is cultivated thirty, fifty, a hundred feet deep." The soil compaction caused by heavy machinery used in reclaiming the site can have an effect "similar to macadamizing the surface." Groundwater infiltration is intentionally minimized during reclamation to prevent water from contact with subsurface pyrites, so runoff is increased instead. The land thus often doesn't get enough moisture, Duvall said, and shallow-rooting crops may not do well; consequently, much reclaimed land is put into pasture with deep-rooting alfalfa.

But to prove that this is not always the case, Duvall drove to Lincoln Felterfaver's farm in Oliveburg, Pennsylvania. The land had been surface-mined and subsequently restored by Dover Spike Coal Company. A good crop of corn was now growing there. And on the hills of the nearby reclaimed Wachob farm, rolls of hay were waiting for baling, and white cows were grazing on restored fields.

Duvall is quick to also point out 150 acres of wasteland ruined by Jefferson County miner Blake Becker, a small operator convicted of numerous mining law violations. Duvall's complaints brought the case to the attention of then-Assistant Attorney General Robert Ging, Jr. Becker was eventually fined $100,000 and given five years' probation, but—with half-a-dozen abandoned mines to his credit—the judge allowed him to go out and mine under someone else's license in order to pay off his fine.

Arrests for reclamation violations are extremely rare, says Duvall, and he has observed that far more substantial violations than Becker's by larger operators in Pennsylvania proceed with little legal restraint. "There's been an attempt both by our administration and by the industry to take the teeth out of the licensing laws," claims Robert Ging. Pennsylvania requires mining companies to post a performance bond to ensure that their mined land will be reclaimed. The state's maximum bonding rate, however, is thousands of dollars less than the actual cost of reclamation. "It's much cheaper to abandon a mine than it is to reclaim it as long as the bonds stay like that," says Ging. The state's maximum bonding rate for most mines is only $3,000 an acre, with somewhat higher rates for mines with exceptionally tall highwalls.

Charles Gummo, former assistant director of Pennsylvania's Bureau of Mining and Reclamation, concurs that the bonds posted are far too little to enable the state to cover its costs in reclaiming nonconcurrent reclamations operations. In reclamation jargon, *nonconcurrent* means costlier reclamation because it is done after mining has already ceased. "I don't think we could bond at a rate which would allow us to reclaim nonconcurrent operations. It would just be too high. We're talking about $10,000 an acre."

Attorney John Dernbach of the state's reclamation bureau says that federal funding is inadequate to pay for reclaiming the backlog of existing abandoned mined lands in the United States. "It's a drop in the bucket. We know that the government's not going to come up with the bucks—ever." Therefore, he said, Pennsylvania is trying to create incentives to encourage mining companies to remine and, in the process, to reclaim abandoned mined lands.

The mining industry disturbs a lot of land in the United States by surface mining. Stone, sand and gravel, bituminous coal, copper, iron, and phosphates are all won from the earth by digging, scraping, blasting, and gouging. All told, about six million acres of land in the United States have been altered by surface mining. Close to four million of those acres still require reclamation. About half a million of those four million acres are surface-mined coal lands where reclamation is legally required. Twice as many acres of surface-mined coal lands need reclamation, but their reclamation is not legally required because they were disturbed prior to the passage of surface mine reclamation laws.

The U.S. Bureau of Mines has estimated that the reclamation of approximately 400,000 acres of unreclaimed surface coal mines would cost three billion dollars (in 1978 dollars), based on a "median" reclamation cost of $7,700 per acre. The bureau estimates that comprehensive reclamation of *all* the nation's abandoned mined lands from deep and surface activities, including leveling waste piles, eliminating subsidence, and extinguishing fires, would cost thirty billion dollars. Some of this land may no longer need reclamation, but the total bill for repairing U.S. surface-mined lands that do need reclamation would be steep. Just correcting the acid mine drainage problems alone on these lands would cost about eighteen billion dollars (1978 dollars).

Reclamation of surface-mined lands is not a labor-intensive process, because it's done largely with massive and efficient mining equipment. Yet David Callaghan, director of West Virginia's Department of Natural Resources, affirms that even in this area of reclamation work, significant numbers of jobs could be created. His department assumes that a million dollars' worth of mine reclamation work creates about fifty jobs. Thus if thirty billion dollars' worth of surface mine reclamation work are commissioned in the U.S., that would mean a million and a half person-years of employment.

The mining industry is now paying thirty-five cents per ton of surface-mined coal into a federally sponsored fund dedicated to mined land reclamation and related activities. A charge of fifteen cents per ton is levied for every ton of deep-mined coal. The U.S. Bureau of Mines estimates that it will collect only four billion dollars through this program before it expires—a fraction of the funds needed. If restoration is not conducted, agricultural, commercial, or recreational resources are damaged and lost. Meadows, woods, wetlands, and wildlife are eradicated.

Observers who have spent time in regions disturbed by surface mining often are categorically opposed to stripping, no matter "how badly the country needs the energy." They would rather see more coal removed by deep mining or left in the ground while the country relied more on other energy sources.

Assuming all the money needed could be found, can devastated acidic mined lands, such as those at Morcoal, ever be satisfactorily repaired ecologically? Opinions differ, but there is some consensus among experts that whereas acid mine drainage can often be prevented, it is difficult to correct once it is allowed to begin. Geologist Robert L. P. Kleinmann at the U.S. Bureau of Mines Pittsburgh Research Center says, "We do not have a good success record in stopping acid mine drainage. . . . For the abandoned mine lands, there are very few cases where acid mine drainage has been successfully halted as part of the reclamation process."

The chance of success is improved when only a relatively small area is covered by acid-producing material and it can be isolated from air and water. "If there's a lot of pyrite," Kleinmann says, "there's no way you can restore an abandoned site and stop it from producing." Current technology is even less able to control acid mine drainage from underground mines. "If we come up with anything, it'll be a revolution in the state of the art," Kleinmann notes. Yet he is hopeful that solutions will be found, and he thinks researchers may be nearing a breakthrough. "In the next few years, you're going to see techniques developed [to stop acid mine drainage]. . . . It's an exciting time to be working with the problem."

Kleinmann has been experimenting on the iron-oxidizing bacteria that accelerate acid production from mined areas. His work has shown that eliminating the bacterial activity can reduce acid production by 75 percent. He is currently testing ways to kill the bacteria by slowly releasing detergents into pyritic soils.

A colleague of Kleinmann's, geotechnical engineer Murray T. Dougherty, has worked on mine reclamations for years and is as pessimistic as Kleinmann about controlling the effects of ongoing acid mine drainage. "We reduced acid mine drainage in the long run, but came up with other problems," he said, "such as high aluminum and heavy metals. We can't control acid mine drainage. We've never cleaned up a stream to the point where aquatic life's come back. The stream bottoms are wrecked due to the coating of iron. Bottom organisms can never get [re]started to support the food chain."

The consequences of acid mine drainage are thus so serious that the problem has upstaged efforts to achieve true ecological restoration of mined areas. As the prominent restoration ecologist John Cairns, Jr., points out in his book *The Recovery Process in Damaged Ecosystems*, "The goals of most mine restorations have been to prevent acid drainage, erosion, and to achieve some . . . ground cover, not to restore the original vegetation or to attain the original species diversity."

Kleinmann believes that while technology for controlling existing acid mine drainage is in its infancy, we do know how to prevent it from occurring in new mines, provided we confine mining to suitable sites low in pyrites. However, the technology for predicting whether a site will or won't produce acid is still under development and mistakes are sometimes made.

Opponents of strip mining are sometimes willing to concede

that reclamation is possible in temperate, well-watered Appalachia when knowledgeable mine operators use discretion in siting their mines and take great care during mining. But the opponents are skeptical about reclamation succeeding in more inhospitable climes where, even under the best of circumstances, vegetation is naturally sparse and new plants are hard to establish.

7

Badlands and Indian Range

Near the Arizona border along Highway 264 in northern New Mexico, the countryside is a pale yellow rangeland of high mesas. Sagebrush, tumbleweeds, and saltbush bristle here despite the harsh desert climate. Tough junipers and rugged piñon pines also wrench their living from the gritty soil. Thus piñon nuts are on sale in the gas stations here: The Indians cook with them; Anglos nibble them; Chicanos bake them into *empanaditas*. A few cattle and horses graze in arid scrub pastures and Indian hitchhikers stand wanly by the road or trudge along it.

As one leaves the main road and winds uphill toward the Pittsburg & Midway Coal Mining Company's McKinley Mine, the booms of giant draglines loom over the hillsides in the distance above the mesas. The steel shafts seem intrusive in this low-hilled terrain. P&M's surface mine is among the top twenty coal producers in the nation, and the company's claim covers 28,000 acres—11,000 owned by the Navaho and leased by them to P&M.

When the New York-based public interest group INFORM

conducted a 1980 study of Western coal mine reclamation practices, P&M, a Gulf Oil Company subsidiary, was the only company that refused to allow INFORM access to its mine site and to
data about its extensive reclamation work. What, if anything, did
they have to hide?

Alan Balok, formerly a teacher of horticulture and at one
time a county agricultural agent, is in charge of reclamation for
P&M. Wearing an orange hard hat, long sideburns, and sun-
glasses, he meets visitors at the company security office, and ne-
gotiates the rough dirt road into the mine in a GMC Sierra
Grande that is dwarfed by hulking 120-ton coal trucks that rum-
ble past. Balok had intended to go into farming with his agricultural degree. Now he supervises the repair of 400 acres of mined
land a year. "There's not much you can do with a degree in agriculture these days," he lamented. "This was as close to farming
as I could get."

Coal trucks are not the only giant pieces of equipment here,
for this is a land of monsters: The mine's draglines weigh fourteen million pounds and can wrest tons of material from the
ground in a single bite of their twenty-five-cubic-yard buckets.
Each dragline dangles its bucket like a toy from its 340-foot
boom—about the length of a football field.

Balok rapidly leaves the mine road and begins traversing a
steep spoil bank in the GMC, which bounces wildly on the un-
even surface. The grade is more than 30 percent (3:1), and it's
fortunate that the truck has a wide wheelbase. High on the spoil
bank, Balok executes a sharp turn to gaze out over a site being
readied for reclamation. The valley below is brown with dust
blowing off the spoils, and the wind booms fiercely against the
back of the truck. "You're working with a fragile ecosystem here
that's been abused and overgrazed for centuries," Balok says. "If
it's not taken care of now, there'll be nothing left."

How is reclamation accomplished at McKinley on these
rough, windswept slopes, where annual rainfall is only ten to
twelve inches per year? Can the land actually be restored for
grazing and wildlife habitat? Balok obligingly discussed the
challenge. First, he explained, careful reclamation studies are

done prior to mining: The land and its drainage pattern are mapped and analyzed in detail. When mining is done on the site's thick multiple coal seams, the huge spoil piles left by the draglines are graded by bulldozers that go over the slopes to reestablish the approximate original contours and drainage of the land. Next, if any topsoil is available, it is spread on the new surface to a depth of twelve inches. But much of the land has little topsoil and even that is low in organic matter. So where topsoil is absent, the company spreads a top dressing, usually a subsoil mixture of shale and sand with fertilizer added later to compensate for nutrient deficiencies. Then the soil is disked to break up lumps and to mix in the fertilizer. The steeper slopes are finally contour-furrowed to slow runoff and aid the soil in retaining moisture.

When the soil gets moist enough for seed germination, an agricultural machine called a rangeland drill drills in and broadcasts seed. The freshly seeded slopes are then mulched with shredded straw. This reclamation cost $5,000–$6,000 per acre in 1981. Unlike some other mining companies, P&M uses no irrigation. Water is scarce and costly here and irrigation would eventually have to cease.

The McKinley mine began coal production in 1959 but the company did not begin land reclamation until required to do so by the federal Surface Mine Control and Reclamation Act of 1977 (SMCRA). In its early reclamation efforts in 1978, the company found the ground cover that sprouted from its first seed mixes was dominated by saltbush. Subsequently, the company increased the diversity of its seed mix and surviving vegetation. An area seeded in 1979 had six different grasses growing. A 1981 plot had nine surviving varieties, including several nonnatives which Balok believes are good for erosion control and for grazing. Yet more than a hundred native plants are normally found in the region. INFORM thus had criticized P&M for seeding mainly grasses instead of a mix of the forbs, shrubs, and grasses found on nearby undisturbed land. "This dominance by grasses does not provide as good forage as undisturbed lands covered with more diverse plant community," the group stated.

Balok says that P&M is now striving to surpass the minimum requirements of the 1977 reclamation law. That law mandates that the land be made equal to, or better than, before. On its own initiative, the company has therefore transplanted 40,000 native trees and shrubs onto the mine site to reestablish them. At the time of a recent visit, it was still too early to assess their long-term viability. But the company no longer seems to feel the need to be secretive and Balok has been the epitome of candor.

What will determine the ultimate success or failure of the McKinley reclamation work and projects like it? New Mexico geologist Stephen Wells believes that the greatest long-term threat may come, paradoxically, from off-site areas. A gully in a nearby valley not even disturbed by mining could progress up-valley from a nick point to cut into a reclaimed area and open the spoil bank to serious erosion. Nick points can travel at rates of several yards per year.

A wide range of external variables, including hill slopes, rainfall intensity, and sediment yields, could affect the site in the short term, Wells notes. Over long periods of time, climatic change, and alterations in bedrock and geomorphology might affect site stability. Wells therefore urges mining companies to look at a proposed reclamation project as part of a complex regional geomorphic system, to gain better understanding of the direct and indirect disturbances to the system that mining might cause.

To a casual observer, the reclaimed land at McKinley looks comparable to the weedy, abused rangeland nearby and demonstrates that replanted vegetation can survive at least in the short run under very adverse conditions. But should the goal of reclamation be just to restore mined land to the caliber of a previously degraded range, or to make it as productive and ecologically diverse as it can be? And if the land is to be wildlife habitat, should it be made as close as possible in diversity and productivity to undisturbed land? These questions raise difficult issues: Can a corporation that buys already impoverished land for mining be required to make the land better than when it acquired the land?

The way society answers this question may determine the fate of thousands of acres of Western mined land.

The road to the giant Four Corners power plant in north-western New Mexico near Farmington leads directly to the headquarters of Utah International's Navaho Coal Mine. This is no coincidence. Much of the coal stripped from the Navaho coal site is used to fuel the adjoining plant, one of the world's largest coal-burning power stations. The Navaho Coal Mine here in San Juan County is one of the Earth's mined sites most inhospitable for land reclamation. It is a large, deep surface mine where multiple coal seams are stripped to a maximum depth of 180 feet. More than six million tons of subbituminous coal were produced here in 1978 alone. Rainfall on the site averages only five to six inches per year, and the topsoil not lost during mining has been badly depleted by overgrazing and erosion. The land is wind-swept and rocky—barren of trees and shrubs—even where un-mined. The tough grasses that do manage to grow here are mercilessly overgrazed by Navaho who are also struggling to survive in the harsh climate and need the threadbare pasturage for their sheep and cattle.

To reach the mine, one leaves U.S. Highway 550 a few miles west of Farmington and turns south crossing a small bridge over the San Juan River. The road then winds through small irrigated farms up to the top of a mesa. The green of the cultivated fields along the way contrasts with the sparser vegetation of the sandy hills. Long before seeing the plant, one can see the smoke from its chimneys staining the skies. Climbing higher into the hills, one can see its four large stacks and the dragline spires poking into the sky behind nearby hills. Just over the last rise onto the mesa, the rest of the Four Corners plant looms into view. Against bright sunny blue skies, it is an ominous black beneath billowing clouds of steam and smoke. Away into the distance from the plant marching like wire soldiers over the arid land are 345-kilovolt lines taking electricity from Four Corners to southern California and elsewhere.

The roads here at the entrance to the plant are covered with coal dust and coal fragments. To keep the dust down, crews spray the roads with water and the resulting black slurry accumulates as a rock-hard coating on the sides of cars.

Utah International is itself a subsidiary of General Electric Corporation. When the former began mining here in 1963, land restoration was not legally required, so the company neither graded its spoils nor saved any topsoil during the first ten years of mining. The firm is now not only trying to reclaim lands it mines currently, but is grading and seeding its previously mined land. In the early 1980s, about half the ten-square-mile mined area had been reseeded, but topsoil was available for only one square mile. Reclamation personnel on site do not think this is an insurmountable obstacle.

Bill Skeet, a slow-spoken reclamation specialist with a B.S. in agricultural engineering, directs reclamation work at the Navaho mine. His straight black hair hangs in bangs against his coppery forehead. Skeet explained that the company has conducted its own research program to determine what reclamation techniques are appropriate for the unique site. When work began here, little was known about reclamation under the harsh desert conditions. Fortunately, as in much of the West, soil acidity and acid mine drainage are not problems here; the main problem is aridity plus poor soil.

After several years of trial and error, Skeet in 1982 was seeding the reclaimed land with a mixture of four native grasses (Indian rice grass, alkali sacaton, galleta, giant dropseed), two native shrubs (four-winged saltbush, winter fat), and a native herb (globe mallow). He plants most seed using modified rangeland and farm drills that broadcast seed and bury it within an inch of the surface. He planted a maximum of fifteen plant varieties in 1982, mulching them with barley straw and crimping them into the soil. These plots are irrigated for a year after planting in a watering schedule that imitates natural rainfall patterns. (Most of the scant rain falls in summer storms between August and October.) The plants receive three times as much water as they naturally would. Skeet has had to plant seeds directly into upper mantle material—ground that is below where topsoil would be but usually above the deeper-lying calcium carbonate layers.

Results after the plants have been weaned from irrigation have varied. The vegetation is surviving, but in some areas it is sparse, with plants separated by bare ground on which running water has left thick rills. In some places where the four-winged saltbush had been particularly successful, survival of other species was reduced and species diversity was low. Thus far, except for some controlled grazing experiments, livestock has been fenced out of reclaimed areas to maximize the plants' chances of establishment. Skeet pointed out that much of the mine site was on badlands, where virtually no vegetation grew before the mining began; conditions there were comparable to those on the premined range. However, from his conversations with "old-timers" who knew the local rangeland before both overgrazing and mining had taken their toll, Skeet had learned that wild native grasses once grew "belly high" on part of the site in a fertile native topsoil.

Reporting on the Navaho Coal Mine reclamation efforts, the INFORM research group said, "The company may show, with much experimentation and innovation, that it can make the desert bloom. But it is just as likely that wretched lands long ago disturbed and rendered useless by coal mining will be impossible to reclaim." Other observers have not been so pessimistic. For its part, the company has provided native seed and all the basic conditions for its survival. Time alone will tell how well the arid lands at the Navaho mine will fare when exposed to heavy grazing and when company gully prevention activities on the land cease. Settling of old mine areas is a hazard: It could lead to surface cracking and to long-term erosion problems on the surface. Difficult-to-extinguish coal fires that smolder below ground also can kill ground cover above. Vegetation might in the future be grazed off the soil; sheet and gully erosion might then leave behind a barren wasteland. Or the ground cover might take root and eventually rebuild a productive topsoil. Despite the many hazards that his reclamation work faces, Bill Skeet is nonetheless optimistic that his desert mine reclamation work will survive.

Whereas many coal mines have been revegetated, it appears that no large open-pit uranium mine has been reclaimed in the United States. To do so, the reclaimer would not only have to contend with physical scars in the earth, but with radioactivity as well.

Anaconda Copper's Jackpile-Paguate uranium mine on the Laguna Indian reservation near Grants, New Mexico, was the largest open-pit uranium mine in North America. Today, the mine is a silent radioactive moonscape of chalky heaps and holes—closed because cheaper uranium can be dug elsewhere.

Mine explosives once boomed across the mesas and heavy trucks carrying uranium ore for nuclear fuel rods once roared along the winding, dusty mine roads over 2,600 acres of open pits, highwalls, waste and ore piles. For twenty-nine years Anaconda mined uranium here, producing 25 million tons of ore from 400 million tons of soil and rock.

But now that the dust has settled, a small Southwestern Indian tribe, a major mining company, and federal resource managers are wrestling over what must be done to repair the ravaged land, which the Indians own. Not only must Anaconda transform this devastated area back into natural-looking desert rangeland (or hire a contractor to do so), but it also must grapple with serious threats to public health and safety arising from the mine's present condition.

If reclamation is to succeed here and set a good example, Anaconda will need to eliminate radiological hazards, such as the radon gas escaping into the air from waste and ore piles, and the potential for radioactively contaminated water.

At the Bureau of Land Management (BLM) in Albuquerque, environmental protection specialists Mike Pool and John Andrews have taken refuge in a motel to concentrate on completing the long-overdue preliminary environmental impact statement outlining reclamation alternatives.

The task has already taken four years, has cost five million dollars, and has required delicate negotiations between the BLM, the Bureau of Indian Affairs, the multinational Anaconda Copper Company (an Atlantic Richfield [ARCO] subsidiary), and the Laguna Pueblo Indians, who have done most of the actual mining on their land.

Although the tribe has received royalties on uranium mined for twenty-nine years before the mine closed in 1982, the Indians have paid a steep price for them. Miners and villagers have been exposed to radioactive dust and gases from the mine, and Indians' homes near the mine may have been damaged by the use of explosives during mining operations. The Laguna Pueblo's village of Paguate is perched on a bluff overlooking the Jackpile-Paguate mine 300 yards away from one of the pits. Reclamation of the mine will be a complex job because of the masses of material removed and because of serious on-site radiological hazards.

Successful restoration might make the terrain less dangerous and economically useful for grazing. After the scarred land is contoured and revegetated, "It'll be somewhat close to what it was before mining," asserts Curtis Burton, ARCO public affairs manager. "Ten years after the reclamation," he says, "it wouldn't stand out from its surroundings," a rough dry land of scrubby vegetation.

Only a few surface (open-pit) uranium mines have ever been reclaimed in the United States, and those reclamations have been accomplished on relatively small mines, since 1980. Yet according to Andrews, a geologist, the small mines in the aggregate add up to a more serious reclamation problem than the relatively fewer large ones.

Although unreclaimed uranium mine lands exist in at least seven states, mainly in the Southwest, no national legislation sets standards for their reclamation, and state surface mine reclamation regulations vary widely in their requirements and enforcement. New Mexico, for example, requires reclamation of uranium mines only if reclamation is called for under a state land lease. Currently, there are over 3,000 active and inactive uranium mines throughout the U.S., of which more than 1,300 are surface mines.

At the Jackpile mine, Anaconda has proposed limited back-filling of its pits to cover the mineralized zones, and selective stabilization of its dumps rather than leveling them. Radioactive materials would be covered with nonhazardous material either in place or after some of the wastes were put back into the mine pits. Anaconda, however, would like to leave its steep highwalls in place. Some of them are a hundred feet in height with forty-five-degree slopes. The Laguna Pueblo would like the hazardous slopes reduced.

Local residents and environmentalists have cause for concern about the thoroughness of the reclamation to come. During the period of active mining, radioactivity was released into the atmosphere on dust particles that blew from the mine onto the village of Paguate and as radon gas from ore and waste piles. Radon (a decay product of radium) readily escapes from disturbed ground and, when inhaled, increases the risk of lung cancer. Radium (a decay product of uranium) is leached from mined areas and enters ground and surface waters. Because radium is a bone-seeking isotope, it will irradiate the body from within once ingested through contaminated drinking water. Unfortunately, for many years the Laguna Pueblo Indians used surface and ground-water flowing through the mine for irrigation, stock watering, and domestic purposes, despite the fact that in 1980 elevated levels of radium were found downstream from the mine.

Given the expenditure of enough time, energy, and money, Anaconda can resculpt the land surface at Jackpile; but coping with water contamination may be more difficult, for streambeds already have been contaminated, and the groundwater could be coming in contact with toxic material over a wide area. By 1982, the company had reclaimed 485 acres and asserted that "species diversity, [ground] cover, and forage production approximate that on surrounding undisturbed rangeland."

During the more ambitious reclamation effort to come—which may last for up to ten years—Anaconda or its contractors will need to route surface water away from contact with disturbed ore bodies. Hydrological detective work will also have to be accomplished to identify underground sources of contamination. Comprehensive reclamation work will be expensive: Estimates have ranged up to seventy-five million dollars. Actual costs might go much higher, depending on the reclamation standards which the company is ultimately obliged to meet.

Anaconda proposed to monitor the site for only three years following completion of the reclamation work. During that time, grazing would be prohibited to allow vegetation to become permanently established. The company states it would like to be relieved of all further responsibility for reclamation when the grazing starts. The BLM would like Anaconda to monitor the site for ten years.

Even if the company meets its reclamation goals, human habitation of the site is to be expressly prohibited, essentially forever, because of radiological contamination. "The Pueblo of Laguna must agree not to allow homes or commercial/industrial facilities to be built anywhere within the disturbed area," a company report said. Thus no matter how well the grass and shrubs grow, land use at Jackpile will be restricted forever.

"The groundwater recovery level is the major issue right now," said Tribal Administrator Ron Solomon. "We want to make sure that we don't have water ponding at the bottom of the pits or soil deterioration due to salt and alkali crust accumulation. Then we would end up with a vast wasteland."

"Because there are no enforceable statutory standards for the reclamation of an open-pit uranium mine," Solomon said, "the entire reclamation project is in many ways left to the whims of the parties involved. The lease provisions are not a solid basis for requiring extensive reclamation. . . ."

As the actual plans for the Jackpile-Paguate reclamation near completion, many people are awaiting the outcome of negotiations between the federal government, Anaconda, and the Laguna Pueblo. The final reclamation plans agreed upon for the Jackpile mine will be a clue to what will be required elsewhere in the years ahead as thousands of the nation's uranium mines eventually close.

8

The Prairie Makers

Whipped by spring winds, the fire roared across the restored Curtis Prairie in Wisconsin sucking air towards the vortex of a firestorm in the center of the blaze. During the two minutes it took the fire to roast the buff-colored prairie, flames leaped twenty-five feet into the air and exploded through the tall dry grasses on sixty acres of land which ecologists had labored for nearly fifty years to restore. Gray smoke billowed high, visible for miles, and then, as the acrid smell of burnt grass drifted away, the Curtis Prairie lay charred and deceptively sterile-looking.

No one, however, was dismayed to see the restored prairie go up in smoke. The Curtis Prairie fire at the University of Wisconsin–Madison's Arboretum had been carefully planned and set. In fact, it is a regular event, reminiscent of the vast, primeval prairie fires that once swept across the American plains, ignited by lightning or by Indians. A prairie fire in those days could race from northern Illinois into Indiana, leaping creeks until the wind turned against it or until it came to a major river. Those huge prairie conflagrations were often visible many miles away on the great plains. Early settlers in the Mississippi Valley remarked on the eerie and beautiful way distant tongues of liquid fire "festooned" the night sky.

Prairie ecologists now believe that fire is beneficial to native prairie and necessary for its survival. Roots and seeds of prairie plants beneath the soil survive the blaze. So do many prairie animals. But fire removes the thatch of dead prairie grass which interferes with new plant growth and shields the ground from the sun's spring warmth. Most important, the fire kills trees, weeds, and other competitors of the prairie community. These conclusions were among the important findings that resulted from ecological research conducted on the restored Curtis Prairie in the 1940s and '50s. "[Ecologists at the arboretum] played a role in the rediscovery of that ancient technology," said William R. Jordan III, who manages public relations for the arboretum. Jordan, a tall, thoughtful man with a Ph.D. in plant physiology, is founder of *Restoration and Management Notes,* the nation's only ecosystem restoration journal. He serves informally as theoretician, chronicler, and *philosophe* for the growing national restoration movement.

The Curtis Prairie may be the world's oldest intentionally restored ecosystem. (Its restoration began in 1935.) Jordan views its re-creation as nothing less than an historic event: the first time anyone ever tried to put a complex plant community back together again on a large scale for scientific purposes. He points out that, in conventional agriculture, the agriculturalist takes a complex native ecosystem, such as a forest or prairie, and simplifies it, eliminating competition so a single crop can be grown. But in ecosystem restoration, simple systems are made more complex. "Restoration is a new form of agriculture committed not to the production of food and fiber, but to the re-creation of communities based upon naturally occurring models. This is a truly historic event," said Jordan, "a new form of stewardship and a new relationship between the human race and its environment."

Few Americans today realize that the nation once had 700,000,000 acres of prairie and that the extensive prairie biome in the United States is now all but extinct. Outside of a few parks and refuges, only small prairie relics still exist. Destruction of the prairie was as sudden as it was complete, and few people mourned the lost wildlife and natural beauty or understood the nexus of prairie and soil. Much of this country's wealth depends on its bounteous agriculture, which in the Midwest and other areas exploits the soils created and enriched by the prairie plants and animals of yesterday. The same prairie vegetation also retained water and protected the land from erosion, even during violent rains.

Hundreds of plant species and countless insects, birds, mammals, reptiles, amphibians, bacteria, and fungi inhabited the prairie. The bison, a prairie symbol, is perhaps the best-known prairie animal, yet prairies were also home to elk, pronghorn antelopes, white-tailed deer, plains bighorns, wolves, coyotes, foxes, squirrels, shrews, black-tailed prairie dogs, prairie chickens, meadowlarks, and prairie falcons. Brooks and prairie pools were filled with sunfish, minnows, turtles, and tadpoles.

Grass grew taller from west to east across the continent along a gradient of increasing moisture. In Illinois, the Prairie State, the grass was ten to twelve feet high and early settlers had to mark their paths with rock cairns to reduce the chances of getting lost.

Settlers told of waving grass stretching to the shimmering horizon. Beneath sunny skies, the rolling land was a sea of shining color—an enormous mosaic of flowers—sparkling pinks, apricots, whites, magentas, reds, yellows, and blues, ever changing as the seasons progressed. The blooms transformed the living prairie carpet from early timid greens through a kaleidoscopic array of rainbow patterns until the russets, tans, and golden browns of fall suffused the land.

A consciousness of what had been lost had already dawned in the minds of several prominent naturalists and ecologists even before the turn of the century. A few very small-scale prairie plant restorations were attempted, such as those by Midwestern landscape architect Jens Jensen, from the 1880s to the 1940s. But in general little attention was paid to the early advocates of prairie restoration and less was known about how to accomplish their goals.

Then, during the Depression, concern about the destruction of native plant and animal communities grew, as widespread ecological damage to the United States became more apparent. The nation's great prairies were almost gone by the 1930s, the virgin forests of the Great Lakes region had been clear-cut, and the calamitous soil losses of the Dust Bowl darkened skies in the Southwest.

These developments were very much on the minds of the ecologists at the University of Wisconsin's Madison campus in 1934. At their arboretum's dedication that year, ecologist Aldo Leopold urged the university "to reconstruct a sample of original Wisconsin—a sample of what Dane County looked like when our ancestors arrived during the 1840s." Leopold and others meant that the arboretum should not merely warehouse individual plant species in a living museum, but should try to actually re-create naturalistic communities. As part of this effort, Leopold in 1936 hired Theodore M. Sperry, a young prairie ecologist, to restore a sixty-acre arboretum field to native prairie.

The arboretum was then the site of a Civilian Conservation Corps encampment, and Sperry directed the unskilled recruits in prairie-making. Corn stubble still stood on the chosen land, surrounded by quack grass and ragweed. Because so little was known about prairie reestablishment, Sperry relied on the results of experiments by botany professor Norman Fassett's students. The best prairie restoration method they had found was to transplant whole sods from existing prairie. Sperry and his crew therefore drove in trucks to the east side of the Wisconsin River opposite Prairie du Sac and began digging up plants from a gravelly native prairie remnant.

By spring of 1936 they had planted twenty-five tons of prairie sod; but a severe summer drought followed, and only three percent of the plants survived. Sperry nonetheless persisted in his restoration efforts, and when he left in 1941, he had reestablished forty-two different prairie species, in segregated single-species stands—a patchwork quilt of prairie vegetation.

Later prairie devotees would deplore the fact that Sperry had ransacked virgin prairie to accomplish his mandate. Some of the prairies he dug up were being destroyed anyway, however. And he was under pressure to produce timely results for his sponsors. He also seems to have viewed his task more as a construction effort than as a scientific experiment. That approach to prairie restoration changed radically as the years went by and the arboretum's management became more sophisticated about restoration.

During the 1940s, further experiments were carried out on the experimental prairie site to learn the best way to reestablish prairie. Grasses and forbs were planted into both de-sodded ground and unbroken sod; various seed mixes and methods of germination, soil preparation, and weed eradication all were tried to learn the prairie plants' requirements and to find ways of reassembling them into a real prairie.

Using the knowledge gained during more than a decade of prairie research, university personnel began a second stage of prairie planting in 1950. More than 150 prairie species were introduced to the prairie over a five-year period by arboretum botanist David Archbald, and a regular burning schedule was begun. This rapidly began to improve the prairie by suppressing weeds and encouraging the spread of the native plants.

The days when the destruction of relic prairies was condoned were now long past. Much of the new planting was done by casting prairie seed into disked ground and using a cover crop to hold the soil and protect the new plants.

By the 1980s, nearly fifty years after the restored prairie was first begun, introduced nonnative species and weeds had been greatly reduced, and parts of the prairie were comparable to, and even richer in species composition than, native prairies; the entire prairie was beginning to biologically resemble a natural prairie. Species which had not been planted in their proper positions on soil-moisture-microclimatic gradients had rearranged themselves by migrating toward their preferred microenvironments. Yet even at this writing, parts of the prairie are still infested with aggressive nonnatives like bluegrass, sweet clover, and wild parsnip, illustrating the difficulty of restoring the native community. To create a prairie *identical* to a natural virgin prairie is impossible today. For one thing, some prairie species are already extinct. For another, the development of a prairie is a slow process. "Only God can make a prairie," says Grant Cottam, a University of Wisconsin professor who has been involved with the Curtis Prairie research for the past forty years. He was a graduate student of the late Professor John T. Curtis, a botanist for whom the prairie is named. Cottam believes, with Sperry, that it would take a thousand years fully to restore a native prairie so that the delicate and intricate dynamic competitive balance between hundreds of species of plants and animals could be reattained.

Apart from the Curtis Prairie, later and more sophisticated prairie restoration also took place at the arboretum, designed and executed by the late Dr. Henry C. Greene, an expert among experts in the seed-bearing plants of Wisconsin and a noted specialist in parasitic fungi. He particularly admired the low prairie vegetation of the Waukesha County sand prairies and therefore obtained permission from arboretum management to begin a long-term prairie restoration experiment.

He began working on a sandy thirty-five-acre site in 1943 and did most of the planting by 1952, continuing into the early 1960s. He had seen the damage that Sperry's unskilled laborers could do by trampling plants or by not placing them properly, so he worked alone; indeed, no one could match his encyclopedic knowledge of prairie vegetation and his ability to recognize them from weeds in all stages of their development.

Greene laboriously collected much of the prairie seed he needed, grew them in flats and, by 1951, had individually placed at least 12,000 mature plants and seedlings where he knew each would do best, skillfully mingling the species together. He also seeded countless thousands of plants directly into the ground to establish over 130 species of prairie grasses and forbs. The result was a magnificently natural-looking prairie, a work of art by a master botanist.

Ray Schulenberg and Professor Robert Betz are two ecologists who have continued prairie restoration and conservation work in the tradition of Greene, Curtis, and Leopold. Schulenberg is curator of Plant Collections for the Morton Arboretum at Lisle, Illinois. In the 1950s he read Curtis's major work, *The Vegetation of Wisconsin*, and in it heard echoes of his own almost lifelong concern for restoring and preserving local flora using local plant stock. After corresponding with Curtis about prairie ecology, Schulenberg visited the Wisconsin arboretum prairies, and they spurred his interest in prairie restoration.

Coming in from the outdoors to his office one day at the arboretum's modern research center at Lisle, Schulenberg sits behind his desk in his white tee-shirt and looks like a Nebraska farmhand. He is muscular, almost husky, and his work-hardened hands have strong fingers and deeply etched palms. His face is tanned, his eyes clear blue, his manner self-effacing, and his cheeks healthy pink. His once sandy hair is now gray. Yet when he speaks, his voice is soft—more like someone of 22 than 63, except when he occasionally gives a word special emphasis by exhaling deeply into it from the diaphragm, the way a Plains Indian might.

Born and raised on a Nebraska farm, Schulenberg still keeps farm hours, and the inside of his modest rented house is spartan, with bare walls and little else besides minimal furnishings and shelf upon shelf of books. He calls this place "my teepee," a fitting abode for a monk or abbot whose monastery was the nearby Morton Arboretum.

Schulenberg rises each morning at four, eats immediately, and studies until nearly 7 A.M. (Over the years he has applied himself to languages, anthropology, drama, history, and religion. His studies of Native American cultures and languages—including Dakota, Navaho, Mandan, Hidatsa, and Potawatomi—have been particularly extensive, but he has also studied Latin, German, Spanish, Chinese, Russian, Finnish, Greek, Czech, and Hebrew.) He then goes to his office and later, with an assistant, does the often backbreaking physical labor of caring for over 2,000 kinds of cultivated woody plants—some 40,000 specimens in all.

Schulenberg grew up during the 1920s and '30s on a remote, low-income farm near Falls City, a small Nebraska town. By his late teens, he had read a lot about nature and American Indians and had developed a strong desire to save nature from destruction. Between 1945 and 1947, he wandered as a lost soul, hitchhiking through each of the forty-eight states then comprising the Union. He "hobnobbed" with the Hopi and the Potawatomi, attended peyote meetings with Plains tribes, but never really felt he belonged with them. Feeling a kinship with Thoreau, however, he borrowed $840 from his father in 1947, bought twenty acres with a shack, and tried living alone in the hills. There, managing frugally on ten dollars a month for all supplies, he practiced subsistence agriculture in a Nebraskan Walden—but with only a well instead of a pond.

When his money was gone, he began working in nurseries. In 1949 he became a museum assistant at the State Historical Society of North Dakota, where he made exhibits of Indian life while intensively studying the local flora, along with linguistics and anthropology. At this juncture, he concluded that it was even more urgent to save plant and animal species from extermination than to save dying Indian cultures, so he decided to get training in horticulture, acquire land, and create a nursery. He wanted to raise the regional native plants and design and reassemble self-maintaining plant communities. He did obtain a B.S. in horticulture from Iowa State, but in 1955, before he could build a landscape nursery, he was offered the job of assistant propagator at the Morton Arboretum, twenty-five miles west of Chicago. Drawn by the arboretum's goal—to maintain a living outdoor collection of all the world's woody plant species that will survive local conditions—he accepted the post.

Next, for seven years, he learned propagation skills and studied the woody plants of the North Temperate Zone in the ar-

boretum's living collection. In 1962 arboretum director Clarence
E. Godshalk asked him to reestablish a prairie community on a
newly acquired tract of arboretum land. These twenty-five acres
presented a tough challenge. Corn had been grown there until
the soil was badly eroded; in some places, no topsoil was left.
The fields were dominated by coarse Eurasian forage plants and
tough, aggressive weeds. The object was to replace this weed
patch with a weedless, self-maintaining community of the prairie
plants native to northern Illinois.

Schulenberg began by hand-collecting most of the original
seed for the prairie in great quantities from prairie remnants
within fifty miles of the arboretum. He was determined not to
use commercial seed that would be genetically different from
native, locally adapted varieties. Most of the prairie relicts where
he collected—along old railroad tracks and on never-plowed, un-
developed land—were destroyed a few years later by development. He cleaned the seeds and stored them cold and damp
during the winter to prepare them for spring germination.
Meanwhile, in preparation for planting them, he kept tilling the
soil repeatedly for about six months to kill as many weeds and
weed seeds as possible.

He used two main methods for planting the new prairie. The
first was to raise seedlings in greenhouse flats in early spring,
then to transplant them one by one into the clean, tilled field
when frost danger was past. This method gave him maximum
control over plant distribution and made it possible to weed with
a hoe. The second method was to broadcast mixed seeds onto the
field, raking and rolling them in, much as in planting a lawn.
This method gave a smoother, more natural-looking prairie, but
allowed less control of species composition, and made weeding
much more tedious. Weeding is the most critical aspect of prairie
restoration, because weeds grow much more rapidly than prairie
plants and can quickly overwhelm a planting.

As expected, the new prairie plants were quickly surrounded
by weeds that had to be removed by hand because the prairie
plants were so close together that machinery could not be used.

Nor could herbicides be employed; the plantings included broad-leafed herbs.

Weeding was done by a team of workers, each person squatting on a plank to avoid trampling the prairie plants. The workers had to recognize all the weed species, which had to be destroyed, and all the prairie species, which were to be left unharmed. They worked with almost surgical precision using linoleum knives and pruning shears, weeding two or three times during the first growing season. After one weeding the second spring, a new planting was usually on its own. By the end of the second growing season, those prairie plants had formed a closed community, not likely to be invaded by weeds if the prairie were burned each spring from then on. Fire is always an essential factor in prairie ecology. Without fire it would be almost impossible to maintain a prairie remnant or to restore a prairie, at least in the upper Midwest. Schulenberg found that late March or early April was the most effective time to burn in northern Illinois for setting back the Eurasian weeds and forage plants and for encouraging the fire-adapted perennial prairie plants.

Today the Morton Arboretum prairie is lush and green in June, a polyphony of flowers through the summer, and a symphony of soft, warm tones in fall as the grasses go to seed and prepare for winter and fire. Under the surface, the soil is turning rich and dark again as it is improved by the legumes and the deep fibrous root systems of the warm-season grasses. "The prairie is building soil just the way it had before the honkies came and plowed it up," Schulenberg said wryly. The land is full of healthy prairie plants, including cream and white wild indigo, rattlesnake master, leadplant, wild hyacinth, yellow coneflower, false sunflower, big bluestem, little bluestem, coreopsis, golden Alexander, shooting star, and perhaps 105 other species Schulenberg introduced. The prairie is used for educational purposes, and serves as a refuge for endangered local plants and insects.

About a year before Schulenberg began restoring the Morton Arboretum prairie, he met Robert Betz, a biology professor at Northeastern Illinois University in Chicago. Betz is a robust, full-bearded man of 61 who likes to wear a short-sleeved white shirt with his khaki pants and cap when plunging into the prairie for a day's work. With the help of Schulenberg and others, Betz initiated and supervised the ongoing prairie restoration at the Fermi National Accelerator Laboratory where he pioneered large-scale prairie restoration techniques. Despite Betz's leadership role, he speaks of restoration as a cooperative effort. "You need a lot of people helping you. I have no illusions that I could do it alone. Don't ever get the idea that one man does it."

He teaches biochemistry, biogeography, ornithology, environmental analysis, and other courses at Northeastern. Though personally modest, he is something of a Renaissance man who holds a bachelor's degree in biology, a master's in bacteriology, and a Ph.D. in biochemistry. He reads six languages, and has also studied Algonkian to learn about the relationship of the Indians to the land's native vegetation.

The son of a Chicago area milkman who delivered milk to the late Mayor Richard Daley of Chicago, Betz was the first person from his district ever to earn a college degree. From an early age, Betz developed an aversion to the city with its dead concrete and asphalt pavements, but he loved the small, weedy neighborhood lots which people then mistakenly called prairie.

Although Betz was delighted by the butterflies, grasshoppers, and wildflowers on these little scraps of land, his childhood was unhappy. Living in the middle of a city in a family with no intellectual interests, Betz just instinctively felt that something was wrong. "I didn't know if I belonged anywhere," he said. "I found solace in nature and animals." It was not until Betz was 37 and already a professor that he learned about prairie.

Dr. Floyd Swink, a plant taxonomist from the Morton Arboretum, was leading a group of students on a field trip in 1960 and Betz, then teaching an ornithology class, decided to go along. "For the first time, I saw a real prairie, and I fell in love with it," Betz said. "Prairie was the thing I was always looking for. . . ." The contrast between what he had in childhood called prairie and the real prairie was a "startling revelation." As soon as he recognized that these were the native plants of the region and that he was seeing what the Indians had seen, he was awed. "You got this feeling," he said, "of something that went back all the way for thousands of years. This was what the real vegetation of Illinois was like, not the thing I had assumed."

Ever since then, Betz has been searching the land for prairie remnants. In so doing, he soon realized that there was little prairie left and that every morsel was in jeopardy. Shortly after seeing that first real prairie, Betz met Ray Schulenberg and a mutually beneficial collaboration began. "Ray not only has the intellect and intelligence, but he has this *fire* that a real prairie person has to have," Betz said.

Betz and Schulenberg discovered their first virgin prairies in old cemeteries where the land was protected by fencing. By experimenting on them, they got their first knowledge of how to manage prairie. Betz found that in some mowed cemetery plots, prairie plants still survived as tiny bonsai. "I began to go there and work and try to take care of them and burn them and pull weeds and so on. Within about two or three years, the prairie came up with a vengeance," Betz said with glee. "The dandelions that had come in when mowed, holy God, the prairie just shoved them out—the dandelions were almost running from the prairie as the prairie came back to reclaim what was theirs. This land is owned by the prairie along with its ally, fire. Just give that prairie half a chance, and the prairie will take it." Betz looked triumphant.

When Betz and Schulenberg discovered that none of the prairie remnants they visited were safe from development, they began trying to save prairies. For Betz this led to more than twenty years of unpaid and spare-time labor on prairie remnants. With some weeding, brush removal, and managed burns, these often degraded relicts could be returned to high-quality prairie. He put in countless hours cutting out blackberry bushes and pulled ragweed from sunup to sundown. "You can't just go to school and read books about prairies. You have to spend time and get dirty and get tired and go home half *dead* working out on the prairies. Ray was the same way. We're partly successful due to the fact that we did this. When you work with these plants, you know every one of them on an intimate basis."

Saving Illinois's Gensburg-Markham Prairie, which has never been plowed or overgrazed, is unquestionably one of Betz's greatest achievements. The prairie at Markham today is similar ecologically to what it was some 8,000 years ago after the recession of the last glaciers.

The Markham preserve is home to rare butterflies like the Aphrodite, to threatened species of orchids, and to rare animals, including the gray fox and a number of fascinating snakes. The prairie also harbors at least 2,000 insect species, including many that are "prairie-linked." Ron Panzer, site manager for Northeastern Illinois University, plans to reintroduce dozens of other insect species that should be part of the prairie community but are already gone. Possibly as many as 200 species of plants can be found here, including Indian puccoon, yellow star grass, bluets, prairie willow, Indian quinine, royal fern, prairie lilies, phlox, shooting stars, Indian paintbrush, and meadow rue.

While at a national prairie conference in 1972, Betz heard from taxonomist Swink that the Morton Arboretum had been approached by Fermi National Accelerator Laboratory (then under construction) to provide the facility some landscaping assistance. Betz's reaction was instantaneous. "You mean to say they're gonna take that thing and plant a lot of biological monstrosities? Why don't they put it back into prairie the way it should be? The soils are all there!" The idea may have had a compelling appeal to Betz, but convincing a national accelerator laboratory run by high-energy physicists that they should not only allow, but actually sponsor, three ecologists with prairie fever to build something as anachronistic as a prairie was another story.

Some months later, Betz, Schulenberg, and the late David Blenz of the Cook County Forest Preserve arranged a meeting with laboratory director Robert Wilson. Betz spoke about prairie, its beauty, and his love for it. It was everyone's heritage in the Middle West, he said, and he talked of its possible scientific and medical value. "Some of these plants may hold a key to solving some of our diseases with their glycosides and alkaloids. They've never really been tested adequately." Betz did not fail to convey his basic motivation for saving prairie: "Ray and I both had this feeling that it was immoral to destroy nature, the thing that gave us birth. To destroy all these animals and plants and the whole community without one whimper was wrong. We were not going to see it go down the drain without a fight!"

The prairie proposal was formally submitted to the lab through the Illinois chapter of the Nature Conservancy and the laboratory granted permission to create a prairie on 650 acres of land right in the center of the laboratory's new proton accelerator ring which is situated in front of the laboratory's main building.

Until that time, prairie had been restored, largely by hand, a few acres at a time. Yet if Betz and Schulenberg worked at that rate, it would have been a hundred years before the Fermi prairie would even have been properly planted. Obviously, a new technology for prairie restoration was needed, and Betz rose to the occasion. He foresaw that the same agricultural equipment that had been used to destroy the prairie could now be used to rebuild it. "This was one of the first times anyone ever actually used agricultural equipment on a large scale to build a prairie," said Betz.

Even with mechanization, the proposed restoration presented enormous problems. Because Betz and Schulenberg insisted on using only locally adapted native prairie seed, they had to organize a major collection program. They therefore mustered over a hundred volunteers who, by 1974, collected about 400 pounds of prairie seed. That seed the following spring was used to plant 8 of the 650 acres at Fermi with forty to fifty different prairie species. After the ground had been repeatedly plowed and disked to get rid of as many weeds as possible, the planting was done with a Nesbit drill (an older piece of agricultural equipment).

At first, said Betz, "The weeds grabbed that land, and we had ragweed towering above the land; we had lamb's-quarters;

we had daisies; we had thistles; we had everything." Betz then gave an informal tour of the project area for state and private-sector conservationists, and he had to get down on his hands and knees to show them the tiny tufts of prairie plants that were just beginning to poke through the soil. Many of the conservationists, said Betz, "just wrote the whole thing off." He knew, however, from over fifteen years of prairie fieldwork that, when getting established, prairie plants grow downward before putting out much above-ground growth. He also knew that the prairie plants, because they had been exposed to the forces of natural selection on the prairie for thousands of years, were far better suited to thrive in the region than nonnative weeds.

"I knew the prairie was working from within, and I said, 'Wait 'til those little ones grow. These weeds don't know what's in store for them.' And sure enough, my God, the second year, all of a sudden these little tiny fellows started to grow, especially the grasses, and within about two to three years the grass got tall and thick; we were able to burn it; and with the fire as an ally, the prairie just rolled over those weeds and cleared 'em all out!" Betz punched the air jubilantly with a clenched fist.

"The next year [1976] we put in seven acres, then nine acres, then we jumped to thirty. Then we jumped to another thirty [in 1979]." During this time he was experimenting continuously with new methods of cultivation. The Nesbit drill was eventually retired for a modified highway salt spreader. After three or four years, Betz and his crew were able to begin collecting seed on their own prairie plot. Despite all the gains, the volunteers on whom the project largely depended for manpower were beginning to become discouraged because of the enormous and seemingly unending labor required. "Why isn't all the seed in?" the volunteers would say after a season of backbreaking toil. And then they'd disappear.

"It looked like the work would never end," said Betz, "and people lost interest and thought it was a failure." But as more and more volunteers defected, Betz's determination did not crumble. "Tony Donaldson worked on this and he and I kept it alive. . . . I told myself: 'We'll *have* that prairie at Fermi if I have to go and push those plants up from the roots!' "

Betz then decided to hold a little reunion to thank all the people who had ever assisted in the project. Way out in the center of the prairie, he gave an informal talk and progress report. "It was in the month of August and the grass stood six to seven feet high with the compass plants blooming. It was a beautiful thing to see. They all began to realize it was going to be a success. And that turned the thing around. They reorganized the committees that had essentially disintegrated, and there was a resurgence forward and it's been moving ever since."

To reduce the human labor required, the project members began harvesting seed by a combine so they could collect seed on 30 or 40 acres instead of just 9. Thus in 1981, they gathered enough seed to plant 90 more acres of prairie, and by 1983 they were planting 120 acres and were collecting 12,000 pounds of prairie seed from their own prairie. More than 300 acres of prairie have already been planted and the project's pace continues to quicken. The Fermilab prairie is now the largest restored prairie in the U.S.

The Fermilab is one of the very few places in the United States today where both wildlife species and habitat restoration are occurring simultaneously. Tough and aggressive Sarus cranes from Asia are already living at the Fermilab in pens to test the pens' integrity before native sandhill cranes are introduced. If raccoons or foxes ever make their way in, the powerful Sarus can defend themselves effectively. They stand about five feet high, and will not hesitate to attack a man by thrusting at his eyes with their strong beaks.

Seven trumpeter swans, a species that once inhabited the Illinois prairie, already have been reintroduced to ponds on the prairie. They have adapted readily to their surroundings and may eventually establish an indigenous flock.

Betz is planning to reintroduce prairie insects at Fermi, especially those without functional wings which might have a hard time returning to the restored prairie. "We're going to actually go and find some of the grasshoppers, the moths, the flies, the what have you—we're gonna have to bring 'em back," Betz says. He also is planning to reintroduce Franklin's ground squirrel, a native prairie dweller, to both the Fermi and Markham prairies. He assumes that many mammals and birds will restock themselves on the prairie.

In the course of his Fermi work, Betz has come to realize that prairie needs to be restored in phases. The first phase of pioneer prairie plants that invades newly disturbed ground is aggressive and competitive. These plants can overcome foreign weeds. Then a second phase of less competitive prairie plants can be interseeded among the first. These could not have survived with the weeds, will not thrive alone on bare soil, but are adapted to grow *with* the other pioneer prairie plants. Each successive phase of the restoration introduces ever more delicate prairie plants. Betz believes that prairie must be long established, with an accumulation of soil fungus (mycorrhizae), bacteria, and natural antibiotics before the more finicky prairie species can move in. "I don't know all the answers," he says, "but we're working on them with our experiments. I may never live to see the last wave go in at Fermi," he said without chagrin.

9

Highway Prairies

The legacy of prairie restoration pioneers from the University of Wisconsin is alive today not only in the work of Schulenberg and Betz, but also in the efforts of others, like landscape architecture professor Darrel G. Morrison and Wisconsin nursery operator Joyce Powers.

Professor Morrison, now at the University of Georgia, is an informal, amiable man in his forties whose face shows the effects of prairie wind and sun. When not teaching, he has restored prairies on industrial sites and has done research on using prairie to reclaim iron ore tailings. Wearing a plaid shirt with orange stripes that looked like a farmer's suspenders, Morrison talked about his prairie work one afternoon in Madison while he was still on the University of Wisconsin faculty; that day his shoes were still wet from a prairie field trip. In 1974, he recalled, he had designed an eighty-acre prairie for General Electric's Medical Systems Division in the Milwaukee suburbs. When he began, the site was still bristling with the stubble of a ryegrass cover crop. Morrison had workers drill grass seed directly into the ground amidst the stubble and then broadcast the forbs. The restoration was mechanized and little hand labor was used following seeding.

Nine years and one burn cycle later, the prairie has eliminated many weeds but still has as many exotic species as natives. Nonetheless, the site is now an attractive expanse of undulating grasses and flowers that bears a strong visual resemblance to prairie. And using prairie instead of lawn here saved General Electric money because the prairie cost only $300–$400 per acre to install versus the $1,000 per acre they paid for a conventional bluegrass lawn nearby. But whereas the lawn requires mowing, watering, fertilization, and weed control, prairie requires nothing but occasional burning. GE's prairie management costs have been less than $5 per acre per year. Park departments around the United States often spend $500 per acre per year to maintain mowed lawn, whereas those with prairie spend less than $50 for managing it, according to Morrison.

Does the prairie look unsightly after a burn? "Immediately, for the first few days, it's blackened," said Morrison, "but if it's burned in April, it's bright green in three weeks."

Morrison advocates using prairie instead of lawn along highway rights-of-way, provided some mowed area is left so motorists can pull off the road. Roadside prairies could be beautiful and would help the prairie region retain its distinctive regional identity. In addition, says Morrison, "the interstate has eight acres of right-of-way for every mile of highway, on average, so when you eliminate mowing, watering, and fertilizer, you cut costs by 80–90 percent. It adds up very quickly." Less labor would be needed for lawn maintenance, but new jobs would be created in propagating prairie plants, in gathering seeds, and in marketing and distributing the plants.

Prairie species may also be valuable in the revegetation of surface mine sites because they can tolerate drought, high temperatures, strong sun and wind, low soil nutrient levels, and relatively high alkalinity. Morrison has planted various prairie grasses and forbs in iron ore tailing deposits of the Jackson County Iron Company at Black River Falls, Wisconsin. The tailings contained essentially no organic matter and surface temperatures on the bare heaps reached 140° F. in summer, but he was able to establish predominantly prairie vegetation there using nitrogen and phosphorus fertilizers. "We've had 90 percent vegetative cover in about a three-year period," said Morrison. "Prairie species produce a really good root network and they have very good cover above ground, which reduces erosion problems, so they're very effective once established. The only drawback is that the establishment period is slower than with some exotic species."

He would like to see parts of public parks in prairie states and some agricultural land returned to prairie. "Certainly in large parks there would often be 10, 20 percent of the site that could be restored to prairie." Morrison recognizes that his desire to return not only pasture but some cropland to prairie is shared by few. But restoring prairie for use as summer pasture for livestock is not so heretical. Some ranchers, particularly in Nebraska, have been doing it for years.

Cattle gain weight when grazed on growing grass. The tall perennial prairie grasses are warm-season grasses that do most of their growing in the summer. By contrast, introduced (cool-season) annual grasses grow most in the spring and fall and are dormant in summer. So cattle grazed on the annuals typically gain weight in the spring and fall but stay about the same, or lose weight, in the summer. Thus the use of reestablished native grasslands for cattle could have economic advantages, as explained by Robert M. Skinner in *Prairie: A Multiple View*:

> For maximum beef production, I believe that ⅓ or more of Missouri's 4,047,000 hectares (10 million acres) of grasslands should be converted to warm season grasses for summer pasture. This means that under proper grazing management the potential exists for creating several million hectares of prime grassland habitat productive of wildlife.
>
> If native grasses are reestablished and managed correctly for long-term sustained production by proper grazing and

fire, then we will obtain again, through management of a natural plant community by natural means, a maximum quantity and quality of all things desirable—birds, beef, and beauty.

Morrison also would like to see prairie plantings used for long-term crop rotation to restore the soil, and he speculates that the farm subsidy program, in which farmers are paid in kind for not planting certain crops, could be modified to encourage prairie restoration. Many people would disagree that it is desirable to take land out of food production to plant prairie, and Morrison himself recognizes "this is contrary to the whole human nature of wanting instant rewards and making the most possible money out of each square foot per year."

Native plants, of course, are not only suitable for industrial, commercial, and public land sites. Rural or suburban residents can plant miniature prairie in their yards, and neighbors with adjoining yards in a subdivision or on a block can remove fences and plant large contiguous areas with prairie. This would provide cover for birds and would help maintain a diverse population of pollinating insects. Morrison, for example, landscaped his family's suburban home in Madison with native plants. The 100-by-150-foot lot has representations of various native Wisconsin plant communities, including dry prairie, dry forest understory, old field, and cedar glade. He raised most of the prairie grasses and forbs from seed. If purchased from Wisconsin prairie plant nurseries, the prairie plants would have cost about $4.50 per square yard in 1982. (One plant costing about $0.50 is used per square foot.)

There are about fifteen prairie nurseries in Wisconsin and northern Illinois, and a number of them, such as Prairie Ridge Nursery in Mt. Horeb, Wisconsin, owe their inception to inspiration or seed gathered from the Curtis or Greene restoration efforts at the University of Wisconsin Arboretum.

Joyce Powers, creator and proprietor of Prairie Ridge, is a

red-haired biologist in her forties with agate eyes. She has been restoring prairie for more than a decade and also consults on the restoration of prairies and other native plant systems, such as wetlands, woodlands, and "edge" communities. Curiously, the story of Prairie Ridge Nursery began in the tropical rain forest of Mexico.

Powers was in Mexico doing research for her master's thesis and visited the tropical rain forest in the state of Chiapas. "I saw it being destroyed before anyone knew what we were losing," she said. "I just drove through days of burned-over land and smoke." Walking from this blackened land into a rain forest was like entering a cathedral. Where the land had just been burned, the torrid sun already had baked the exposed soil to a bricklike consistency, cleaved by ugly fissures. Stepping into the rain forest, Powers experienced a sudden change: The temperature was cool, the humidity pleasant. The first animal Powers saw in the forest was a magnificent Blue Morpho butterfly, six inches of turquoise from wingtip to wingtip, floating through the shade and streams of forest light like a living stained glass window against the ancient trunks of 150-foot-tall mahoganies.

Mexican biologist Miguel Alvarez del Toro of Chiapas drove Powers to visit a favorite remnant forest. They reached the place where the forest should have been and there was nothing left but desolation—a burned and ruined zone that would never regenerate. "I saw this man get out of his car," Powers said, "and he stood and cried. The tears were just pouring down his face."

She returned to the States deeply depressed that she could see no effective way to stop the destruction of the tropical forest. "I really started growing prairie plants as my own therapy," she said, "just to feel that I could do something about this little piece of land I owned." Powers had read Curtis's *Vegetation of Wisconsin* and thus knew that the land on which her house stood had once been prairie. "My goal was really just to put prairie back where it used to be and see what that would have looked like. . . . The system that needed work here was the prairie, 'cause we were in danger of losing it." But Powers also took a course in tropical biology in hopes that if she learned how to restore an ecosystem in Wisconsin, she might someday help restore the rain forest.

As a graduate student at the University of Wisconsin, Powers visited the arboretum's restored prairies, studied Greene's and Curtis's prairie publications, and became friends with naturalists Rosemary Fleming and Jim Zimmerman from the arboretum. The naturalists were troubled that people were going out into the scarce remnant prairies to dig up the nearly extinct native vegetation, in part because few people knew how to grow it or where to buy it. Zimmerman and Fleming suggested that Powers get a nursery license and sell the plants she didn't need. So Powers started Prairie Ridge.

Once she became knowledgeable about prairie plants, she found a most pleasant surprise on her property. On careful examination of her land, she discovered a small prairie remnant that had never been plowed. The prairie was only a tenth of an acre along the ridge of a hill where the soil was shallow; but it proved to be a useful asset as a seed source.

Powers raises all her plants from locally collected native seed. Her neatly planted rows contain hardy well-known prairie species as well as the more delicate plants of the mature prairie. Powers is proud of her pale lavender-and-white shooting stars with flowers shaped like upside-down hanging darts and her pinkish orange columbine and her asters, gentians, and orchids. "Most of the wildflower plants available in this country are dug from the wild," Powers explained. "I have a real ethical problem with that. I think we need to learn to respect systems. Even if we can move a plant successfully, that doesn't give us the right to do it." Although she has hundreds of shooting stars in her woods, they are not dug. Powers painstakingly raises shooting stars from seed for three years in shallow boxes and then transplants them into rows. "A lot of our really lovely flowers are being exterminated by people who love them and are really subsidizing their destruction," she said sadly.

Because of a concern for wildlife, Powers is most interested in working on the re-creation of native ecosystems rather than in landscaping with native plants. She wants to keep "as many different things with us on the planet as we can." Returning people's yards to prairies in developed areas has value, she believes, as a way of giving people an opportunity to experience replicas of whole natural ecosystems. If we could thereby gain a better appreciation of our own interdependence with other living things, Powers contends that we would probably not "tolerate the kinds of things that are being done to our environment."

Prairie Ridge Nursery is not yet able to pay its founder a salary, but the company keeps four employees busy and two Powers children have paid their college expenses by working in it. Meanwhile, Powers offers 125 species of prairie plants and is expanding the nursery in hopes that it will soon become profitable. Her son and a daughter have become excellent botanists, and in addition to the prairies she herself has installed, Powers has provided enough seed for hundreds of acres of prairie statewide. Though she had never done physical work before, she has personally enjoyed the effort and now misses the fact that business commitments keep her away from fieldwork. "It's been really hard work," she says, "but I love every minute of it."

10

The Toxic Temple

Many specialists on toxic waste problems believe that the contamination of groundwater by toxic chemicals is such a grave and intractable problem that it cannot be rectified in our lifetime. No toxic waste sites have been "restored," in the sense in which that word is used in this book. Yet people are struggling to mitigate the effects of toxic water and toxic land. And successful mitigation may eventually make restoration possible. The story of the toxic temple—a case widely represented as an unqualified success in toxic waste management—reveals how hard it is to clean up and control toxic substances. The case concerns the travails of one Michigan community, an internationally known chemical company, and environmental regulators in conflict over how to cope with a major release of toxic wastes.

Summer homes, year-round residences, docks, and a marina cluster around the oak-and-maple-bordered shores of White Lake in Montague, Michigan. This lightly industrialized community of 2,300 people is situated near what once were sites of

Ottawa and Potawatomi villages. Montague's downtown area, in fact, is just yards from an ancient Ottawa burial ground.

In the late eighteenth century, the region was part of John Jacob Astor's fur-trapping and trading empire, but trapping soon gave way to lumbering and sawing. When most of the local timber was cut by the end of the Civil War, steam-powered sawmills along White Lake consumed millions of logs floated down the White River from the extensive clear-cutting operations in western Michigan. Tanneries were built on the lakeshore, too, to use its clean water in tanning leather with ground hemlock bark.

A paved two-lane road called Old Channel Trail now extends along the north side of White Lake and runs over the old Ottawa graveyard connecting the Hooker Chemical and Plastics Corporation plant site with downtown Montague. The community wooed the firm (then called Hooker Electrochemical Company) to its township in the early 1950s. Montague was in economic doldrums and saw a major chemical facility as an important source of jobs and an exciting new source of revenue. For its part, Hooker was attracted to the town by the plentiful high-quality groundwater near the lake and by the presence of subterranean mineral brines, which the company hoped to use in manufacturing chlorine and alkalis.

When Hooker received permission from Michigan's Water Resources Commission in 1952 to use White Lake for disposing of wastes from its planned chlorine and caustic soda facility, local officials and residents strongly favored the new plant, subject to one major condition. Former Montague town supervisor Clare E. Munson spoke at the time for a number of townspeople when he said, "One of the first questions we asked was, 'Would they harm the lake in any way?' and they gave us assurances that they wouldn't. We had confidence that those assurances would be carried out." The permit was granted, the plant was built, and the company quickly went into production.

Thus did Montague's citizens unwittingly begin the process of trading their clean, safe community with its pleasant wooded lake for an expanded tax base, a hundred jobs, and deadly poisons in their air and water. Before the company was through, hundreds of pounds of lethal polychlorinated hydrocarbons would find their way into the soils of Montague and into a sloping aquifer that delivered its toxic burden into White Lake and thence to Lake Michigan.

It was not long before the community's naïve trust was violated. An internal Water Resources Commission memo on September 9, 1955, expressed concern that Hooker was discharging "rather large quantities of brine" to surface pits near the wells and that serious groundwater pollution could result. That same year, J. A. Tardiff, Hooker's Montague works manager, wrote to the commission of company plans to manufacture "some new products" at Montague, and asked for an opportunity to discuss "problems we expect to face as regards waste disposal. . . ."

The new products were to include C-56. C-56 (hexachloro-cyclopentadiene) is a deadly chlorinated hydrocarbon. This pungent yellowish substance is persistent in the environment and is highly toxic: Some occupationally exposed workers had experienced nausea, skin and eye irritation, sore throat, fatigue, and liver malfunctions. In one study, rats exposed to high levels of airborne C-56 for four hours died within two days after showing severe hemorrhaging of lungs and hydrothorax. Their skins were gray or cyanotic, and they had nasal discharges. Guinea pigs, mice, rabbits, and rats exposed to C-56 vapor in another study had breathing irregularities, weight loss, and mucous membrane irritation. Pathological examination revealed degenerative changes in their adrenals, brain, kidneys, and liver.

The Michigan Department of Natural Resources regards C-56 as not only acutely toxic by ingestion, inhalation, or skin absorption, but as carcinogenic and teratogenic (causing birth defects). It is used commercially as a chemical intermediate in making plastics, dyes, fungicides, and pesticides, including the now banned Mirex and Kepone. The U.S. Army reportedly rejected C-56 for use as a nerve gas in World War II because it was too dangerous to be employed as a defensive weapon.

A memo from Hooker dated January 12, 1956, appears in the Water Resources Commission's files entitled "Estimated Composition of Plant Effluent Including Hexachlorocyclopenta-diene." The memo plainly set forth the "estimated maximum effluent from the plant to White Lake. . . ." Six compounds were listed, including carbon tetrachloride, hexachlorobenzene (HCB), hexachlorobutadiene (HCBD), and C-56. Hooker's maximum projected discharges of these substances was based, said Hooker, on study and research the company had done "upon toxic effects of various organic chemicals."

A commission inspector, Chester Harvey, soon had a conference with Hooker about the company's new plans, and in a memo he stated: "Most of the discussion concerned itself with the wastes possible through the production of C-56." That June the commission gave Hooker the permission it wanted to expand its chlor-alkali facilities and to begin C-56 production. In the expanded use permit, the commission stipulated that Hooker's discharges must not "create conditions in the receiving waters toxic to human beings, wild animals . . . or aquatic life. . . ."

By 1961 Hooker was discharging twenty-five times more chloride than its permit allowed. The commission expressed polite concern, but relied on the company's voluntary compliance and good faith. Commission personnel took pains during these years to maintain a cordial relationship. The company, however, salted the lake with millions of pounds of chlorides during the sixties; contrary to its repeated promises to reduce pollution, it actually increased its discharges. By 1969, Hooker was discharging 220,000 pounds of chloride to the lake every day. The previous year, a commission employee who took a "grab sample" of Hooker wastewater reported that it had "a strong chemical odor" and that "a 10 percent concentration was fatal to fish within 15 minutes." Fish tested in 1970 died in a 2-percent solution of Hooker effluent.

During the 1960s and early 1970s, the commission apparently was so preoccupied with the chloride discharges and with water pH that it failed to monitor regularly for the other chlorinated organic pollutants that Hooker had announced it would be discharging. Effluent samples taken by a commission inspector at Hooker in 1961, for instance, revealed that Hooker was discharging 1,369 pounds per day of unnamed "volatile solids." Apparently these were not analyzed further.

Not until 1972, apparently, did the commission begin paying serious attention to Hooker's chlorinated organic waste discharges. That was the year a commission official wrote to Hooker that the commission had found "elevated levels" of PCBs along with highly toxic HCB and HCBD in fish specimens from White Lake. Referring to HCB and HCBD, the official wrote: "Your industry is the most likely source of these materials." As with C-56, long-term exposure to HCB can damage the liver, thyroid, adrenals, and bone marrow. HCBD has a high acute toxicity: "Systemic responses," a commission staff report later stated, "include motor stimulation followed by incoordination, spasms, convulsions, paralysis and death. Gross morphological changes occur in the liver and kidneys."

Once HCB and HCBD were found in Hooker's effluent, rigorous monitoring of the plant's effluent and stiff enforcement action might logically have been expected. But the state continued to be patient with Hooker, despite further damning evidence. In March 1972, the commission found HCB in Hooker's effluent again, but the company claimed it had been collected in a "dirty" container. The commission found even higher levels of both HCB and HCBD in Hooker's discharges that June, and ended a letter informing the company of its findings with a polite request to Hooker for its "comments and plans for corrective program." The company called the sample data "inconclusive" and promised to initiate its own investigation. The commission meanwhile withdrew its claim that Hooker was releasing "PCBs."

While the commission and Hooker shadowboxed, word of Hooker's pollution was spreading, and the county health department's Julian Szten wrote to the commission in August 1972 "that today we have learned from a chemist that Hooker Chemical Co. is discharging Hexachlorocyclopentadiene [C-56] in their waste water." The commission still did not impose fines and abatement orders on the company until after citizens' complaints dragged evidence of Hooker's pollution into the open.

Marion Dawson, now a nursery-school owner and teacher, lived a mile from the Hooker plant for three years during the 1970s. Mrs. Dawson, blond and winsome, was then a young mother raising a preschooler. Periodically, she was bothered by "very strong noxious fumes from the plant that would make your eyes and nose water and make you feel very uncomfortable." Chemical vapors strong enough to turn nearby trees brown and occasionally to defoliate them were wafting off the company property. Some of Mrs. Dawson's neighbors closer to the plant had complained to the company that their trees had been killed. The company paid for a few trees but did not install monitors to measure these airborne chemical releases, analyze them, or warn of their occurrence.

Mary Mahoney, who lived less than a mile from the plant, remembers: "My kids would come in and say, 'Mom, it's those chemical smells again,' and you'd have to get your kids in and get the windows all closed." The smells burned the Mahoneys' sinuses and gave Mrs. Mahoney "a real bad headache." Severe headache is one symptom of C-56 poisoning. Mahoney's concern about the plant grew as her relatives across the street contracted cancer. Father, mother, grandmother, aunt, and the family dog all developed various gastrointestinal forms of the disease. They and Mahoney had drunk water for years from a well that Mahoney later learned was contaminated with Hooker chemicals.

When the fumes came, Marion Dawson and other townsfolk would call the plant to complain. "They always gave you the impression that they thought you were imagining it," Dawson said. Things might have gone on in this vein for a long time had it not been for two frightening events: Dawson was riding her bicycle one day on a public road not far from the plant with her two-year-old son in the back when, at a dip in the road, she found herself engulfed in an invisible cloud of toxic gas. "We were in the middle of it before we had time to stop, and so I just went on through." The vapors were acrid and the little boy's nose and eyes ran as he gasped for breath.

Yet Dawson was still reluctant to make a big public fuss and get into a struggle with Hooker. The plant was by now a major employer in town and had powerful friends. "If I do something," Dawson wondered, "will I be sacrificing my husband's job or my position? Will I be subjecting my child to ridicule?" She decided to be quiet. Then came the second incident: a winter morning when—though the house was tightly closed against the cold—she awoke to find her home full of chemical fumes. "That was the breaking point. I said, 'That's it—we're going to do something and let the cards fall. What they're doing is wrong, and I feel so threatened by it that it's more important than these other considerations.'"

Dawson contacted her fellow citizens, surveyed the complaints of twenty-five families near the plant, held a meeting with about fifty people, and collected petitions asking the state's Department of Natural Resources (DNR), which had absorbed the old Water Resources Commission, to look into their air pollution complaints. In response to the citizens' meeting, the plant manager tried to convince Dawson that what she was smelling was her neighbors' chlorine bleach. He urged her not to follow through on plans to complain to the state's air quality board. Dawson nonetheless presented the citizens' complaints to a meeting of the Michigan Air Pollution Control Commission at Muskegon in May 1976.

Dawson told the commission that nineteen of the twenty-five households she had surveyed within two miles of the plant reported smelling chemical fumes resembling chlorine, or asphalt-like and insecticide-like odors. The residents' most common complaints were breathing difficulty and irritation of nose and eyes, but people were also suffering nausea, headaches, throat irritations, and sleep loss.

At the hearing, a local industrial chemist, James Cousino, said if Hooker were making a substance known as C-56 at its plant, then fumes were a serious matter. (He evidently knew the compound was being made, but spoke hypothetically to avoid antagonizing anyone.) Neither Dawson nor most of the townspeople and officials had ever even heard of C-56, nor did they have any idea of its effects on people and the environment. The

Department of Natural Resources officials at the hearing, said Dawson, "behaved as if" they were unaware that Hooker was making C-56.

After the Air Pollution Control Commission hearing, "The air got better," said Dawson. "The DNR started really cracking on this," and both the agency and the county began taking air samples. The DNR already had fish from White Lake stored in freezers and now decided to analyze them; they found chlorinated hydrocarbons. For the first time findings of Hooker's pollution at Montague received wide publicity. Now DNR subjected Hooker's wastewater to further scrutiny. The results shocked the community and the state: Hooker was discharging up to ten pounds of C-56 into White Lake every day in its wastewater. Aquatic life in the lake was surveyed and the findings were compared to survey records made in the early fifties; the results confirmed that serious widespread pollution had occurred. Many people now assumed that the mollycoddling of Hooker by DNR was over. The DNR and the attorney general's office conferred, and the DNR, in a June 1976 meeting with Hooker, firmly told the company either to prove that its chlorinated hydrocarbon discharges would not harm the environment or eliminate them altogether. Hooker submitted a toxicological literature review that did nothing to allay the DNR's concern, and so they asked Hooker for immediate action to cease its organics discharges.

But instead Hooker signed a consent order with the DNR that year allowing the company to continue contaminating the lake until pollution control equipment could be installed. The following year, 1977, the DNR entered into a general release agreement with Hooker that absolved Hooker of responsibility for damage done to White Lake and to groundwater beneath the plant site: the company got a release from any and all claims, damages, penalties, fines, and causes of action that the statemight later have brought against Hooker in those specific regards. The release did not cover groundwater contamination beyond the plant site. Hooker in return paid the DNR $135,000 for damaging the fishery, although the company did not officially admit any liability. Eager to portray itself as a defender of aquatic life, the company said in the consent decree that it desired its funds to be used to rehabilitate or enhance the fishing in White Lake and to protect the quality of Michigan's aquatic resources.

Attorney A. Winston Dahlstrom of nearby Whitehall appeared before the DNR in March 1977 to argue against granting the release to Hooker on two grounds:

1. DNR had no legal authority to grant releases which would have the effect of preventing the state of Michigan from enforcing its laws in the future against the same violator whose case gave rise to the granting of the release in the first place, and,
2. a release from Michigan to Hooker would be used, rightly or wrongly, by Hooker in the future as a defense against any actions by a private citizen *or* by Michigan seeking damages, restitutions, fines, or injunctive relief against Hooker.

Dahlstrom later commented:

All Occidental Petroleum [Hooker's parent company] wants is the release so it can use it as a legal springboard to protracted litigation when they are inevitably again sued over the continuing problems they created in the first place. [The release] is a company-inspired legal device aimed at protecting private corporations against criminal and civil enforcement actions. . . . It's cheaper for the Oxys and Hookers of the world to hire a high-powered law firm to fight these cases indefinitely than it is to address the environmental problem—which they already know cannot be solved no matter how much money is spent or allocated for that purpose. They plan the legal game right down the line procedurally and they don't give a damn about the merits of the case or the substance of the law. . . . It's by going down the procedural route for years on end that [they win] the case through attrition.

Indeed, when Hooker was sued by the state of Michigan two years later, the company's defense brief asserted that the action was "barred by a general release given by the State of Michigan and the Plaintiffs to the Defendant May 17, 1977."

Nonetheless, having at last been caught polluting the lake and groundwater and faced now with adverse publicity, intensified regulatory scrutiny, and an impending absolute ban on C-56 discharges, Hooker in a tactical move closed the C-56 plant. Predictably, most of the laid-off workers and their families rallied to Hooker's side. But meanwhile, the DNR was at last getting firm: It issued a formal abatement order in 1977 fining Hooker $75,000 for water pollution and ordering it not to discharge any of the C-56–related compounds. The company was also ordered to bring all of its other chemical discharges into compliance with its permit. If deadlines were not met, large fines would be imposed.

By coincidence, the plant's water discharge permit for its chlorine and caustic soda facility came up for renewal in April of that year. The issue posed for Montague was jobs or the environment, and the permit-renewal controversy polarized the community. "It was a big hearing and everybody filled up the high school gym," Marion Dawson said. "You could just cut the tension with a knife. There were still a lot of local people who felt that the company was justified and—a little smell, what the heck—it's the jobs that count." Hooker's Montague plant manager came to the meeting and said the odors were probably due to "pine needle decomposition." Arrayed against the company's economic boosters were those who felt they might be paying with their health or their lives for the company's prosperity. The company, too, had jumped into the battle for public opinion. According to Cathy Trost in *Detroit* magazine and Michael Brown in *Laying Waste*, company representatives responded to the citizen opposition by harassing and intimidating the local newspaper publisher and disgruntled citizens. The company also mounted a newspaper advertising campaign to vindicate itself. A local resident from the plant vicinity complained at the meeting that his well water was so badly contaminated with Hooker chemicals that it nauseated his family to shower in it.

Organized labor from nearby Muskegon supported the company. The commission renewed Hooker's discharge permit, subject to stricter effluent limits, and it required the company to have a hydrogeological study done to delineate its groundwater contamination.

The pollution controversy intensified that summer when Warren Dobson, a conscience-stricken Hooker employee, signed a dramatic affidavit drafted by Dahlstrom, his attorney, attesting to unsafe waste disposal practices at the Hooker plant just as Hooker was seeking DNR approval to restart its C-56 plant. The Dobson affidavit mentioned a secret dumping ground on site and stated:

that [Dobson] participated under instructions from his employer, viz., Hooker Chemical and Plastics Corp (Occidental Petroleum) in the disposal of C-56 wastes by emptying the contents of the so-called "still" . . . into 55 gallon drums which had been opened at the top with an axe; that he witnessed said 55 gallon drums which had been filled with C-56 wastes loaded onto Hooker-owned trucks . . . and hauled to a location on Hooker's land in Montague Township northerly from the plant where, he was informed and believes, said drums filled with toxic C-56 wastes were dumped upon the land; that the contents of said drums leaked onto the surface of the ground where it was permitted to soak into the soil and evaporate into the atmosphere; that deponent is informed and believes that said toxic C-56 wastes have penetrated the soil and have entered the groundwater beneath said premises and have migrated beyond the boundary lines of Occidental Petroleum's premises and have contaminated the water table on adjoining lands.

That he has personally witnessed highly concentrated vapors, containing C-56 and other toxins, escaping from open drums and containers and from the surface of the ground on Hooker's premises into the atmosphere; that he has personally witnessed highly concentrated vapors containing C-56 and other toxins escaping from pipes and drains; . . . that he was instructed by . . . his foreman that in the event residents of the White Lake area should complain about escaping vapors . . . he should act as though he thought the white vapors escaping from said pipe was steam . . . that the escape of C-56 vapors and liquids was permitted . . . repeatedly and frequently during the time deponent was employed by said company as a routine production method.

That in addition to highly toxic C-56 wastes, chlorine gas was frequently and routinely discharged from the smoke stack on Hooker premises; that sometimes the emissions from said stack were green in color—indicating a high concentration of toxic chlorine gas. . . .

That chemical wastes containing high concentrations of C-56 and other dangerous chemicals were dumped onto the ground near the fine chemicals department until all the trees in that particular area died . . . that the area was referred to . . . as the "dead lake"; that no effort was made to prevent said dangerous and toxic chemicals from reaching the groundwater aquifers or from evaporating into the atmosphere. . . .

That . . . high concentrations of C-56 fell onto the floor of the building where the fine chemical department was located and that said leakage went directly into the drain where it emptied into the retention pond . . . and that as a result of such overloaded condition of said pond, high concentrations of C-56 and sulfuric acid, along with other toxic chemicals, were discharged into the water of White Lake. . . .

That he personally witnessed C-56 draining through the floors above him from leaky drains and onto the floor of the operating room where deponent had to work; deponent complained to his foreman about this condition, but his complaints were ignored. . . .

That said company routinely had prior knowledge of inspection visits from the Michigan Department of Natural Resources.

After signing this affidavit and releasing it at a press conference, Dobson fled Montague with his family. One might think that the nature of his charges would have induced the DNR to investigate them with all deliberate speed, but the agency was in no apparent hurry. It was to be six months before the DNR went to the plant to see what Dobson was talking about.

About the same time as Marion Dawson appealed to the state's air pollution board, a memo mentioning C-56 happened to cross the desk of Andrew Hogarth, the DNR's regional water quality administrator. He had never heard of C-56, nor even that Hooker produced it in Montague. He now began asking questions about C-56, and his inquiry eventually led to further evaluation of the company's discharges into the lake. "My experience with the company was that they were always extremely secretive and protective about what was going on," he said. Once when he was at the plant to sample their wastewater discharge, a malfunction occurred and a cloud of white gas escaped. Hogarth began to photograph this, but company employees demanded his film and he relinquished it. Hogarth's studies helped confirm that C-56 and many other related compounds were in Hooker's effluent. The DNR entered an order requiring Hooker to do a groundwater study and to identify their on-site disposal areas.

In the late 1970s and early 1980s, groundwater contamination was beginning to attract nationwide attention. The United States already had about 15,000 uncontrolled hazardous waste sites, and as many as forty states were suspected of having dozens of toxic organic chemicals in their drinking water, according to the President's Council on Environmental Quality. Yet as serious, costly, and widespread as the problems were, little was known about how to clean up contaminated groundwater. Groundwater often moves very slowly—sometimes just a few feet per year—deep below the surface in underground reservoirs or streams known as aquifers. Contamination may thus persist in an aquifer for hundreds of years or more.

When the DNR's Andrew Hogarth rejected one of Hooker's written reports as inadequate because "it didn't define the scope of the [groundwater] problem," he received a phone call from the company telling him that he "better come out and look at it."

A company employee then led him to a remote wooded site at the back of the company property. There he witnessed a "mind-boggling" scene that had been missed during years of routine DNR inspections. The scene was the secret dump that Warren Dobson had revealed six months earlier in his affidavit, and its "discovery" caused a scandal. Hogarth found 20,000 rusting barrels containing C-56 production waste scattered on the ground, lightly covered with ash. The thick syrupy contents of the barrels had been deliberately drained directly onto the sandy soil above the underground stream from which local residents drank. The aquifer discharged into White Lake and thence into Lake Michigan. Hooker had used the site as a dumping ground for fifteen years, until 1972, when it began shipping its C-56 wastes off-site for disposal.

Hooker's prior knowledge about the risks it was taking with residents' water and White Lake while it manufactured a billion pounds of C-56 are a matter of record. The earliest warning dates from 1952, when Hooker was studying the Montague site prior to construction of its facilities. A study done then for the company by Carl A. Bays and Associates pointed out that the sandy site was highly porous and warned Hooker to dispose of its chemical wastes carefully because of its proximity to White Lake and to public drinking-water supplies. An internal company memo three years later stated again that disposal of chemical wastes was a problem on the site. Groundwater contamination with brines was documented in a study by Deep Well Pollution Control Company at Hooker in 1963.

After the Hooker barrel dump was discovered in 1977, the hydrogeological study DNR had required Hooker to obtain was completed. It showed that hundreds of pounds of toxic chlorinated hydrocarbons were flowing into White Lake daily through the groundwater. In addition to C-56, there were about two hundred other chemical compounds in the water which shouldn't have been there. Still, the DNR did not file suit against Hooker until 1979 to recover damages and force a cleanup.

"At Hooker," says Assistant Attorney General Stewart Freeman, "it took the Department of Natural Resources about twenty years to get the evidence together and get over here. The problem was known to the DNR at the levels of the field investigators for about twenty years. It came to our attention as a result of a segment of '60 Minutes,' the TV show." The show Freeman saw dealt with toxic wastes at Love Canal and elsewhere.

The next morning, Freeman discussed the issue of hazardous wastes with Michigan Attorney General Frank J. Kelley and began inquiring whether some of the same types of chemicals that caused problems at Love Canal and in the James River were being made in Michigan. Yes, Freeman learned, the chemicals were being made by Hooker, and DNR field investigations had reported problems. The attorney general's office demanded information from the DNR. In response, the DNR assigned Dr. James Truchan from its environmental enforcement division as investigator. Within several months, the investigation led to the filing of a lawsuit by Kelley against Hooker. "This rapidly became one of the most complex pieces of environmental litigation ever brought in an American court," said Freeman. The state soon was embroiled in ascertaining where responsibility lay within Hooker, Occidental Petroleum, and the DNR. This could have started the legal war of attrition referred to by attorney Dahlstrom. The company could afford to retain a large staff of high-priced lawyers to tie the suit up in court for years and exhaust their adversaries. Hooker's immense financial resources would naturally stack the deck in its favor. The multinational firm produces more than a hundred chemical products and is a subsidiary of the multibillion-dollar Occidental Petroleum Company.

The attorney general's office, which had recommended granting Hooker its general release, now found it expedient to reach an out-of-court settlement. The DNR outlined the state's cleanup demands and technical performance standards for the attorney general with the help of the hydrogeological study required earlier. Final details were negotiated in the New York apartment of the well-known trial lawyer Louis Nizer, counsel to Armand Hammer, chairman of Occidental Petroleum. Periodically during the negotiations, Nizer would phone Hammer directly to obtain approval for specific provisions of the agreement.

Like the barrel discovery, the Hooker settlement in the fall of 1979 made headlines and set a constructive precedent for the later settlement of other complex environmental pollution cases. According to records of the state circuit court of Ingham County, the consent judgment constituted "a full restorative program for eliminating any threat to the lands and waters of [Michigan]." The attorney general called it "one of the largest chemical waste remedial programs ever." Hooker agreed to construct an impermeable clay vault to contain and isolate almost a million cubic yards of toxic chemical waste forever. The ten-foot-thick clay walls—double the federal requirements—were to be compacted so tightly that moisture could travel through them at no more than a ten-millionth of a centimeter per second. At that rate it would take a molecule of water at least a hundred years to pass into or out of the vault.

The vault was to be built at least eight feet above the highest point ever reached by the water table and was to be equipped with "internal leachate collection systems." Thus any moisture draining from the wastes within the vault would be collected inside it and safely piped out to a purification plant before discharge. The vault would also have an internal venting system so that if gas pressures ever built up inside due to chemical reactions, the pressures would be relieved by filtering the gas before it reached the external environment.

The agreement called for the construction of a groundwater collection and purge well system to remove toxic substances from the groundwater by activated carbon filters operating twenty-four hours a day "under court supervision for however long it takes to clean up the aquifer." The agreement carried with it a two-million-dollar guarantee by Occidental Petroleum Company and required the payment of a million dollars by Hooker to the state of Michigan, to settle the state's claims for fines, penalties, and damages and to reimburse the state for its costs. A restrictive covenant was attached to the deed for the Hooker site to prevent its transfer to different owners or users without state approval.

Assistant Attorney General Freeman refers to the agreement as one of "the ten most important environmental settlements of recent times." The case, he said, is used in legal education courses. "We've got a complete cleanup. And as far as we know, no human health involvement."

Dr. Howard Tanner, who was director of the Michigan Department of Natural Resources when the settlement was made, called it "the most technically comprehensive program ever developed to solve a toxic waste disposal problem. . . . No shortcuts or compromises of environmental or public health protection were taken by the parties." Tanner expressed state officials' satisfaction when he said, "We have a total package that not only permanently contains the wastes but also stops any subsurface migration of chemicals into White Lake." As future events were to demonstrate, these laudable goals were easier to announce than to achieve.

Today the lightly grassed sloping walls of a massive, engineered clay burial vault rise abruptly from a sandy flat about a quarter mile from scenic White Lake in Montague Township. Two permanent granite markers stand sentinel, inscribed with the words, "Hexachlorocyclopentadiene production wastes. . . ." Still closer to the vault is a metal fence with yellow signs that read: Warning, toxic material burial area. Keep out.

Shaped like a tan pyramid with its top sliced off parallel to the ground, the forbidding earthen structure has no doors or windows and rests upon a square base 800 feet on a side—the area of thirteen football fields. As provided in the consent agreement, Hooker not only built this vault as specified, but also dismantled the C-56 production facility and buried it in the vault along with all the soil beneath the facility to the depth of the water table. The areas beneath the facility and beneath the waste barrel dump were major sources of the groundwater contamination by C-56. Hooker spent fifteen million dollars on loading and building the vault and paid the one million dollars which the state of Michigan had demanded.

The Hooker agreement looked good on paper and the towering pyramid several stories high certainly seemed solid and unbreachable. But knowledgeable observers wondered how well the containment technology would work and how rigorously the attorney general, the DNR, and the circuit court would enforce the agreement.

One of the first people to smell a problem was Hooker's old antagonist, Winston Dahlstrom. He was riding a bicycle south of the Hooker plant one summer day in 1982 with a local doctor when both men "detected the highly pungent odor of C-56 in the air. That toxin was coming from Hooker's waste dump," said Dahlstrom. "When one can smell C-56 in the air," he added, "the concentration is already thirty times above the threshold limit value. We were five miles away, and the smell was heavy. . . ."

About 100,000 cubic yards of C-56–contaminated soil from a buffer area around the waste disposal site was belatedly "discovered" after the Hooker vault was already too full to accommodate it, and that soil is now the subject of a dispute between Hooker and the state. "Hooker quietly allowed [the vault] to be closed and capped off knowing full well that there was a hell of a lot of C-56 contamination still out there poisoning the community," Dahlstrom charged. "It is incredible to believe they wouldn't know about it, since it was on their land right near the location of their former C-56 'fine chem' building."

Dahlstrom has tried to get the Circuit Court of Ingham County and the attorney general to force Hooker to enlarge its vault, but Judge Michael G. Harrison—who had pledged to intervene aggressively to uphold the consent order between Hooker and the state—was now reluctant to act: "The Court," wrote a member of Harrison's staff, "does not have adequate staff or resources to investigate complaints concerning Defendant Hooker Chemical, nor is that the Court's proper role; that is the role and responsibility of the Plaintiffs in this case, the At-

torney General and the Department of Natural Resources." As
of April 1985, however, the attorney general's office had still not
filed a motion for enforcement of the consent order, although the
DNR had requested action. Members of the state's environmental enforcement division currently are insisting that Hooker en-
capsulate the remaining contaminated soil, even if it means
building an expensive annex to the vault.

Almost four years after the settlement, a visit to the Hooker
site revealed that indeed, despite significant accomplishments,
more work still remained to be done. James Kolanek of Hooker
Chemical supervises the day-to-day monitoring of the Hooker
vault and groundwater purging system. He holds a bachelor's
degree in chemistry with training in industrial hygiene, and
maintains his headquarters on site in a laboratory-equipped
trailer. The company, said Kolanek, took all material that "we
thought was significant. . . . Our position is that the purge well
system will handle what was left" when it reaches the groundwater.

A radio transmitter is mounted near the vault's leachate collection system to automatically sound an alarm if any of the
leachate pumps or filters fail. Monitoring wells downhill from
the facility are used to warn of any leakage from the vault. The
system was collecting four or five gallons of leachate per minute
for storage and subsequent treatment in the summer of 1983.
The treated water is then discharged into White Lake, and Kolanek says that water meets or exceeds federal clean water guidelines. "I have no qualms about eating the native fish" from White
Lake now, he said.

The site's purge well system for cleaning up the groundwater
taps directly into the contaminated aquifer and creates a "cone of
depression" or suction area designed to collect all the groundwater passing through the aquifer to the lake. Kolanek explained
how the contaminated water is piped into a separate building
where it is fed into tanks, each containing 20,000 pounds of activated charcoal. But during that summer of 1983, the groundwater purge well and filtration system did not operate for at least a

month and contaminated water flowed unimpeded into White Lake while the purging system was being tested for effectiveness.

Although Kolanek discussed the site and its cleanup technology in great detail, he never mentioned that Hooker and DNR are in conflict over the system's performance. However, William Iverson, chief of remedial design in the DNR's Groundwater Quality Division, said that even when operating, the Hooker purge wells were capturing only about 50 percent of the contaminated groundwater. At DNR's request, Hooker since then has doubled its groundwater pumping, but the DNR's calculations indicate that the system is now getting only 60 percent. And Hooker officials have not agreed to enlarge their vault.

The ongoing dispute in what many people regard as a model remedial program illustrates the expense and difficulties that a comprehensive cleanup of toxic substances presents once poisonous chemicals have escaped into the environment. Until the toxins are cleaned up and contained, little thought can be given to revegetating or to reintroducing native fauna.

Dahlstrom does not see the Hooker cleanup as an encouraging development:

I have heard naïve people say that Michigan has taken a large step in the right direction by suing Hooker and actually getting a consent judgment, but I am not impressed by "steps" in the right direction if the steps don't continue until the end is achieved. I suppose it can be said that a surgeon takes a step in the right direction when he surgically removes diseased tissue from an ailing patient, but if that surgeon walks out of the operating room leaving diseased tissue remaining in the patient and without closing the wound or making proper arrangements for post-operative supervision, the "step in the right direction" becomes a horrible joke. It looks to me as though that is what is now happening. . . . The purge wells are not effectively keeping the poison out of White Lake and Lake Michigan, and now we have 100,000 cubic yards of additional highly dangerous poison on our hands which Hooker obviously has no intention of taking care of without vigorous intervention.

Whether the Hooker cleanup will be completed expeditiously or at all is as yet unclear. All that can be said with certainty is that five years of very costly and complex cleanup work have not fully cleansed either the soil, the groundwater, or White Lake. Hundreds of millions if not billions of gallons of groundwater still remain to be treated to remove compounds like carbon tetrachloride, chloroform, trichloroethylene, and C-56.

Though the cleanup technologies used at the Hooker site still leave much to be desired, they nonetheless represented recent state-of-the-art treatment for widespread land and water contamination. Unfortunately, secure landfills like Hooker's vault are no panacea for coping with the nation's toxic waste problems. Secure storage areas consume scarce land, cost a great deal of money, require perpetual care, and could be gradually breached by slow degradation over very long time spans, or ruptured by catastrophic earthquake, or by engineering miscalculation that allowed stored chemical waste to crack the vault's clay walls. Land-based disposal of chemical wastes should be avoided wherever possible, because landfills ultimately leak and release wastes. In Dahlstrom's words, "To the best of my knowledge, there is not one single example of such a vault in the world today which has not leaked sooner or later—and usually more sooner than later."

Solutions to toxic waste problems must be site-specific. In the Hooker case, because large volumes of soil were contaminated, the incineration or chemical treatment technologies that might be preferable in other situations were not realistic options in Montague. The Hooker case does illustrate that waste encapsulation and groundwater purging, if done correctly, can help cope with badly polluted toxic waste sites once a Pandora's box of contaminants has been opened and the well-nigh impossible task of closing it is attempted. The Hooker case also attests to the need for far, far tougher environmental regulation of chemical polluters and for citizens to take an active, organized role in prodding environment regulators to enforce the laws.

"What would the DNR have done regarding Hooker had the citizens not complained about air and water pollution and had the attorney general not requested state action from DNR?" Dr. James Truchan of DNR was asked recently. He replied succinctly, "Probably nothing."

"Without the citizen complaints," DNR enforcement chief Jack Bails acknowledged, "the Hooker issue may have lingered a very long time and the consequences would have been much more severe. But DNR's failure to react sooner was not due to incompetence. It was our naiveté towards industry and, initially, our incomplete understanding of toxic waste hazards. The most positive thing here is that citizens can get legitimate environmental concerns resolved. When citizens tell us we're not doing our job well and the facts support them, we'll take action." So Montague-area citizens may have to renew their complaints and political action before the Hooker cleanup will be completed.

Many people would like to forget that toxic chemicals were ever found in fish from White Lake or that the whole Hooker fiasco ever happened. Marion Dawson, for example, has moved farther away from the plant, and she is devoting her time to running a nursery school rather than to health politics. Mary Mahoney still lives by the plant on Old Channel Trail and continues to hope that all the poison near her home will finally be cleaned up. Those who promote tourism to Montague would also like to be able to forget the Hooker problem: The company's toxic temple does not appear in local tourist brochures. At a roadside rest stop east of nearby Muskegon, Michigan, a poster for tourists reads, "Experience Muskegon County, Fishing Capital of the Midwest." The ad describes White Lake as a "beautiful inland lake off Lake Michigan" with "sport fishing, public boat launching, and lakeside dining facilities. . . ." Below that is a color photo of two trout on a stringer entitled "Typical catch from White Lake. . . ." No mention is made, of course, of what those fish have been swimming in or the extra chemical baggage they may bring to the dinner table.

. . .

It would be comforting if Montague's appalling experience with Hooker's wastes were an anomaly. But evidence is accumulating today that that experience is probably just a harbinger of numerous difficulties to come for many other U.S. communities which in good faith loaned their resources to chemical companies or to other firms using hazardous compounds. The difference between Montague and the other problem areas is that at Montague the process of making amends is under way.

III

WILDLIFE
RENEWED

11

Falcon Fervor

Kurt Stolzenburg and Merlyn Felton clung to a two-and-a-half-foot-wide ledge on the sheer granite cliff 2,500 feet above Yosemite's Hetch Hetchy Reservoir, uncertain how to reach the peregrine falcon aerie a dozen feet above them. A quarter-mile away along the cliff, a roaring stream swollen with snowmelt charged down the mountain over masses of sun-baked granite and plunged off the heights to the valley below in a brilliant arc. The peregrines had chosen their mountain fortress well: The vertical rock face beneath them offered no handholds.

A fresh spring breeze was blowing. Stolzenburg gazed somberly up at the smooth rock wall. Felton waited. Their climbing rope was of no help here. Suddenly, two furious adult peregrines defending their young swooped toward them from the sky far above with piercing screams. The men ducked, covering their heads. The birds veered away at the last instant to avoid striking them.

Recovering and closing his mind to distraction, Felton planted his feet firmly on the ledge, and squatted with his back flattened against the cliff. Fine mist blowing from the waterfall made little rainbows over thousands of feet of space. Stolzenburg gingerly climbed onto Felton's shoulders. Felton rose in slow motion to a full standing position. Stolzenburg straightened up slowly from a crouch and carefully reached toward the aerie ledge above. Seizing it with outstretched arms, he suddenly projected all his strength into his arms and hands, catapulting his upper body up above his wrists onto the ledge. With a breath of relief, he turned and pounded in a ring eyelet anchor to tie himself in and helped Felton up.

Three young peregrines there were now in a panic, and one ran to the edge. Too young to fly, it cowered inches from death. Yet it had no real reason to panic. Stolzenburg and Felton are with the Santa Cruz Predatory Bird Research Group (SCPBRG), an organization helping peregrines recover from near-extinction. After quickly banding two peregrine chicks, the men left the third terrorized chick alone.

On another occasion the two climbers landed by helicopter on the cliff tops above Crater Lake in Oregon, site of the state's only remaining active peregrine aerie. (Oregon once had thirty-nine active peregrine aeries; today, there is only one, and the pair occupying it have been unable to raise young unassisted.) They rappeled 150 feet down a cliff, surmounting a 25-foot overhang to reach the peregrine aerie.

In the aerie were four brown speckled American peregrine falcon eggs (*Falco peregrinus anatum*) badly contaminated by pesticide residues. Once found throughout most of the forty-eight contiguous United States and deep into Mexico, the *anatum* subspecies was in trouble. If left here with their mother brooding them, the eggs would soon crack, dehydrate, and die.

Stolzenburg and Felton carefully transferred the sensitive, thin-shelled eggs to a specially designed insulated carrying case and left a plastic set of imitation peregrine eggs before departing quickly. The adult birds continued to soar around the cliff for a long time after the climbers left before finally returning to their "scrape"—a hollow in the earth. (Peregrines do not build nests.) Guided by instinct, the female peregrine then began brooding the dummy egg clutch. Stolzenburg and Felton later would return with her chicks—safely hatched in a Santa Cruz, California, incubator and ready for her to raise. Hatching under optimal conditions increases the eggs' chances of survival. The artificial eggs left behind stimulate the birds' brooding behavior and keep them hormonally receptive to the returned chicks they must nurture.

Cliff-hanging approaches to aeries in California, Oregon, and Washington are all in a day's work for Stolzenburg and Felton, who frequently risk their lives to assist the peregrine in its struggle for survival. The peregrine project they are with is assisting the American peregrine falcon population on the West Coast as part of The Peregrine Fund, a national organization based in Ithaca, New York. The Santa Cruz project works with peregrines and other raptors (birds of prey) in captivity and in the wild. Its program affects all stages of the birds' life cycle— courtship, mating, egg laying, brooding, hatching, fledging, and maturation.

Three subspecies of peregrines exist in North America: the tundra peregrine, Peale's peregrine, and the *anatum*. Tundra peregrines (*Falco peregrinus tundrius*) inhabit the Arctic and Alaska and migrate to Central and South America. Peale's peregrine (*F. peregrinus pealei*) is found in a nonmigratory population on the Queen Charlotte Islands and elsewhere in the Pacific maritime zone off the British Columbia coast. The *anatum* or American peregrine falcon (*F. peregrinus anatum*) is found in the western U.S. A distinctively different subpopulation of this same subspecies once existed throughout the eastern U.S., but that subgroup became extinct in about 1960.

Peregrines have a superb aerodynamic design, telescopic eyesight, and a magnetic presence that commands respect. These two-and-a-half-pound feathered missiles with a bluish-gray back and barred undersides can dive on prey from thousands of feet above at more than 220 miles an hour. The bird's body actually whistles like an artillery shell as it streaks down from the sky. Like stunt pilots, peregrines can execute a long series of spellbinding loop-the-loops, rolls, and sudden dives. The bird uses its stupendous flying ability to court and to hunt, generally stunning its prey by striking it with great force at high speed. Peregrines kill more than two hundred other bird species—even some that are three to four times larger than itself. They use several modes of attack, including flying underneath prey and rolling upside down suddenly to snatch it in midair. Usually peregrines administer a quick *coup de grâce* by biting prey on the back of the neck with a notched beak specially adapted for severing or disjointing cervical vertebrae. The killing is usually all over in five seconds or less.

But peregrines are more than hunters. They form a lifelong pair bond, faithfully returning over thousands of miles to their mates and to natal cliffs where they raise young with extreme devotion. The name *peregrine* is from the Latin verb *peregrinari*, to travel in foreign lands, from the Latin *peregrinus*, meaning foreigner. The peregrine is not only a wanderer, it is the world's most widely distributed bird, found on every continent except Antarctica.

The bird's remarkable speed, agility, complex hunting behavior, dramatic courtship displays, great stamina in migration, and regal dignity have made it a source of fascination to humans for thousands of years. But falcons and other raptors mysteriously began disappearing from their native aeries in the late 1940s on both the European and North American continents. Biologists and ornithologists who began studying the birds in the 1950s to solve the enigma soon noticed an abnormally high loss of peregrine eggs during incubation in the wild. They also saw abnormal behavior: Some adult peregrines were eating their own eggs.

Whereas many U.S. observers had noticed that peregrines in their localities were failing to rear young, people were slow to realize how serious and widespread was the bird's plight. Some peregrines still occupied their native territories in the United States and peregrines from other regions still passed through these territories on their way elsewhere. To the casual observer, the peregrine population did not seem to be in crisis. But in fact it was in grave danger. "What is surprising—indeed shocking," wrote David Zimmerman in *To Save a Bird in Peril,* "is that fifteen years would pass during which breeding peregrines would practically vanish in the United States, outside of Alaska, before the correct explanation first was advanced authoritatively and an alarm was sounded by ornithological experts. Perhaps," Zimmerman said, "as with every disaster, natural or man-made, no one believed it would happen." By the mid-1960s, the birds were 90 percent extinct in some northern European countries and in the western United States. East of the Mississippi, where there had once been nearly 200 nest sites, not a single breeding pair remained. Some northern and northwestern maritime populations in the United States and Canada remained viable, but Soviet and even Japanese peregrine populations were also vanishing. Whatever force was wiping out the birds had arisen suddenly and was affecting wild falcons everywhere.

As early as 1962, British researcher Derek Ratcliffe of the Nature Conservancy had found high levels of chlorinated hydrocarbon pesticide residues in peregrine eggs and had voiced his strong suspicion that the species' decline was somehow connected to those residues. But what *was* the connection? The peregrine's sudden disappearance coincided exactly with the widespread use of two chlorinated hydrocarbon pesticides in agriculture: DDT and dieldrin. But neither Ratcliffe nor anyone else knew of a mechanism to connect pesticide exposure with the birds' reproductive failure. Thus the scientific community generally greeted his hypothesis with reserve, refusing to be convinced unless the mechanism could be explained and reproductive failure could be demonstrated under controlled laboratory conditions.

The mystery went unsolved and Ratcliffe remained curious. Then about 1967, while handling some recently collected peregrine eggshells, he noticed that they felt unusually thin and weak. In a simple scientific study, he weighed and carefully measured peregrine eggshells preserved in museums and private egg collections from 1900 to 1967. He found that, starting in the

late 1940s, a rapid decline in shell thickness perfectly corre-
sponded to the start of massive worldwide applications of DDT
and dieldrin in agriculture.

The findings were confirmed in North America by others.
Professor Tom J. Cade, a Cornell University biologist studying
the eggs of Alaskan peregrines, found a direct correlation between the amounts of DDE—a breakdown product of DDT—in
the egg and shell thickness. Cade also observed that many peregrine nestlings had died of starvation or exposure from lack of
parental care, as though the parents' hormonally mediated
brooding behavior was not being properly activated. These results were soon replicated under controlled conditions in laboratory experiments. Skeptical scientists now became believers.

Further scientific studies established that DDE stimulates
the production of an enzyme that inhibits the bird's estrogen
production, which, in turn, governs the transfer of calcium from
storage in the bird's bones to the shells of its eggs. Studies also
revealed that peregrines are much more sensitive to chlorinated
hydrocarbons than ducks, doves, and various other species. As a
predator, the peregrine absorbs trace quantities of pesticides
from its prey; the pesticides then accumulate in the peregrine's
fatty tissues. As little as 1 to 3 parts per million (wet weight) of
DDE in the peregrine's diet will thin its eggshells by 15–20 percent. That is enough to cause reproductive failure: The thin-
shelled eggs break under the brooding mother's weight. The
bird's response sometimes is to eat the broken egg; the egg's met-
abolic energy can thus be reused by the mother in another try at
reproduction.

Many people who knew of the peregrine's plight in the 1960s
were afraid that the bird would soon become extinct throughout
the entire United States. DDE is persistent in the environment,
and it looked as if the peregrine would be gone before the DDE.
Not even a vestige of the species would have remained in zoos
because the peregrine had rarely bred in captivity. Americans
faced the prospect of watching helplessly as the last generation
of wild peregrines in the continental United States disappeared.

Undeterred by the peregrines' long-standing refusal to breed in captivity, biology professor and falconer Heinz Meng in 1964 began breeding experiments with peregrines in New York State. The story of his extraordinary work is well told in *Peregrines Return*, by Meng and John Kaufmann. For six years Meng was unable to get the birds to reproduce. Professor Cade at Cornell in 1970 decided to put the resources of Cornell's Laboratory of Ornithology and its Division of Biological Sciences to work on the problem. He persuaded the division to allocate funds for a breeding barn in which he could develop captive breeding techniques for peregrines and other endangered raptors. He wanted nothing less than to restock peregrines on their native range. Lots of people doubted that the wild sensitive creatures could be reliably bred in captivity at all, much less on a large enough scale to have a significant impact on their huge native range again. The peregrine was a lost cause for them. But working in New Paltz, New York, Meng finally succeeded in breeding peregrines in captivity in 1971. Cade that same year bred related predators— hawks and prairie falcons—in his new Cornell breeding barn; he had no success with peregrines. Meng then gave Cade his breeding pair in 1972 and, by 1973, Cade and falcon expert James D. Weaver had raised twenty young peregrines.

Despite this promising start, many people remained doubtful that Cade would succeed. First, he was working mainly with Peale's peregrine and the tundra peregrine. No one even knew if birds raised in captivity could be successfully returned to the wild, or if the nonnative subspecies would adapt to the Eastern *anatum*'s range. If so, would these foreigners establish territories in the eastern United States and then return to breed? The tundra peregrine in particular is genetically programmed for life in the Far North. Even Cade feared that these birds after migrating south would overfly the United States for the Arctic.

To garner funds for a restocking program, Cade in 1974 set up The Peregrine Fund, Inc., a nonprofit group. His restoration strategy was to be a combination of captive breeding, restocking, and manipulation of the remaining wild stock. He wanted to take the wild birds' doomed thin-shelled eggs from wild aeries, hatch them successfully in incubators, and return the young to their parents, to other peregrines, and even to the nests of prairie falcon foster parents for rearing.

Cade soon put the project's first young produced in captivity into the aerie of a wild peregrine pair in Colorado, and he reintroduced other young to the wild by hacking—an ancient falconry technique he adapted for turning birds loose without parents under controlled conditions. He also negotiated a cooperative agreement with the Colorado Division of Wildlife to build a peregrine breeding facility at Fort Collins, Colorado, so as to restock the Rocky Mountain states with peregrines. This facility has since been relocated to The Peregrine Fund's new World Center for Birds of Prey near Boise, Idaho.

Using eggs from the wild and from the few captive breeding pairs, the fund released sixteen young peregrines to the wilds in New York, New Jersey, Maryland, and Massachusetts during 1975. Two of the young, lacking parental protection, were immediately killed by great horned owls, but most grew to adulthood as wild birds. Much to the breeders' delight, five returned the next year to the vicinity of their release sites.

While falconers and ornithologists were working to save the peregrine in the East and in the Rocky Mountain states, Westerners, too, went into action to help save the Western race of peregrines. James C. Roush II is a Santa Cruz veterinary surgeon and falconer noted for his skillful surgical repairs on wounded eagles and falcons. He was deeply distressed by the disappearance of peregrines from the wild, and when he heard about Meng and Cade's work about 1972, Roush concluded that if it were possible to breed falcons in captivity in the East, "we'd better look at the idea of doing it on the Pacific Coast." Western peregrine populations at the time were down to only 10 percent of their historic numbers.

Roush began by proposing a peregrine restoration program at the University of California's Santa Cruz (UCSC) campus, but the plan quickly ran into stiff academic opposition. Professor Kenneth Thimann, a developer of the herbicides 2,4-D and 2,4,5-T, was the main opponent. The university should be exclusively for basic research, he contended. The peregrine project was merely wildlife management. Pesticides were not a major cause of the peregrine's decline. UCSC marine biologist Kenneth Norris, however, lobbied the biology studies board for the project, and thanks largely to his support, Roush was able to convince the university that the project offered genuine opportunities for behavioral research and field biology. Thus the project became a university organized research group, and the school made land available in an abandoned limestone quarry to house the project.

In his spare time, Roush and student volunteers erected a simple plywood building there for a "falcon factory" in which to breed falcons and rear young. Its rooms opened onto a long hall, each chamber equipped with perches and nesting platforms beneath a lattice of wood slats open to the sky. As the facilities took shape, Roush sought money and breeding stock, but both the state and federal government initially refused collection permits and the university did not provide any funds to the project. At first, only bird clubs, individuals, and a hunting organization donated to it. "[Money] came in very small bits and pieces for a very long time," said Roush. Two years of hard work and constant struggle now passed. Foundation money gradually began to trickle in.

About this time, Brian Walton, a young field biologist known for his work on raptors, took over the project leadership. But funds, a support staff, a proper facility, and governmental cooperation all still were lacking. For the first eighteen months, Cheryl Walton supported the couple on her salary as a biologist at Stauffer Chemical Company. Brian Walton soon realized that to get the state's permission to work with endangered peregrines, he would have to prove his proposed peregrine management techniques on prairie falcons (*Falco mexicanus*). They are biologically similar to peregrines but much more common. Thus, while trying to raise funds, promote the project, coordinate volunteers, and physically construct buildings, Walton also had to conduct a prairie falcon field biology program.

For their trials, Walton and Carl Thelander, another raptor specialist, took the eggs of a wild prairie falcon pair in central

California. After hatching them and raising the young in captivity, they returned them to the aerie and the hatchlings fledged successfully, meaning they learned to fly well enough to leave the aerie, living and hunting independently without their parents. That same year (1976) the California Department of Fish and Game gave the Santa Cruz group two young prairie falcons for breeding purposes, and by 1978 the project succeeded in breeding them in captivity. Climbers placed young bred in captivity in wild prairie falcon aeries and the foster parents fledged all of their adopted offspring successfully. Then the project began raising Harris's hawks, a bird that was already extinct in California. Walton began releasing them in substantial numbers in habitat along the Colorado River restored under Bureau of Land Management auspices. Eventually he returned more than fifty hawks to the wild.

Based on the prairie falcon work, in 1977 the department granted the project permission to take a small number of peregrine eggs from the wild and to keep ten of the adults raised between 1978 and 1980.

The Waltons, however, were exhausting their personal savings while struggling to keep up the project's momentum. Their modest two-bedroom rented house was filled with incubators and other bird hatchery equipment. Spare floor space had become a falcon nursery. In addition to normal project management tasks, a myriad of bird husbandry chores fell to the Waltons. Eggs had to be watched and weighed to ensure they were kept at the proper temperature and humidity. Their growth had to be monitored by candling—holding the egg up to a light—and the eggs had to be turned frequently to prevent the embryo from attaching to the shell. During the breeding season, bird rearing became a twenty-four-hour-a-day occupation. And once the eggs hatched, the Waltons had to ensure the birds' parents were caring for their young properly. Untended hatchlings had to be fed with fresh minced quail and chicken. Whatever could be spared from Cheryl's salary went to pay for construction of the project's campus facility.

As more and more peregrine eggs were hatched by the

project, the prairie falcons came in handy. When the small over-worked staff found it physically impossible to feed all the young birds themselves, peregrine chicks were entrusted to the care of prairie falcon foster mothers. Each can tend as many as twenty or thirty chicks in a breeding season. The prairie falcons stuffed the young peregrines diligently and the young peregrines grew strong and healthy.

The project passed a major milestone in 1978 with the arrival from the Fort Collins Peregrine Fund station of some young peregrines for breeding stock. "When they arrived, there was a good, good, good feeling," said James Roush. "Here was the future of the species on our coast! That was a very thrilling time."

As the months went by, the "chup, chup, chup" of the young adult peregrines could be heard in the Santa Cruz falcon factory. The Waltons and others had high hopes that from these maturing youngsters, eventually a West Coast peregrine renaissance would begin. Historically, 200–300 pairs of peregrines had resided in California. The Santa Cruz peregrine recovery team wanted nothing less than the return of 150 pairs of peregrines throughout the Pacific states. But because of their pesticide contamination, the wild peregrine eggs the staff collected often arrived in Santa Cruz for hatching in poor condition with thin weak shells and occasional pits, cracks, and small holes. Brian Walton became an expert at sanding, gluing, and waxing the living eggs to keep them from dehydrating.

"The eggs must be kept at precisely the right temperature and humidity as a mother falcon would keep them, so that on the day of hatching, they have lost just 15 percent of their weight in water and gas to the environment through their shells," Walton said. The mother falcon can normally regulate the eggs' temperature and humidity perfectly with her body and the moisture in her feathers. She even has a well-warmed breast patch infiltrated with a rich blood supply. The patch loses feathers during the breeding season so it can serve as a heating pad for the eggs. Thus healthy falcons are usually better at hatching eggs than people with machines.

Despite all the project staff's care in incubating the eggs, some chicks with heavy pesticide contamination are simply too weak to break out of their shells after pipping at hatching time. To save these young, Walton then must act quickly before the embryo cools off. "We break the shell off piece by piece," said Walton. "Blood vessels have to be tied off and sometimes the yolk sac has to be tied off with sutures and the chick has to be helped out and [into] a warm spot in a brooder."

The staff makes a great effort to prevent illness by keeping the birds' food fresh and by constantly cleaning everything. "It's easy for the young to get dehydrated or too hot or too cold, and [then] they get bacterial infections," said Walton. If a bird does get sick, it takes as much work to care for that one bird as it does to care for the whole population. Yet during the rearing season, the staff is already on call twenty-four hours a day. Chicks must be fed every two to three hours. Once pointing during an interview to a sick young peregrine resting in his living room, Walton said, "Gail Naylor [a project staffer] has to take care of that thing every three hours until it's better. That might take weeks. She devotes her entire life to curing that bird."

Although hatching, healing, and feeding baby peregrines is physically taxing, neither Walton nor his staff seems to mind. "It's very easy for me to be up all night," said Walton. "From mid-March till end of June, you never know when the eggs are going to hatch. Every one is so critical, you have to monitor them all the time. I take great joy in that. I would almost pay somebody to be able to raise baby peregrines."

Although he has seen many eggs hatch, Walton has never lost his sense of wonder that a perfect and complete peregrine can materialize from a yolk and egg white in the embryo's thirty-three-day development cycle. "If you ever get the opportunity to watch an egg go through that whole process, it's just mind-boggling. Even as a biologist, I find it hard to believe that it actually happens."

For the project to succeed, events have to happen on time with respect to the birds' biological needs rather than in accordance with human wishes. On its thirty-fifth day of life, the young peregrine on its way to the wild must be placed in its hack box. (Hacking is a falconry technique originally developed to teach captive falcons to hunt in the wild and then return to their masters.) The Peregrine Fund uses hacking for gradually acclimating birds to the wild prior to their release. The release of hatchery-raised birds must occur when they are forty-two days old. At that age their plumage is not fully developed and they don't venture far from the hack site. "If you keep 'em till fifty or fifty-five days, the whole year's a waste," said Walton. "When you release 'em, they fly away and die."

For the first week of hacking the birds are fed in their box; then the whole front door is removed, and they are allowed to fly around, learning to hunt. They are still fed daily for another six weeks and are monitored by radio telemetry devices attached to each bird. Finally, seven weeks after being placed in the hatch box, the free meals stop, and the birds are forced to fend for themselves. They normally disperse six to nine weeks after hacking starts.

The Santa Cruz project's greatest challenge has been actually getting the fickle peregrines to breed in captivity. For years Walton and staffers watched their intended breeding stock through one-way mirrors. "Essentially," Walton said, "they were doing nothing—eating quail every day, living happily ever after, and not knowing they were supposed to produce young to help save a wild species." Finally, in 1981, two birds showed courtship behavior. Walton and staffer Karen Burnson then spent thousands of hours observing the birds very closely. Burnson was the first to see the birds mating. Walton watched for several hundred more hours until he saw another pair mate.

Thanks to the practice the project staff had had first with prairie falcon eggs and then with the eggs of wild peregrines, they were now able to hatch all the fertile eggs that the captive birds laid.

As soon as falcons are able to focus their eyes—at eight to ten days of age—they recognize adult birds of their species and look to them for food and protection. At this imprinting stage, hatchlings also seem to establish their avian psychological identity, and normally reach the conclusion, "I am a peregrine." When mating time approaches, the bird will normally be attracted to a peregrine of the opposite sex. So as not to disturb this process, most peregrines raised at the Santa Cruz facility are handled as little as possible by the staff. In some cases, the young are initially hand-fed by peregrine-like puppets and then later fed remotely through a chute so that they do not come to associate humans with food.

Not so the project's human-imprinted birds. Karen Burnson has to court these birds all year round as though she were their mate—to try and stimulate the females to lay eggs and entice the males to become semen donors. "With the females I bow to them and 'e-chup' at them as if a male falcon was doing the same thing, and I feed them like a male falcon would do." However, since in nature the male peregrine brings food offerings to his prospective mate during courtship, Burnson presents food to the male falcons and then takes it back—as if the males were feeding her.

As Burnson repeats this process twice a day, the birds' sex hormone production increases and their breeding behavior intensifies; usually they eventually start to view Burnson as their mate.

For the artificial insemination procedure, Burnson first dons a floppy-eared military surplus hat specially adapted for the purpose of collecting peregrine semen. Male peregrines in the wild mount the female's back to copulate. Human-imprinted peregrines want to copulate with people. Thus the imprinted male peregrine flies to the highest possible point on his surrogate—her head—and ejaculates on the hat. Semen is then collected in a tube from the hat rim for injection by specially designed syringe into human-imprinted female peregrines.

Because Burnson is so intimately involved with the birds, she rarely leaves Santa Cruz. Instead, she arises every morning at 4:30 or 5 A.M. to tend them as she has done virtually every day for five years. "The birds are used to me and it sets them off their usual schedules to have anybody else do it, so I don't usually go anywhere. . . . The birds always come first here."

Burnson's dedication seems to be shared by other staffers like

Jamey Eddy, 27, a recent poultry science graduate of California Polytechnic State University of San Luis Obispo. Eddy is now in charge of raising 40,000 quail a year for the project. His co-worker George Patracuola, a former research chemist, now raises, kills, and cleans up to 1,000 chickens a month seven days a week to feed the project's peregrines. And it does not seem possible that anyone could be more devoted to wildlife restoration than staffer Gail Naylor who lives with an owl in a trailer at the project site. She supervises the egg incubation process and raises the young every spring. She found it easy to get used to the twenty-four-hour-a-day routine of feeding peregrines every two to four hours for several months a year after her previous job raising baby hummingbirds for the Living Desert Reserve of Palm Desert. (Baby hummingbirds have to be fed every twenty minutes from sunup to sundown.) While she admits that getting up at all hours of the night to check on an unhatched egg can be tiring, she finds it rewarding. "I love to see those birds flying free," she said.

While the Santa Cruz project was moving from demonstration stage to full-scale implementation, The Peregrine Fund was active in raptor restoration at Cornell and Colorado. By 1981, The Peregrine Fund had produced more than 1,000 peregrines and more than 500 falcons of other species at the fund's three centers. But because of natural mortality in the wild, only 500–650 of the birds were expected to survive. Of the 400–500 birds in the East, only 75–100 may be in pairs, and, of these, only 9 pairs are known to have fledged young; but many other young birds are now nearing sexual maturity, and the breeding population will soon be increasing exponentially. More than 100 birds were released in California by 1982, and California now has about 50 known pairs. Two-thirds of them are successful breeders. Also by 1982, adult birds were nesting in Virginia, and others had taken up residence on artificially constructed tower nesting sites in the eastern coastal zone. So much progress has been made in the coastal zone that The Peregrine Fund has now begun repopulating cliff sites in the interior of New England and New York. During 1983 alone, The Peregrine Fund produced 260 peregrines in its three hatchery facilities.

Some peregrines released in the East have chosen major bridges as well as skyscrapers for their aeries. Pigeons are the main diet of these urban peregrines in places such as New York City, Los Angeles, Oakland, and Washington, D.C.

The peregrines released in the East are not all of the native *anatum* subspecies: The fund also releases Peale's peregrines, brookei peregrines from Spain, and tundra peregrines, as well as Western *anatum*. Staffers are not concerned about mongrelization of the population through interbreeding because variations between the subspecies are often slight. In fact, variation within a subspecies is frequently greater than the variation between it and another subspecies. Some hybridization occurs naturally in the wild.

Despite their successes, none of the fund's three major projects has any cause for complacency. If, for example, the Santa Cruz project were to cease operations, the peregrine would resume its decline toward extinction in the West because of DDE remaining in the environment. "We know from our own data on the Monterey coast," said staffer Carl Thelander, "that they are unable right now to hatch their own eggs."

The fund's critics are dismayed by the high cost of saving peregrines—$1,500 per bird returned to the wild—and also fault the project for concentrating attention on the temperate zone while, in absolute numbers, more species extinctions are going on in the tropics, primarily through deforestation. Other critics say the fund directs its attention to the symptoms of the peregrine's plight rather than to the underlying causes. Thelander admits that "we put birds back into a situation knowing that they're going to get DDE pollution. There's nothing we can do about that. It's best to keep the wild population going as best we can in the hopes that the DDE problem will subside. . . . Manufacturers of DDT are no longer producing in California or the United States, but they indeed go down to South America and produce. It's used real heavily on cotton in northern Mexico, on bananas in South America, and for malaria control." Economic pressure could be applied by the United States to deter DDT use, but sufficient political clamor for that pressure has not arisen.

From its new World Center for Birds of Prey in Boise, Idaho, The Peregrine Fund is now extending its operations throughout the world. The fund will conduct scientific research on raptors and will work to preserve rare or endangered raptors and their habitats. It will apply techniques used with the peregrine to other endangered raptors. "As many as 100 of the 200 species of diurnal raptors may be in serious jeopardy by the year 2000," a fund publication says. "Several raptorial species are already threatened with extinction or are extremely rare.... Action must be taken soon to preserve their natural environments and to increase their numbers."

Although the cause of the peregrine's distress remains ever present, the recovery of the population is exhilarating, especially to people like peregrine workers Kurt Stolzenburg, Merlyn Felton, and Brian Walton. Felton and Walton flew by helicopter one day along the majestic Big Sur coast of California to search for and survey peregrine populations there. When they had begun their work in 1976, they were aware of only two nests on the entire eighty-mile Big Sur coast. On their journey in 1982, however, they saw the graceful soaring silhouettes of wild Western *anatum* peregrines riding the thermals and swooping down along the rocky cliffs at every suitable location on the entire eighty-mile coast, against a background of frothing surf.

IV

HUMAN
SETTLEMENTS

12

Optimal Suburbia

For many people, the prospect of living in a modern suburb is part of the American Dream. Successful suburbanites can own their own split-level or ranch house, swim in their own pool, relax with color TV in Tudor bedrooms, or tinker in the two-car garage. Ideally, a pelt of flawless lawn bordered by bright flowers surrounds the castle.

Typical new tract homes are strategically located near highways or major arterials that take most breadwinners to work. The car is king here—vital to reach Safeway, the children's swimming lesson, and other activities. Despite all the affluence, a subdivision's standardized model homes, its fifty-foot-wide streets, and its predictable layout can lend it a dull, impersonal character.

Yet by modifying existing suburbs and completely redesigning new ones, suburbs can not only be made more congenial, but stresses in the form of resource demands, which human settlements place on ecosystems, can be partially relieved. In this respect, although strictly speaking it is not restoration, the ecology-conscious redesign of suburb and city could restore some harmony between built and natural environments. But can ecologically sound and energy-conserving suburbs be built profitably under current economic and political conditions? Michael N. Corbett, for one, has reason to believe they can.

Corbett is a tall, obliging man of 44 with straight brown hair, heavy eyelids, and a hint of Scandinavia in his features. Soft-spoken and modest, he seems part of an earlier era when a handclasp was still as good as a signed contract. He works today as a licensed contractor, builder, and planning consultant, and is the author of *A Better Place to Live: New Designs for Tomorrow's Communities* (Rodale Press, 1981).

Corbett began working on a unique eighteen-million-dollar suburban development called Village Homes in 1973. He was then an unknown small builder with a net worth near zero. His dream, however, was to build a villagelike solar subdivision in Davis, California, a university town twelve miles west of Sacramento. Corbett did not even have an architect's license, and he initially estimated his chances of success as minuscule. But he resolved to try.

The design for Village Homes was painstakingly thorough; Mike and Judy Corbett, his wife, had thought intensively about model communities and how the design would influence residents' daily lives. The Corbetts wanted to create a place where residents could develop close relationships and integrate the process of earning a livelihood with living, learning, and playing together. They also wanted Village Homes to be affordable for the average American.

To accomplish all this, Corbett proposed to mix agricultural, residential, and commercial land use in one subdivision. The houses were to use passive solar energy systems for space conditioning and solar panels for hot-water heating. It is hard today—now that passive and active solar heating systems have become commonplace—to remember that, even a dozen years ago, solar heating was regarded as a radical, highly experimental idea. Moreover, Corbett also wanted his homes in groups of eight clustering around a third of an acre of commonly owned land instead of on the usual rectangular grid. When he first showed the subdivision plans to Davis's city planning director, he recalls, "she just laughed and laughed." But, however inexperienced as a developer, Corbett had confidence in his design work and he began a two-year struggle to realize his dream. In addition to battling with city planners, Corbett had to contend with the city engineer, the police, and even the local fire department, over the development's innovative features. No doubt, some people wondered why he committed himself to this arduous struggle with an uncertain outcome when, given his exceptional energy and talent, he could probably have earned a large income building conventional tracts. Corbett, however, believed that an architect has to understand people's fundamental needs, and that most architectural firms did not really understand the people for whom they were designing. He therefore chose to build more individualized homes as an independent designer.

The Corbetts, moreover, were deeply concerned about environmental problems, including air and water pollution and the loss of agricultural land and natural areas. Michael remembered the beauties of the Sacramento countryside of his boyhood when what is now Interstate 80 was an ordinary road that went for miles through rich alluvial fields of the Sacramento River Valley. Rivers and streams, shaded by willows and oaks, flowed gently and birds alighted on natural marshy areas while foxes stalked through the woods and bushy grass. Then he saw armies of bulldozers turn fields and meadows into housing tracts. The Army Corps of Engineers straightened the American River where once he had played as a child. "Streams flowed through concrete channels beside the road," Judy Corbett remembers. "The wildlife was gone. There was man-made stuff, and it was ugly."

By the early 1970s, the Corbetts' environmental concerns extended to energy problems. They became convinced not only that fossil fuels were being wasted but that their use was destroying the ecosystem. Then came the Arab oil embargo and the energy crisis of 1973. The Corbetts had previously started a discussion group of people interested in designing and building living environments for themselves that would not cause an ecological breakdown. During one of their meetings, someone suggested that Corbett look into solar energy as an environmentally sound way of building. Corbett went into action, experimenting with solar energy and building solar houses. "At the time," he said, "I was probably one of ten solar experts in the country who had built solar water heaters and produced basic passive houses." The group also produced many ideas which the Corbetts later incorporated in Village Homes, confirming their belief that ordinary people should be active in designing their own environments. To Corbett's disappointment, the group disbanded without proceeding to find land on which to build a community.

Corbett began laboring on his own to convert the dream of Village Homes into reality. Initially all he had was a vision of a community that would use land, energy, and building materials frugally. He wanted Village Homes to minimize air and water pollution, preserve natural resources, and incorporate desirable features of village life into a suburban setting. In case it didn't work, Corbett planned to write a book about it, showing what "an environmentally sound neighborhood design would be."

Despite his thoughts of failure, Corbett began going to Davis realtors only to discover that most of them didn't take him seriously. Finally, one realtor seemed willing to take a chance and sold Corbett an option for a suitable seventy-acre subdivision site. Corbett later suspected the realtor did it only to get the property rezoned. Davis had a construction moratorium in force, and the realtor may well have surmised that Corbett's project would appeal to Davis's liberal and environmentally concerned city council.

As soon as Corbett got the option, however, he produced a design that reflected more than a decade of intensive discussion with Judy. Next Corbett immediately began seeking public support for the design, inviting people to open houses where Michael and Judy told people what the prospective community would be like. In addition to generating enthusiasm for the project, the open houses gave Corbett additional feedback on the plans and helped him make the design more acceptable.

With the property option and design in hand, Corbett undertook to win acceptance from the city of Davis and backing from investors. The Corbetts first tried the Bank of America. Judy caricatured their initial approach: "We've got this wonderful project. It's going to solve all these social and ecological problems—you can't resist it." The bank, however, proved quite capable of resisting.

"Most banks didn't like it because of the narrow streets and the solar applications, and because it was untried," said Michael. "They just didn't want anything to do with it." More than twenty banks turned the Corbetts down.

From about 1973 to 1977, Corbett worked sixty to seventy hours per week on the effort to create Village Homes and did little independent building. Judy Corbett supported the family by working as a medical technologist. These years were fraught with anxieties for the Corbetts about whether they were going to get a loan or meet impending deadlines.

Finally, in desperation over his inability to finance the project, Corbett went to Sacramento Savings and Loan, where his stepfather, Alan Hensley, banked. Hensley was also a builder and was in good standing with the bank. Based on his commitment to build the first fifty homes in Corbett's subdivision, the loan was approved. These initial homes were to be conventional in appearance, but would incorporate passive solar design features.

Although Corbett felt a rush of excitement as the loan papers were signed, his exuberance was guarded: Many big hurdles remained. The city was resisting the proposed subdivision. Every innovative feature created a struggle. "But we kept writing arguments to the staff reports," Corbett said, "and just outwrote and out-logicked them. . . ." He eventually got the variances he needed.

Meanwhile, he was raising investment capital in a limited partnership to take possession of the sixty-nine-acre property. Each investor would put up between $6,000 and $13,000. Corbett's option on the land expired twice while he doggedly corralled investors. "I got the last one or two just six months prior to actually breaking ground." At the last minute, the realtor who had given Corbett the land option failed to put up his own money, and it looked briefly as though the whole project would fall apart. The rezoned land would then have reverted to the realtor. At that crucial juncture, however, the title company expressed its confidence in Corbett. They closed the sale of the property even though the down payment was $13,000 short, on Corbett's personal pledge to get the remaining funds immediately, which he did.

About half of the funds Corbett raised through the partnership now went to pay for the first ten acres and the other half went for engineering and loan fees on it. The Sacramento Savings loan paid for installation of streets and utilities. Once the first fifty houses were built by Michael's father-in-law, they sold rapidly. "After that," said Judy, "financing was never a problem again."

Corbett himself sold some of the lots in the subdivision to generate an immediate cash flow, and he custom-built houses to order and on speculation. Eventually, he deeded the common areas of Village Homes to the homeowners' association under a restrictive covenant that ensured they could not be sold simply for profit; the covenant provided that after any first deeds of trust were paid to banks, any profits would belong to the Audubon Society.

While he did not want Village Homes to benefit middle-class people exclusively, Corbett was leery of subsidized housing programs. "Where houses were heavily subsidized," he said, "the degree of care of the house went way downhill—the people never really felt part of the neighborhood. We decided, 'Let [low-income people] get in, but let them work for their equity, so they really feel pride of ownership.'"

He initially hoped to build 15–25 percent of Village Homes via a "sweat equity" program for low-income people. But neither California Housing Finance, a state agency for low- and moderate-income families, nor FHA would make the necessary loans. "It just turned out that if you're Mexican-American and don't speak English very well, and have a background as a farm worker—even if you've had an ongoing job for two years and a good employment record and enough down payment for your house," said Corbett, "you won't get a loan. It was probably the saddest part of the whole project."

Confronted with disinterest on the part of banks and social service agencies, Corbett himself recruited and interviewed families for a much-reduced sweat equity program. He first hired participants for six-month trials as construction workers at Village Homes, and was able to help three of them to obtain bank loans. A fourth worker dropped out of the program voluntarily, and two others who were qualified lost their houses because they were unable to get financing. The three families who did complete the program took pride in their homes and changed their status in society. "There could have been many more had [banks] made the loans," said Corbett. "For me, the important thing is that I got houses to people who otherwise couldn't afford them."

The houses in Village Homes began selling in 1976 for $28,000–$45,000, with most priced in the mid-30's, which was average for Davis at the time. Some of these homes are now selling for up to $170,000. Many of the once low-to-moderately priced solar homes have appreciated by nearly 400 percent. Village Homes' commercial investors have made an average annual rate of return of 28 percent on their investments.

Today, multicolored flowers are everywhere along the narrow foot and bicycle paths weaving through Village Homes' more than 270 units with their red-to-brown tiled roofs and near white stucco walls. Backyards are unfenced and adjoin large grassy common areas.

Unlike other subdivisions which are diced into rectangular blocks by broad streets and sidewalks, Village Homes uses roads sparingly. They are narrow—twenty to twenty-five feet in width instead of thirty-two feet or more—and without sidewalks, and end in cul-de-sacs. The land saved is open space or housing, making Village Homes seem spacious even though its density is greater than the average Davis neighborhood's. Bicycles are more evident here than cars, and children play in the

streets in safety. Corbett used a unique system of natural drainage that retains 85 percent of the rainfall on the site in pleasant
streams and ponds. Water soaks into the ground, minimizing
erosion and the need for watering. Wild cherry trees grow along
the stream banks, and compost piles can be seen fermenting for
use on residents' vegetable plots and on a community garden.
This also reduces the subdivision's refuse collection. Manure
rather than chemical fertilizer is used on the land, and pesticides
are taboo on the commons. Corbett was concerned to maintain
some of the agricultural productivity of the prime farm land on
which he built. Thus almond, apricot, plum, and tangerine trees
are growing in the community's orchards, and an abundance of
wine and table grapes grow in Village Homes' ample vineyard.
A variety of birds—woodpeckers, killdeer, hawks, and hummingbirds—are familiar visitors, and people come from all over
town just to jog along the pleasant, tree-lined lanes.

The community is democratically managed by a nonprofit
homeowners' association which now owns the village's green-
belts and other common areas. All residents are automatically
members. The association also owns stock in a profit-making
corporation set up to own the commercial property amidst and
adjacent to Village Homes. The homeowners' association runs
the project's co-op boarding house, miniplayground, and Saturday morning farmer's market, community center, and pool. It
also publishes a monthly newsletter that serves to encourage
neighborhood cohesion and was used to coordinate a neighborhood crime-reduction program. When a notorious Sacramento
rapist moved his theater of operations to Village Homes after
committing thirty-five rapes in other neighborhoods, commu-
nitywide citizen night patrols stopped him. At Village Homes,
the cul-de-sac design and the ownership of land and other resources in common encourage residents to get to know each
other. This increases their awareness of who is in their neighborhood and why, enabling them to watch out for themselves.
The community has a 90-percent lower crime rate than other
residential neighborhoods in Davis, even though the police don't
patrol it.

Village Homes already has a small office complex with six offices—mainly for residential professionals—and is planning adjacent buildings for neighborhood shops, a restaurant, and an inn that should be ideal for overnight guests. There is space for a small medical facility. Corbett looks forward to a day when the homeowners here will have made enough money from their joint commercial property to own a large agricultural reserve, their own summer camp, and their own energy supply (possibly a woodlot).

The average house in Village Homes uses less than two-thirds the energy of a conventional house. Many of the houses rely on passive solar designs—massive insulation, southern orientations, roof overhangs, concrete slab floors for thermal mass, solar greenhouses—and require no air conditioning even though summer temperatures often top 100 °F in Davis. Solar water heating produces about three-quarters of each home's hot water for the year. "The passive houses, the ones with the least amount of solar," said Corbett, "are producing about 40 percent of their energy needs through the south glass; the better ones probably produce 70 to 80 percent of their needs. . . ." Corbett has won a solar design award for Village Homes from the Northern California Solar Energy Association and received the Living Lightly on the Land award from the state of California. Whereas close to half the energy consumed in California is used for transportation, Village Homes' integration of residential, commercial, and agricultural land uses plus supporting social services and educational facilities makes much car travel unnecessary.

Corbett himself has done well by doing good. He earned an average of $35,000 to $45,000 a year for the decade 1973 to 1983, thanks to Village Homes. Moreover, both Corbetts had fun creating Village Homes and found it as exciting as running a political campaign.

13

Soldiers Grove

The year was 1975 and the state of Wisconsin in cooperation
with the U.S. government had just in effect demanded that
the hamlet of Soldiers Grove, Wisconsin, sign its own death
warrant. The village's ensuing struggle for survival has implica-
tions today for other communities hoping to transform themselves ecologically. This is what happened.

In the mid-seventies, Soldiers Grove was home to about 500
people. Having passed its prime economically shortly after
World War II, the town was a bit battered and scuffed, like a pair
of old shoes—no longer elegant, but very comfortable. Along its
broad main street stood the one- and two-story buildings of a
farming center community: a feed store, a meat locker, and The
Electric Theater, a movie house of crumbling brick built a century ago. On a sunny day, locals in their farm caps and overalls
socialized on the bench outside the post office. People didn't
bother locking their doors. Deer hunting, morel collecting, and
berry picking were popular pastimes.

In the town's heyday during the late 1940s, Saturday night

dances at the high school were major social events. The Electric Theater and a place called Danceland did a rollicking business, and several taverns flourished. Now, although the prosperity was gone, the American Legion still put on an annual fall festival at harvest time with tractor pull contests down Main Street to see whose machine could drag a heavy cement slab the farthest. Dairy Day, with its Dairy Queen and parade to honor local dairy farmers, was an even more popular local celebration along with the family picnics and water balloon fights on Memorial Day.

Soldiers Grove lay in an elbow-bend embrace of the Kickapoo River, surrounded by the limestone uplands of hilly southwestern Wisconsin. The Kickapoo normally is a greenish little garter snake of a river that winds docilely about its business. The town was trustingly built more than a hundred years ago right in the river's floodplain, for in those days, the river rarely flooded.

The Kickapoo watershed is a land of marginal corn, tobacco, and dairy farms: Wisconsin's Appalachia. These steep hills have been intensively farmed and logged. Topsoil which eroded from the uplands has raised the Kickapoo valley floor a whole fence post in height during the past half century. Siltation gradually reduced the Kickapoo channel and its capacity to retain floodwaters.

Floods began in 1907 and increased in severity until a flood disaster struck the village in 1935, and Soldiers Grove petitioned Congress for a U.S. Army Corps of Engineers dam on the Kickapoo. But Congress did not protect the village, and in 1951, Soldiers Grove was devastated by an even larger flood such as experts thought likely to occur only once in a hundred years. Deep muddy water moved in everywhere and people watched helplessly from high ground as their livelihoods and property were once again destroyed. Virtually no one in town had flood insurance; it was just too expensive. But with federal disaster relief, the sodden disheveled village dried out and rebuilt. Residents were determined not to be driven from their homes. Some villagers, evidently misunderstanding the concept of a hundred-year flood, believed that since the town had just been inundated, it would enjoy immunity from flooding for the next ninety-nine years.

In the fifties, although the government still offered the town no protection, it did move U.S. Highway 61 around Soldiers Grove so that the road would not be flooded. Cut off from its commercial lifeline, the village languished.

Finally, twenty-seven years after the town first asked for help, in 1962 Congress authorized the corps to build the La Farge Dam upriver on the Kickapoo along with a levee to protect the village. Levee maintenance and other costs for which Soldiers Grove was liable would have doubled the village's tax assessment.

Meanwhile, in Washington, D.C., officials were growing restive over rising flood-disaster relief bills. The total was more than a quarter of a billion dollars in 1965 alone, and it was projected to reach five billion in 1985, so Congress passed the National Flood Insurance Act in 1968. The act contained a zoning ordinance which the people of Soldiers Grove felt was more likely to kill the town than even the worsening floods. Under its provisions, Soldiers Grove was offered subsidized insurance for existing structures in return for the local adoption of a zoning ordinance that would have prohibited new construction in floodways (land directly in the flood path). It also would have made it illegal to spend more than half the value of existing floodplain property to maintain the property.

Virtually all the commercial buildings in Soldiers Grove were in the floodplain, and they were old enough to need expensive renovation. If the village adopted the zoning proposal, business expansion would have stopped and the merchants soon would have had to stand back and watch their property fall to ruin. Yet if the town refused the ordinance, it would lose the right to participate in federally insured loans. The business community would have been cut off from most commercial credit.

As the town's fortunes ebbed and the pace of commerce slackened, the town merchants reacted by becoming suspicious and closed-mouthed toward their equally hard-pressed rivals. A feeling of meanness and failure insidiously set in where friendliness and cooperation had been. Time crept by, leaving the town in its backwash.

While the village fretted, the corps began building the La Farge Dam in 1969, and Wisconsin put increased pressure on Soldiers Grove to adopt the floodplain ordinance. Then, in 1973, a feisty, optimistic, city-bred outsider named Bill Becker appeared in town.

Becker is a confident man of medium height who seems tall in his Western boots and jeans and speaks with a natural ease and grace. Behind lightly tinted glasses and beneath dark brown bangs, his eyes are good humored yet determined. If ever anyone from out of town could charm a community of crusty and conservative small-town Wisconsinites, it was Becker with his dynamism and informal, reasonable manner. People were even inclined to forgive his neatly trimmed beard.

Becker bought the village newspaper and became champion of an idea that had started as a joke: moving the whole town instead of trying to subdue the river. He mobilized local support and helped persuade the army corps in 1975 that it had nothing to lose by helping the town move instead of building levees for it. Shortly after, however, construction of the La Farge Dam was halted after environmentalists raised objections to it which were sustained in an environmental impact statement. Since the entire project was stopped, the corps rescinded its offer of assistance to Soldiers Grove, and the town was once again plunged into crisis.

Was Soldiers Grove even worth saving? The villagers, particularly the elderly, felt passionately that it was. But its assessed valuation was only $3.2 million and, even if it could be preserved, the task would be expensive. Money, however, was not the whole story. Wiping out the town meant destroying the world where Aunt Jess and Uncle Will Ward, in green visor and rimless glasses, left the neighborhood kids a pitcher of lemonade and cookies on the porch and told them entertaining stories. It was also the world of John Hansen, the oldest barber in Wisconsin, and that of W. A. Sannes, the town physician. Sannes made house calls for more than forty years and had delivered every-

body's babies and comforted the dying and had been everything
you could want in a family doctor.

Naturally there were also practical economic reasons for
keeping the town afloat. If Soldiers Grove went under, nearly
fifty businesses and the jobs that went with them would be lost;
dozens of homes would be abandoned as people without access
to basic community services would move.

The debate about whether to give up the fight or continue
the struggle was prolonged and intense. Gradually, however, the
community leaders forged a consensus: Soldiers Grove would
fight for its survival despite the unfavorable odds. The Village
Board recommitted itself to the struggle.

Once this was decided, Becker worked relentlessly. He had
been impressed by energy expert Amory Lovins's assertion that
virtually no building in the United States should be built without solar heat. Why not rebuild the town as a solar village?
Becker wondered. Yet it seemed like such a radical idea even to
him that he didn't even broach it to people in town until it got to
Soldiers Grove through an interview he did with the *Chicago
Tribune*. His phone had rung soon after, and to his dismay it
was the town's elderly and conservative mill owner, Wilfred
Burkum, demanding, "What's this I hear about solar stuff?"

"Gee, Wilfred," Becker replied, "you know, some people talk
like it would be a good idea." Becker held his breath, expecting a
torrent of objections.

To his amazement, the old man at the other end of the line
said, "Well, you know, I don't think we ought to do this move
unless we do something like solar. This town isn't worth the
trouble unless we can show the rest of the country something."
Other citizens were interested, too: They were paying onerous
utility bills for fuel oil and propane, and they believed in
old-fashioned values like self-reliance. They also liked the idea of
breaking new ground and becoming a model solar community.
But would solar work? And could it be done economically?

The answers to these questions had to wait, however, because the town's top priority was relocation. The Village Board
hired architect and town planner Tom Hirsch to find the means

to relocate and to coordinate relocation. He recognized at once that it was a formidable task. In Chicago, where he had lived and done political organizing, he had often seen local neighborhood desires "squashed by centralized government." In Soldiers Grove, he was impressed by the village's will to survive, and he saw an opportunity to help the people build a better life for themselves. Throwing himself into his new job, Hirsch soon acquired small grants to study the feasibility of relocation. The first study affirmed that relocation was indeed the community's best alternative. It identified potential relocation sites, and suggested turning the site of the old business district into a municipal park planted with native floodplain vegetation. Another study came to the awesome conclusion that relocation would cost six million dollars. Raising that much money seemed almost impossible: It was nearly double the town's entire assessed valuation, and village tax levies brought in only $10,000 a year. But the Village Board refused to be overwhelmed by the amount and at the end of 1976 passed a brash resolution declaring its intent to move. Written by Hirsch, it read in part: "The Board hereby directs the governor of the State of Wisconsin, its state senator and state representative, its U.S. congressman and senators, to so represent the interests of the Village, actively and aggressively taking the necessary steps to ensure the timely and successful execution of the relocation proposal. . . ."

Hirsch had used forceful language because the village was in a desperate situation, and a new flood could happen virtually any time. In addition, he felt that he had to be "outrageous" to get distant decision-makers' attention. He also knew that this explicit policy statement by the village's elected representatives would provide legitimacy to state officials' efforts at assisting Soldiers Grove to raise funds.

With the village now emphatically on record in favor of moving, Hirsch arranged numerous meetings at which villagers were encouraged to discuss how they wanted to re-create the town. "We never allowed any of the various consultants or technicians to tell anyone what to do," said Becker. "We made it very clear to every official and [relocation consultant] who came in that they were simply going to serve the people's wishes. Soldiers Grove was going to live or die on its decision to relocate—there was no assurance the project would succeed—so it had to be the people who made the decisions to do that and take those risks."

Nevertheless, Hirsch in 1977 boldly urged the village leaders to buy a 190-acre relocation site for $90,000. It lay along Route 61 above the floodplain, half a mile from the old downtown. The town would also have to spend anther $300,000 to outfit the site with water and sewer facilities. The Village Board nonetheless agreed. The decision was risky; the village by then had already been vainly struggling for two years to raise relocation money.

Responding to the village's determination and commitment, the state of Wisconsin gave Soldiers Grove a $110,000 grant to help it extend water and sewer facilities to the new site. But that was only a tiny fraction of the millions needed, and so gradually people again grew despondent. Shortly after the state's grant for utility extension arrived, the CETA grant that paid Hirsch's salary expired. He continued to work without pay, but hope for financial aid to the village dwindled.

Then, during the last week of June 1978, Nature interceded and torrential rains began. Creeks and tributaries to the Kickapoo filled. In the early hours of July 2, the Kickapoo topped the temporary levees built by the corps in 1969, and the worst flood in Soldiers Grove's history began. "All you could do," said Hirsch, "was watch as the things that the townspeople had labored for were destroyed."

The flood caused $500,000 damage in Soldiers Grove, and the village was declared part of a larger federal and state disaster area. "It now became clear that we had a substantial propaganda [advantage]," Hirsch said, and he urged the town to take the unprecedented step of refusing traditional disaster assistance.

Over coffee and snacks at a Sunday meeting, Hirsch and village president Ronald Swiggum confronted a puzzled representative of the Federal Disaster Assistance Administration (FDAA), then a branch of HUD. "What is this I hear about your not wanting to take our disaster assistance?" the official asked. Hirsch and Swiggum patiently explained that the town just didn't want any more disaster aid—they wanted help moving out.

About this time, Senator William Proxmire of Wisconsin went on a tour of the disaster area, met Hirsch, and later invited Hirsch and Swiggum to Washington for a meeting of high-level officials from a dozen different federal agencies. Most notable were officials from the Federal Disaster Assistance Administration, which Proxmire oversaw as chairman of the powerful Banking, Housing, and Urban Affairs Committee. Hirsch and Swiggum contended that it would be less expensive for the government to help the town move than to continue paying it disaster assistance after every flood. The town was willing to pay its share of the costs, they emphasized, but one after the other, the officials presented reasons why their agencies couldn't or didn't want to help. The usual response to flooding had always been disaster relief and reconstruction, but Proxmire now directed the agency representatives to report to him on what they could do to assist Soldiers Grove. Within twenty-four hours, nearly a million dollars had been committed to relocation.

In jubilation the Village Board now retained consultants to prepare a land use plan, an energy use assessment, a legal options review, and an analysis of the new town's financial prospects. Villagers participated extensively in all the planning decisions. Relocation was happening. The Board hired the Hawkweed Group Ltd., solar architects, to design the municipal buildings and assist in setting up zoning requirements which included energy management standards. Hawkweed concluded that energy-efficient buildings costing no more than comparable conventional ones could economically get 75 percent of their heat from the sun, even in Wisconsin's rigorous climate.

After reviewing the experts' advice on relocation, Soldiers Grove chose to set up an informal partnership between the town and the business community so that the town would receive federal grants and manage the move under the terms of a Planned Unit Development (PUD). This master plan allowed the town government to control building placement and landscaping while retaining all land except the ground directly beneath each new building in municipal ownership. The board incorporated the Hawkweed study's solar energy recommendations into the PUD master plan. All the new commercial buildings would have to be effectively insulated and would have to get at least 50 percent of their heat from the sun. Soldiers Grove in 1979 thus laid claim to becoming the first U.S. community to require solar heating.

The new business district was designed so that vegetation would block cold winter winds and summer breezes could cool the community. Local building materials were used and structures were situated so they received ample sunlight, with shady areas reserved for parking. Residential and commercial units were combined in irregular clusters of buildings so the unique small-town character of Soldiers Grove was not entirely lost. The new design also provided citizens with informal gathering places for socializing as in the old town.

Homeowners whose houses were in the floodplain and who wanted to move were enabled to do so. "Flood fringe" homeowners who wanted to floodproof their homes in place were offered zero-interest deferred payment loans from HUD Community Development Block grants. These homes were raised about two feet above the floodplain on gently sloping earthen fill beneath new foundations.

The relocation site itself was designated as a Tax Incremental Financing (TIF) district: Whereas new property tax revenue is normally shared by a variety of taxing districts, several states including Wisconsin have laws allowing communities to retain all property tax revenues generated by a new development in a TIF district to finance needed municipal public works.

As of 1984, the town's Office of Community Development had successfully purchased forty-eight commercial floodplain properties in Soldiers Grove. Only two property owners, referred to locally as sticks-in-the-mud, refused to accept the offers made to them. Most of the old business district has now been bulldozed, and the desolate, empty buildings still standing will soon follow. The old downtown has become a floodable riverside

park for villagers and visiting canoeists. Eventually the town
plans to landscape it with native floodplain vegetation.

The entire move eventually cost more than $6 million. Of
that total, the village government contributed $2 million, which
it borrowed from the Farmers Home Administration. Individual
merchants made additional investments so that, overall, the local
contribution was about 40 percent. On balance, relocation was
cheaper than staying put. A recent formal cost/benefit analysis
comparing relocation costs with the cost of the corps's levee
found that the discounted net present value of the levee cost plus
the cost of continued federal disaster relief would have been $8.1
million as contrasted with $7 million, the net present value for
the relocation expenses. In addition, the move redirected federal
aid from relief and flood protection to flood prevention. Soldiers
Grove now has a new enthusiasm for the future and a pride born
of participation in a locally controlled and democratically managed redevelopment effort.

Around a bend on a nondescript stretch of rural Highway 61
today in southwestern Wisconsin, you will suddenly come upon
a group of about twenty oddly shaped new solar buildings forming a small business community. West of the road is a solar IGA
supermarket, a solar post office, a solar bank, a solar tavern, a
solar pharmacy, a nursing home, and a medical clinic inter-
spersed with solar apartments and a sixteen-unit solar senior citizens housing complex. The village's solar library and meeting
room with attached greenhouse has recently been completed. To
the east is a solar-heated Mobil gasoline station, a solar-heated
fire station, a solar-heated woodworking shop, and a solar
American Legion Hall. All the buildings are carefully oriented
with respect to the sun and to prevailing winds. Several use external earthen berms as insulating windbreaks. Almost all are
solar "hybrids," with both active and passive solar features.

The $200,000 solar IGA supermarket, for example, uses its
shelved canned goods as thermal mass to absorb and store solar
heat. The insulated concrete slab floor also stores heat. Refrigera-
tor compressors and other machinery that emit waste heat are

consolidated in a single, well-insulated utility room from which the heated air is vented and circulated by fans, as needed, to the rest of the 7,000-square-foot supermarket. So far, the owner's fuel bill is zero, despite three harsh Wisconsin winters, and his solar system paid for itself in three years. Thick insulation also keeps the building at about 70 °F when outside summer temperatures are more than 100 °F.

From the front, the solar fire station looks like a typical industrial building, but an entire side wall is made of a transparent reinforced polyester glazing. Heat sensors automatically control aluminized cloth curtains on the inside of this giant window, opening only when the building needs heat in the winter and closing to reflect sunlight in the summer.

Like the IGA, the two-story residential and commercial Schoville Building employs a triangular attic area as a solar hot-air collector. Heat is also collected in a thermal wall and is stored in the concrete floor as well as in cans of phase-change salts. Said Gerald Schoville, "What we wanted was to build into the twenty-first century as far as energy was concerned. We wanted to build a village that was so unique that it would attract industry and people."

The population of Soldiers Grove has grown by nearly a third since 1975—and the assessed valuation has more than doubled, to ten million dollars in 1984. Some of the increase is due to inflation, but most of it is due to new investment; about sixty new jobs have also been created.

Thanks to the relocation, the village has left the disaster relief rolls, and it has prevailed over a forty-year-old federal policy of treating flooding as an engineering rather than an environmental problem. By leaving the floodplain, Soldiers Grove, as Bill Becker points out, quietly struck a blow at the conventional wisdom that "when nature and people conflict, nature should yield." No longer a dying village, Soldiers Grove is today a proud and optimistic community with a fighting chance at an economically rewarding future.

Although no community can count on the substantial federal and state aid that Soldiers Grove mustered thanks to its shrewd leadership, the town's experience with long-range strategic planning and grass-roots participation illustrates that environmental protection and economic development can be compatible. If one very small low-income community can eliminate flood danger, decrease energy waste and attendant pollution, prepare its floodplain for native plant restoration, and simultaneously lay groundwork for its economic survival, then certainly other communities, too, can use their collective economic power as leverage to obtain necessary financing for ecologically oriented redevelopment and restoration.

14

Future Cities

For most of the 170 million urban Americans who make up 74 percent of the U.S. population, redwood forests and trout streams, northern lakes and salt marshes, prairies and desert surface mines are far from daily experience. Thus, the challenge of making settled areas better places to live is often more relevant for city people than saving natural systems. However, although cities can of course be improved, it is not quite so clear that they can be "restored." Yet if their restoration is not construed to mean the wholesale removal of artificial structures and a return to presettlement conditions, ecological restoration is possible.

Restoring cities means transforming them to minimize the ecological damage they do, thus restoring a harmony between city or suburb and countryside. As suggested in Chapter 12, cities that use raw materials and energy thriftily minimize the stress those cities inflict on the hinterland whose resources they require. Relieving the ecological strain affords the hinterland a respite during which time natural resource restoration can succeed.

In addition to reducing ecological damage, urban restoration means restoring certain villagelike qualities to the city and its people—qualities such as self-reliance, a sense of stewardship for the commons, and a strengthened commitment to place, an essential requirement for stewardship. The urban transformation ideally will also restore clean air and clean water, useful plants, and native wildlife—all characteristic of the pre- and early-industrial village environs.

In part because ecological stability and social stability are interrelated, the ecological restoration of the city may also help restore some desirable small-town conditions, such as friendly relationships between neighbors who share long-term interests in their community.

Naturally, urban restoration does not mean trying to return the city to an earlier idealized time, nor does it mean bulldozing long-established neighborhoods to make way for hotels, highrise office buildings, or condominiums, in the name of urban renewal.

It would indeed be nice to be able to visit a restored city as we've done with restored natural sites. However, nobody has as yet restored an American city. Therefore, what follows is a description of an imaginary city where existing restoration technology blends with potential future technology (and a dash of whimsy) to create a restored metropolis named Croyden. Our guide for a one-day tour there is a fictional character named Reuben who appeared one day at my home in California.

"Croyden," he said to me, "is one of New York State's oldest industrial cities. We've done comprehensive restoration there, although it seemed beyond redemption. People elsewhere are still starting new cities from scratch, assaulting new land, building everything new, but you run out of virgin resources and land eventually. Instead of just letting old cities decay, we at Croyden believe in repairing and conserving them. Our restoration council wants you to see what we've done."

Together we boarded a small private jet in Oakland for Croyden. We were the only passengers; otherwise the flight began normally enough. But after an hour or so, I began to feel a queer sense of time distortion and the sky outside the cabin seemed to fade. The next thing I knew, the engines were quiet and we were cruising at about 1,000 feet over a huge urban landscape reminiscent of a well-tended Mayan city.

The clarity of the air was stunning, and so great was the profusion of greenery that it was hard to believe I was gazing at a metropolitan area. Every spare inch of land seemed to be sprouting with vegetation. Some of the streets were themselves green but all were lined with beautiful, healthy-looking trees of infinite variety, some in bloom or in fruit, others laden with cones. Low-spreading plants grew on rooftop gardens and made green borders on roof edges. Small intensely cultivated fields and woods no bigger than a single-family home lot could be seen throughout the city. The edges of these tracts were gently scalloped and the crops grew in complex mixtures instead of in straight one-of-a-kind rows. Large stacks and vents were built into what otherwise appeared to be normal residential buildings, apparently for some industrial facilities. Glass enclosed the south-facing walls of tall buildings and there seemed to be greenery inside. "Passive solar apartment houses," said Reuben.

Traffic flowed smoothly along the streets and bicycle paths beneath us in an ever-changing mosaic of multicolored electric buses, vans, and trolleys. Bicycles, some with three-wheeled trailers or sidecars, carried people in great numbers to and fro. Trolleys, evidently equipped with retractable tires, moved freely from rails to merge with street traffic. Lovely creeks meandered through downtown Croyden, traversed by footbridges and overpasses. The thickets along their banks gave them a native appearance. Here and there creeks formed little ponds with ducks and geese. "Eastern bluebirds and wood ducks are back," Reuben said. "Wildlife thrives around the creeks."

He pointed out other ponds used for aquaculture as well as solar ponds and saline ponds for energy storage and electric power generation. "The aquaculture ponds are not quite so essential now that we've halted overfishing. For a while, ocean fish catches were declining everywhere. We've also stopped acid rain, by the way." While he spoke, flights of Canada geese and clusters of shore birds headed along coastal flyways. "The birds are well protected," he explained. "Their habitat is pesticide-free."

To the east of the city was a small forest interrupted by meadows etched with a footpath network. A pair of deer grazed in a glade and a flock of cranes fed in a nearby small field. "Our municipal park," Reuben said. "Only twenty years of restoration and we've now got a facsimile of native forest. We put everything back, even microorganisms. The wildlife's so rambunctious we have to keep the park double fenced on top of subsoil barriers to prevent escape."

Our jet was swooping toward the ground. The words *City of Croyden* were spelled out in flowering bushes. As we stepped off the aircraft, I saw that what I had taken for green asphalt was a tough, spongy ground cover with tiny broad leaves a quarter of an inch in height. I bent down and tried to pluck a leaf but it was of a rubbery, rough texture.

"Runway plant," Reuben said. "Like street plant, it's genetically engineered. We prepare the ground, hydrospray the stuff on in a seed and fertilizer emulsion, and it quickly forms a dense impermeable ground cover. Excludes weeds and never needs tending. Blooms with a tiny purple-white flower—a most beautiful sight. In autumn," he added, "we mow it and process the clippings to extract complex hydrocarbons with which we fuel planes and trucks and make plastics."

"You're kidding!"

"Perhaps I am."

From the airport we took a short trolley tour of downtown landmarks including the city's Restoration Congress Hall from where a working congress had launched the city's restoration two decades earlier. We also visited the main branch of the Restoration Bank and the headquarters of the Restoration Research Institute. "It conducts economic studies on restoration impacts and drafts major restoration plans," Reuben said. A stop at the city's Urban Agriculture Office and at the University Ecologia completed our formal tour.

We then strolled about the city amidst crowds of commuters and shoppers, with Reuben explaining the restorations to me and occasionally stopping to greet people he knew. At one point he said to me, "Synergistic planning was our approach. Synergism in ancient times meant regeneration through the cooperation of divine grace and human activity. We now use the word to mean systems working together to their mutual enhancement. In Croyden we comprehensively redesigned all our resource supply systems: food, water, energy, raw materials, transportation, communication, waste processing.... Efficiency and self-reliance were our bywords, so as to minimize the strain on the natural resources that support us. Thanks to the co-design of these systems, virtually nothing is wasted."

After waving to a group of schoolchildren, Reuben turned to me and continued, "What does it mean to restore a city? At first no one understood. They doubted it was possible. Did we at Croyden advocate razing the skyscrapers and apartments, then sowing grasses and forests because that's what used to be there? Did we mean to eradicate the ports and replant salt marshes? Did we want to destroy human settlements—places with great cultural significance? I laugh about it now, but it wasn't funny back in the 1980s.

"We had to explain, no, no, we mean synergistic planning, thrifty use of resources, recycling, cascading uses, matching resource quality to need, partitioning the resource stream. In rebuilding Croyden, we tried selectively and pragmatically to use principles of nature that were relevant for our task. Nature is efficient. Nature recycles: Outputs from one system are inputs for others. What once was waste from our food system, for instance, becomes useful raw material for our energy and transportation and agriculture. Agricultural and domestic wastes become energy feedstock, transportation fuels, and eventually return again as nutrients to agriculture. We no longer scramble all garbage together the way you did. Garbage that once stuffed landfills has almost been eliminated—it's now a resource."

We strolled along a street closed to traffic and paved with turf blocks—hollow stone blocks filled with earth. Prairie grasses and forbs flowered in the street. "These paving blocks can support a fire engine and emergency vehicles," said Reuben. "They allow the soil to soak up water so runoff's controlled. Water just perco-lates right into the ground. That eases the load on our storm sewers and municipal water treatment plants. The water table's up, too, and our trees are doing better." The trees indeed were thriving everywhere, often protected naturally at their base by roses, berries, or other thorny plants. "We simply replaced most ornamental plantings in town with edible trees and shrubs, pref-erably natives. These marvelous plants," he said, gesturing to some hickories, "provide us food and oxygen and shade and niches for wildlife and even some employment, plus they're lovely to look at. Native trees grow well without pampering and they support native birds and insects. The nuts are gathered and processed. The prunings are used for firewood or chipped and added to our compost piles or gasifiers. Occasionally large trees are removed for lumber and replaced with healthier young ones."

We paused to watch a sanitation worker in an electric truck emptying material for recycling from a large curbside receptacle with compartments for glass, plastics, paper, cardboard, alumi-num, steel, and other metals as well as a small sealable cylinder for toxics. "We have similar smaller receptacles in all apartment buildings," said Reuben. "It's a voluntary program but tenant participants get rent rebates."

We came to a massive apartment house. "Remarkable thing about this complex is that it's sited above our first hot rock geothermal energy plant; energy's no problem here, and the building raises much of its own food. There's a small livestock production facility near the roof and a great many other food-processing facilities."

We entered the lobby and glanced at the large liquid crystal building directory with illuminated letters. In addition to apart-ments, the complex had many industrial, cultural, and educa-tional facilities. "You could live here and never have to leave," I said.

"True," Reuben agreed. "Travel as a necessity is largely outmoded. That's meant enormous energy savings for Croyden. Of course we still indulge in travel for pleasure and education."

Deciding to make a lightning tour of inspection, we visited the food production units on the thirty-sixth floor where a winery, a cheese-making plant, a bakery, and a brewery were active. All but the cheese-making operation used locally produced products. Small fowl were raised in an odor-free facility on the thirty-seventh floor, with wastes continuously removed by a conveyor belt to a high-pressure spray cleaner where they were sluiced into a compact and well-isolated fertilizer-producing unit. "Don't be misled by the ducks and chickens or by the fish we raise," said Reuben. "Most Croydenites are largely vegetarian—meat has become a condiment and a luxury food. We supplement our diets with vegetable protein from soy, alfalfa, and other sources. *VP*, it's called here; comes in flavors and textures indistinguishable from the once common meats."

We walked up a few flights to the roof for the view and beheld the great diversity of buildings in every conceivable shape and color spread out below.

Although the roof was uncluttered, every space was intensively utilized—from the sophisticated greenhouse to the outdoor plots and the large commercial fish tanks covered with floating aquatic plants. "These are the troutapia ponds," Reuben said. I peered in at a fish resembling the tropical tilapia and the American brook trout. "Genetic engineering again," said Reuben. "The fish adapts to crowding and cold water yet it multiplies rapidly, grows quickly, and thrives on urban roofs."

"Does everything except sing lullabies at night," I ventured.

"We're working on that," he answered. "Growing our own food means we can substitute pest management for pesticides and we minimize transportation requirements to get perishables on the table quicker in better condition at lower fuel and energy costs—with less transportation and packaging."

At another corner of the roof he showed me large flats filled with what looked like a dark, rich humus. "Worm castings," he said. "We adopted John and Nancy Todd's ingenious system from *The Village as Solar Ecology*. Vegetable trimmings from the greenhouse and restaurant downstairs are fed to the worms. They are fed to the fish and chickens. We use the worm castings meanwhile to grow more vegetables which we water with sterilized effluent from the aquaculture unit. After we process our fish, the scraps are fed to the chickens, the chicken manure goes into the fertilizer mix, and duckweed from the pond surface is dried and used as green manure and livestock feed supplement. We produce so much good fertilizer here that we sell the surplus in our co-op downstairs and combine the rest with the in-house wet organic garbage for composting in the building's methane generator. It's sealed and vented out that stack above our heads. Another portion of the organic waste stream is fermented for alcohol production. And elsewhere, in our biotechnology manufacturing operation, we produce various kinds of yeast and algae."

We paused on the roof to admire one of the building's huge wind turbines on a tall tower far above the roof. "Hydraulic shock absorbers dampen vibrations," said Reuben. "We don't even need the power for this building, with all the geothermal energy we get here, but it'd be a shame to waste the electricity, wouldn't it? So we sell it back to the municipal utility. You know," he added, "the blades on large wind turbines used to break years ago because of the tremendous forces on them. Now because of the astounding advances in materials science, the strength-to-weight ratio of new ceramic, plastic, and metal alloys enables us to make huge blades that are light and strong."

We rested briefly at a small rooftop cafeteria, dining under colored umbrellas on smoked troutapia, house pilsener, homemade Stilton cheese, and miniature loaves of freshly baked wheat bread. Reuben enjoyed a piece of roast guinea hen from the thirty-seventh floor and some almond butter made from nuts of the trees in the building's courtyard. We concluded the meal with fresh pear compote from the Croyden orchard, served with homemade yogurt. "I feel restored now," he said contentedly.

"So," I proposed, "when you began using your resources widely, you began to enjoy abundance?"

"Yes."

"I'm surprised you don't recycle the air you breathe and the water."

"Well, indeed, let me show you how we handle water. We'll visit an apartment."

Soon we were graciously being shown a medium-sized suite by a proud tenant named Stuart who did engineering design work from his living room computer console. "I rarely need to visit my main office," he said. "My colleagues and I can project complex design problems on the screen and often work on them simultaneously. Many heads are better than one. We've used this approach on previously insoluble engineering problems." However, the much more mundane features of his kitchen and bathroom plumbing interested me more than his computer. "How do you ensure efficient water use?" I asked.

"As you may know," said Reuben, "80 percent of the domestic water in your day was used in the bathroom. Here in Croyden, wastewater is partitioned into what we call 'gray' and 'black' water—gray after it's used for washing; black after toilet flushing. Gray water is all collected downstairs, filtered, and given primary treatment before it's recycled for uses that require only low-quality water—uses like washing the garage floor or flushing toilets. To prevent contaminating the recycled water, it's against the law here to dump photochemicals or other household toxics down the drain."

In the kitchen next to the sink I noticed a switch. Reuben caught my eye and said, "The building's designer planned raw materials, energy, and waste handling systems together. This garbage disposal, for example, automatically sends all the organic wastes from the kitchen to the building's methane digestors by means of a vacuum line." Thanking Stuart for admitting us to his home, we then took leave.

"A couple of other things," said Reuben, leading me to an elevator and downstairs again to the basement. "The building's laundry," he announced, opening a door to a cool, clean room with shiny banks of machinery. "Most of the heat from the washers and driers is recovered and stored in a phase-change salt system beneath the laundromat.

"Several floors beneath us is the geothermal wellhead, encased in its soundproof bunker. Also on this floor are the computers that regulate the building's heat balance. And we keep the composting toilet here in the basement as well. It's a totally enclosed unit. Solid human wastes are decomposed bacteriologically inside. The unit destroys toxins in the digestion process. The wastes enter at the top. Later a dry granular product—greatly reduced in volume—is removed at the bottom of the unit in a continuous batch operation. A complete cycle takes a few months. After the trace heavy metals are removed, the refined organic product has many uses in outdoor revegetation. Shall we go now?" he asked.

"Well, could we just have a quick look around at the main floor market?"

We entered the co-op upstairs and Reuben said, "Large appliances were labeled in your time as to their energy use. Now we label all important commodities with their embedded resource and energy values. For example, you can read on these paper plates how much wood was pulped for each hundred pounds of the paper. Or how much petroleum or jojoba oil went into your plastic picnic utensils and Styrofoam cups; how much electricity was consumed for your aluminum pie plate. If you're still eating hamburger, you can tell how many acre-feet of water and how many acres of land it took to raise each pound of beef. There's a computer console at the front of the store that has all this data plus other useful information about each product and its manufacturer."

Leaving the market, we rambled through a residential neighborhood on a loop destined to return us eventually to the airport. People were bustling along the street or caring for their gardens. Children were still enjoying jacks and other sidewalk games as they have the world over. We soon came to a district of older single-family homes converted to multiple-family dwellings with various additions. We visited one unit that had a greenhouse and aquaculture system, and was, in microcosm, almost as self-sufficient as the large apartment complex. There were also rabbit pens and beehives. I paused to admire the sheathing of solar cells that covered the roof of the house and southern walls like shingles. "The thinnest of the solar cells come in rolls and are adhesive-coated so they can be pasted on," said Reuben. "We also use composite collectors in Croyden. They're extremely efficient and convert sunlight to electricity while simultaneously trapping infrared radiation for space heating."

"Where do you find the time to care for all this—this agribusiness complex here in the backyard?" I asked the homeowner.

"We belong to the urban agricultural co-op," she explained. "In return for produce and poultry, they maintain the production units and make regular service calls. This program's an outgrowth of Croyden's urban harvest project. We inventoried and collected all the food that would otherwise have gone to waste in the city. It's supplied to the needy now and to small food-processing co-ops. Mobile food-processing vans also come by here when needed."

"How do you avoid the usual barnyard smells and flies?" I asked.

"The co-op cleans constantly," the owner said, "and we use sophisticated traps to keep flies under control. Those two hanging containers you see—like cardboard milk cartons—are baited with a powerful chemical attractant. Flies find it irresistible."

On leaving the yard, I marveled to Reuben at how settled the whole city looked. The people seemed amiable, and the neighborhoods looked safe and well cared for.

"A result of planning," he replied. "People no longer move as much as they used to. We gradually but deliberately discouraged transiency because it contributes to a lack of environmental concern—an indifference to one's surroundings. When residents know they'll be moving out soon, they have little incentive to work toward environmental improvement. In publicly owned housing, we freeze people's rents so long as they stay put. This gives them a financial incentive not to move. Plus, we offer lower rents and preferential public housing access to families without private cars and to families that work in the same neighborhood as the public housing. Obviously this reduces commuting.

"We also impose differential property taxes on buildings

according to the degree of resource and energy conservation practiced. Wasteful, inefficient buildings pay more. Because recycling and efficient resource use cut environmental costs, we rebate these savings to residents. The state provides generous tax credits to induce further investment in resource efficiency."

Walking on to another neighborhood we came to an extension of the main city park. It was fenced, so to cross it we had to let ourselves in through a tall gate. Though only about a hundred feet wide here, the park formed a buffer between adjoining urban neighborhoods and served as a wildlife corridor so that small game could travel from one main urban park node to another. The small nodes formed a larger continuous wildlife refuge area, and salmon were running in the corridor's creek. People were taking urban hikes along the creek. Noticing my interest, a park attendant struck up a conversation about the wildlife. "We've just found a family of foxes here," he said, "and, of course, there are lots of raccoons. They're at home along the water." The tall grass and reeds and the hollow trees looked so natural it was hard to believe that all the vegetation had been planted within the past decade. Yet the whole community was now self-sustaining, just like a balanced aquarium. "Creek restoration is labor-intensive and it provides jobs for city youth and unemployed adults," Reuben explained as we moved on across a footbridge. "We have a job training program in resource restoration skills."

In another ten steps we were back in the city, but it was not an unpleasant transition. The air was fresh, and traffic flowed without congestion yet at reasonable speed. I noticed here that trolley rails could be slid in and out of grooves in the streets. When I inquired about it, Reuben explained that an entire track system could be modified overnight. Advanced electric buses that could be operated along fixed routes without a driver provided intercity transport and were controlled electronically through a guide rail. "Much of our long-distance travel now is by high-speed train, though. They're suspended by electromagnets over the rails and then electromagnetic repulsion propels them

like rockets at 500 mph. But in the city we rely mainly on the bicycles and on ultralight electric cars and carts. And, of course,
there's the public transport you've seen."

"You haven't given up private cars entirely, have you?" I
said.

"We still use them occasionally. Each large apartment building has a few in a motor pool and cars can be rented from stands
on the street. A valid credit card will activate them and they can
be returned to any station.

"To keep traffic in check, we link transportation planning
with land use and energy planning through our comprehensive
urban plan. We try to encourage development around transit
corridors to ensure systems are fully utilized.

"Transportation is a major energy consumer and private cars
in the past sabotaged all efforts to make cities livable. Cities in
the 1980s devoted up to 50 percent or more of their land to
cars—for streets, gas stations, parking lots, and so on. You paid
quite a price for the internal combustion engine, with its smog
and noise and lead and its leaky oils and asbestos brake linings.
Those vehicles siphoned away an awesome proportion of your
resources. Think what a public transit system you could have
built with those billions. Think of the millions of acres of prime
land you could have saved! And don't forget all the dreadful automobile accidents you could have avoided! We put a halt to it in
Croyden. We saw we had to control cars or they'd control us. It
wasn't easy because people considered it an inalienable right to
hop impulsively in a chrome horse and roar down the road
spewing out pollution.

"Some cities reacted by squandering billions on ill-conceived
public rail systems without coupling transit planning to land use
planning and growth management, so they just aggravated urban
sprawl. And those systems often foundered—draining public
funds—while people ignored them for freeways and private cars.
Your planners tended to respond to congestion with a wider
bridge or a new freeway or an inflexible multibillion-dollar rail
system. But this fragmentary planning just led to more urban
congestion, and more defections from mass transit. It always

seemed cheaper to people to use the car for one more trip rather than pay for public transit in fares and inconvenience. By contrast, our transit system is free and it's first class.

"At first we tried incentives to keep cars out of town. We set up free bridge toll lanes and express lanes for carpoolers and buses and we gave free lottery tickets to bus and train riders. Next we restricted parking. At that point many people voluntarily gave up driving to work. Then we went for high taxes on private cars and fuel so we could compensate the rest of society for the air pollution, energy waste, and congestion the cars caused. Ultimately, by rapidly depleting fossil fuels, drivers were raising energy costs to all of us. After a struggle, we made sales and registration taxes progressively greater for large private cars with fuel-inefficient engines. We also raised tolls and parking fees. We spent the money raised on the fast, widely available public transit systems that you now see.

"Finally we even had to resort to inner city permits simply to exclude most private cars from congested parts of the city. The penalties were traffic citations and fines. We pioneered the carless neighborhood, where residents get preferential rents or property-tax relief."

"How did you pay for all of these incentives?"

"We reordered our priorities a bit and moved environmental restoration and protection higher up on the list. Government has the resources to do this kind of thing if people demand it, you know. Also we couldn't afford *not* to fund incentives. We just compared the costs of providing decent transit and these measures to the full costs of not controlling cars and growth—the acid rains to which smog contributes, the loss of prime land, and so on. We saw that, even in economic terms, controls on cars ultimately were the only way to go.

"Restraining growth wasn't easy. Capital for infrastructure reconstruction was often less available than it would've been for new highways. We financed our long-term urban development in part by ecological restoration bonds, in part on a pay-as-you-go basis.

"As we redesigned the city, we also tried to prevent private commercial interests from capturing the increased land values that resulted from our sound public investments. We felt the public, not just real estate developers, should benefit from public investment. Previously a primary force for the new transit development had been private developers who held inner-city property. They lobbied for the kind of mass transit and freeways that they thought would drive up the value of their properties regardless of the social consequences. Then, once mass transit was oriented toward their holdings, they built high rises far beyond an area's capacity to absorb the growth. So now when we create mass transit systems with major impacts on central-city real estate, we sometimes place part of the affected land under public corporations' control. Thus windfall increases in land values can be captured as rents by the public. The new wealth can then be used to create jobs and affordable housing for those whose housing costs rose due to the increased land values."

By this time I felt I could scarcely absorb any new information. "It's been a fascinating trip," I said.

"Yes, I thought it would be," Reuben said. "And you're welcome to come back anytime." He then escorted me back to the Croyden Interchronological Airport, we shook hands, and I boarded my jet.

Once settled in my seat, I realized my head was spinning with visions of how a hundred other cities I knew would look if restored. I leaned back and closed my eyes to meditate on the day's extraordinary experience.

V

CONCLUSIONS

15

Modest Proposals

Throughout this book we have seen how greatly restoration depends on the initiative and determination of individuals like Tony Look, Tom Hirsch, Fred Ulishney, Michael and Judy Corbett, or Cheryl and Brian Walton. They owe their successes mainly to the drive and persistence that comes from passionate commitment to environmental causes.

Like most resource restorers, they generally started on a small scale, often in isolation, with little money or experience. Usually they began by working on their own time without pay, and slighting other commitments. As they learned about restoration and achieved small symbolic victories, people joined them—sometimes spontaneously, sometimes because the organizers deliberately cultivated support; thus Francis Smith and Bill Becker publicized their efforts, Ray Schulenberg and Robert Betz taught restoration techniques to others. The essential point is that restoration work may begin alone, but eventually cooperative effort and financing are crucial for success.

The presence of a supportive legislative mandate—such as the Clean Water Act, the Clean Lakes Program, and the Surface

Mine Control and Reclamation Act—is also very helpful. If a project falls within some public agency's area of responsibility, the resource restorer who builds an effective political coalition and commands that agency's attention may be able to attract its financial assistance.

The resource problems tackled by the Marion Stoddarts and Bill Guckerts of this book are widespread. Creatively conducted local repair efforts directed at these problems can be wonderful tools for educating the public and decision-makers about restoration. They can also attract corporate, foundation, and government support. Model local restoration projects, even little ones, may thus ultimately lay the groundwork for a national restoration program capable of transforming the American landscape and providing millions of new jobs.

With so many claims on its resources, however, government is unlikely to begin any large-scale restoration program voluntarily. Grass-roots initiative and continual political pressure are necessary if government is to become committed to a coherent national program. But even if and when government funds are forthcoming, the task of designing and implementing that program cannot be confidently left to government. Major restoration projects are complex and often experimental, and they require people with strong motivation, knowledge, and ingenuity—unusual qualities that the average government bureaucrat cannot be assumed to possess. Therefore, skillful independent leadership is another prerequisite for a successful national restoration program.

One useful early role for government might be the creation of a national "Restoration Corps," loosely modeled on the New Deal's Civilian Conservation Corps (CCC).

The CCC proved that concerted environmental repair efforts can protect and improve resources on a massive scale. From 1933 to 1943 the Corps revegetated more than 800,000 acres of rangeland, protected 154 million square yards of stream and lake banks, and reclaimed additional millions of acres of damaged land. The CCC planted more than two billion trees, created forty-four wildlife refuges, and gave work to three million people. More recent experience with state and county conservation corps projects has reaffirmed the contemporary value of such work. With today's ecological knowledge and a technology far beyond what the CCC had available, a national Restoration Corps could accomplish a great deal more.

The Restoration Corps could repair native habitats and restock them with native species. Hundreds of native plant nurseries could be established for the trees, shrubs, and wildflowers needed. The corps could apply anti-erosion measures to millions of acres of agricultural lands. It could clean up thousands of miles of lake, river, and stream frontage. It could leave behind productive resources and permanent jobs in maintaining and extending the restorations.

In 1984, Congress passed a bill to establish an American Conservation Corps, but the measure was vetoed by President Reagan. Even had the bill become law, the Conservation Corps as contemplated by Congress encompassed many activities wholly unrelated to restoration, such as constructing recreational facilities and maintaining roads. Moreover, it was designed as a training program for unemployed (often unskilled) youth and young adults. An ecologically oriented Restoration Corps will also require *skilled* workers—people versed in biology and botany as well as construction trades.

The scale if not the success of U.S. restoration efforts will no doubt depend heavily on the intensity of popular support for restoration. The necessary broad constituency for this (and for environmental causes in general) can be built if restoration programs are clearly linked to the fulfillment of people's legitimate needs for clean air, clean water, healthful food, meaningful work, and better overall living conditions. This linkage can indeed be demonstrated: All the economic progress and energy development in the world will not sustain us if the air and water are unfit to consume and the soils are too depleted to grow healthful food. Restoration can reconcile the sometimes conflicting social impulses to improve the condition both of the "natural world" and of humanity.

One way to launch a popularly based restoration movement

would be at local and regional restoration assemblies. Economic studies could precede these meetings, to prepare projections of the resource and employment impacts of local programs. These economic assessments could estimate the area's ecological and economic restoration potential in the form of new jobs and of sustained yield income from restored resources. The studies should be based on an understanding of the area's pristine (pre-development) resources to provide a sense of what is ecologically possible. The local/regional assemblies would then use the completed studies as a basis for planning specific restoration programs.

Strong local consensus throughout the country on the need for nationwide restoration could eventually lead to the adoption of federal and state restoration incentive programs. These would encourage farmers, fishermen, lumbermen, miners, and others well acquainted with resources to bring them up to national or local standards. Incentives could include tax deductions, individual tax credits, loans, public insurance benefits, and grants.

A simpler but less populistic way to begin systematic planning on the local level would be to work with county boards of supervisors. They could establish citizen advisory councils on restoration to study the costs and benefits of local projects. The councils' recommendations could be reviewed by resource specialists and such panels could include people with backgrounds in economics, life sciences, and engineering. Restoration plans could also be drafted by regional councils of governments and other existing regional organizations. Successful local and regional efforts would make passage of statewide restoration programs more likely.

Since restoration spending is often a long-term investment, we need to study ways of funding it. Many possible financial mechanisms exist, including sales of long-term bonds. The basic thing to remember is that the resources needed for a massive U.S. restoration program are certainly available if we can muster the political will to use them. As a nation we need to reexamine what we now spend our money on. A small fraction of the wealth spent on space probes and military weaponry could buy the U.S. a restoration program beyond compare.

The nation needs less emphasis on resource-destroying exponential growth, and more emphasis on stewardship of Nature. With respect for all life and a mobilization of young and old to care for our shared resources, we can help the wounded Earth to heal itself.

Acknowledgments

Scores of individuals contributed information to this book. Virtually without exception they gave their time and knowledge generously without thought of personal reward and often at considerable inconvenience or hardship. I am deeply grateful to them all and would like to thank them collectively for their assistance. This book is truly a collaborative effort, although responsibility for any errors is exclusively mine.

I owe a special debt to the people about whom this book is written, for the public spirit that has animated their works, and for the unfailing graciousness with which they assisted me in my research. Without their unstinting help, this book could certainly not have been written. I am also especially grateful to my parents, whose support and faith in me sustained this project through its difficulties.

Several foundations assisted me in meeting the expenses of conducting my research on restoration. The primary support came from the Max and Anna Levinson Foundation. I am particularly grateful to Sidney Shapiro of the Foundation and to Carl and Linda Levinson. Other vital research support came from the

Evergreen Fund, the Foundation for National Progress, the Frank J. Weeden Foundation, the Island Foundation, the Jewish Endowment Fund, and from Clarence E. Heller, Stanley K. Sheinbaum, W. M. Roth, L.T.T., and O.H.T.

A number of people critically read this manuscript in whole or part. The comments and editorial advice of James N. Frey, David K. Dunaway, David Lenderts, and Lester Gorn were particularly valuable. I also thank the following readers for their suggestions: Vincent Berg, Marguerite DiGiorgio, Mary Jean Haley, William R. Jordan III, Jeanne Lance, Robert H. Masterson, Marilyn Maze, Steven Mayer, Joe Miller, Ginny Morgan, Larry Riggs, Nancy Robinson, Sara Schwartzbord, Michael Shuman, Nina Wallerstein, and others.

I'm indebted to William R. Jordan III for his article, "Hint of Green," in *Restoration and Management Notes* (1, no. 4, [summer 1983]), which I used freely with his permission to update the chapter on marsh restoration, and to Bill Becker for his thoughts and writings on Soldiers Grove, Wisconsin, and to the citizens of Soldiers Grove whom I interviewed there.

Thanks to the Chinook Learning Center on Whidby Island in Puget Sound and participants in the Center's 1983 Planetary Village Conference for ideas, inspiration, and encouragement.

Thanks to Robin Wolaner, Elena Vasquez, Ellen Bailey, and other members of the Foundation for National Progress staff.

Thanks to my editor at Knopf, Lee Goerner, for his patience, skill, and tact; to my agent Keith Korman of Raines and Raines; and to Peggy Harrison, Chris Pomroy, and Linda Gaede for tape transcriptions and to Linda Gaede for her meticulous, accurate, and unusually conscientious typing (and for catching some of my worst bloopers).

I am grateful to the following individuals for information about specific restoration projects and other assistance. In "Mother Nashua": Ann E. Breen, the Waterfront Center, Donald Crocker, Richard Cronin, Massachusetts Division of Fish and Wildlife, Ed Himlin, George Keyes, Barry Lawson, Lorna Levi, Joe McGin, Evelyn Murphy, Nashua River Watershed Association staff, Zig Plater, and Katheryn Preston, Massachusetts

Department of Environmental Quality; in "Lake Revival": Jeff Dennis, Maine Department of Environmental Protection, Robert Johnson, Tennessee Valley Authority, James Jowett, U.S. Environmental Protection Agency, Wendy King, Cobbossee Watershed District, William MacDonald, Tyler Libby, U.S. Soil Conservation Service, and Craig Vassel, U.S. Environmental Protection Agency; in "Sea-Run Brookies": Mike Arritt and Al Brewster; in "The Marsh Builder": Joanna Garbisch; in "Redwoods Rising": Deborah Bloch, John DeWitt, Ellie Mansfield, and the Sempervirens Fund staff; in "The Land Skinners" and "Badlands and Indian Range": Richard G. Brittain, Mining and Mineral Resources Research Institute, University of Arizona, Tucson, John Cairns, Jr., Virginia Polytechnic Institute and State University, David Callaghan, West Virginia Department of Natural Resources, Maurice Deul, U.S. Bureau of Mines, Murray Dogerty, U.S. Bureau of Mines, J. Anthony Ercole, Pennsylvania Department of Environmental Resources, Bruce Ferguson, Department of Landscape Architecture, Pennsylvania State University, Bud Frederick, Pennsylvania Department of Environmental Resources, Benjamin C. Greene, West Virginia Surface Mining and Reclamation Association, David Hamilton, U.S. Office of Surface Mining, Wayne Hilgedick, Peabody Coal Co., Roger Hornberger, Pennsylvania Department of Environmental Resources, David Kohler, Bureau of Land Management, Zoe Mankowski, California Division of Mines and Geology, John McFerrin, Appalachian Research and Defense Fund, Motts Myrhnan, University of Arizona, Marc Nelson, Bureau of Land Management, Jeffrey Radford, Bureau of Land Management, John S. Seely, Vipond and Vipond, Inc., Greg Smith, U.S. Geological Survey, Neil Tostenson, Ohio Mining and Reclamation Association, Chester Truax, American Mining Congress, Peter Warshaw, Rick Webb, Braxton County Environmental Action, Joe Yancik, National Coal Association, and Lauri Zell, Mining and Reclamation Council of America; in "The Prairie Makers" and "Highway Prairies": Roger C. Anderson, Grant Cottam, Francis Hole, University of Wisconsin–Madison, and Virginia Kline, University of Wisconsin–

Madison Arboretum; in "The Toxic Temple": Michael Beck, Michigan Department of Natural Resources, Phil Cole, New Jersey Department of Environmental Protection, Jeffrey L. Dauphin, Waste Systems Institute, Tony Farro, New Jersey Department of Environmental Protection, John Hesse, Michigan Department of Natural Resources, Thomas J. Hickey, Malcolm Pirnie, Inc., Larry Holcomb, Hugh Kaufman, U.S. Environmental Protection Agency, Joe J. Mayhew, Chemical Manufacturers Association, Peter Montague, Princeton University, Keith Onsdorf, Mike Rios, Dow Chemical Corp., Bill Schroeder, John M. Shauver, Michigan Department of Natural Resources, Robert Stephens, California Department of Health Services, and Mary Ann Thompson; in "Falcon Fervor": The Peregrine Fund staff; in "Soldiers Grove": Tim Bacon, Kathy Fairchild, Steve Hinker, Audubon Society, Gerald Scoville, and Cecil Turk; and for general advice: Peter Behr, Robert Jenkins, The Nature Conservancy, Huey Johnson, California Resources Agency.

Bibliography

SELECTED REFERENCES

CHAPTER 1

Annual Report of the Town of Lancaster, Massachusetts. South Lancaster, Mass.: The College Press, 1963.

Division of Water Pollution Control, Massachusetts Department of Environmental Quality Engineering. *The Nashua River Basin Water Quality Management Plan 1981.* N.p., n.d.

Dyer, Thomas S. "Riverside Revitalization," Report to the Fitchburg Conservation Commission, River Subcommittee, Fitchburg, Mass., 1978.

Federal Water Pollution Control Administration, U.S. Department of the Interior, 1966. *Report on Pollution of the Merrimack River and Certain Tributaries—Part V: Nashua River.* Lawrence, Mass.

Harreisen, Mary L. "The Nashua River Clean-up." *Massachusetts Wildlife* (May–June 1970).

Harris, Charles D. *The Nashua River Canoe Guide.* Groton, Mass.: Nashua River Watershed Association, 1976.

Kirkpatrick, Doris. *The City and the River.* Fitchburg, Mass.: Fitchburg Historical Society, 1971.

"Nashua River Cleanup," *Soldiers* (March 1982).

Nashua River Watershed Association. *Preliminary Regional Plan for the Nashua River Greenway,* rev. ed. Groton, Mass., 1971.

———. *NRWA Program Plan Summary 1982.* Fitchburg, Mass., 1982.

———. *Water Resources Program 1982.* Fitchburg, Mass., 1982.

Nielsen, Nancy L. "The Nashua River Greenway: Pepperell Pond Area." Prepared for Rich Tree Farm Task Force, Nashua River Watershed Association, 1979.

President's Council on Environmental Quality. *Environmental Quality—1980.* Washington, D.C.: U.S. Government Printing Office.

Roy Mann Associates. *Plan for the Nashua River Watershed.* Groton, Mass.: Nashua River Watershed Association, 1970 (rev. 1972).

CHAPTER 2

Foster, Charles I., ed. *The History of Winthrop, Evolution of a Maine Community.* Kennebec, Maine: Town of Winthrop, 1971.

"Gordon Testifies for Clean Lakes." *Lake Line* 2 (June 1982).

Gordon, Thomas U. "Local Commitment to Lake Restoration: The Cobbossee Watershed Example." In *Restoration of Lakes and Inland Waters, International Symposium on Inland Waters and Lake Restoration,* September 8–12, 1980, Portland, Maine, EPA 440 / 5–81–010. Washington, D.C.: U.S. Government Printing Office, 1980.

Johnson, Bob. "Clean Lakes Needs Your Support." *Lake Line* 1 (January 1982). North American Lake Management Society, P.O. Box 68, East Winthrop, Maine 04343.

Merrill, Daphne Winslow. *The Lakes of Maine.* Rockland, Maine: Courier-Gazette, 1973.

U.S. Environmental Protection Agency. Center for Environmental Research Information, "Lake Restoration in Cobbossee Watershed," Capsule Report EPA 625 / 2–80–027. Office of Research and Development: Cincinnati, Ohio, July 1980.

U.S. Environmental Protection Agency. *Economic Benefits of the Clean Lakes Program.* EPA 440 / 5–80–081. Office of Water Regulations and Standards, Criteria and Standards Division: Washington, D.C., 1980.

Uttormark, Paul D. "General Concepts of Lake Degradation and Lake Restoration." In *Lake Restoration, Proceedings of a National Conference*, August 22–24, 1978, EPA 440 / 5–79–001. U.S. Environmental Protection Agency: Minneapolis, Minn., March 1979.

CHAPTER 3

Pero, Thomas. "New Life for the Quashnet." *Trout* 20:32–36.

Smith, Jerome V. C. *Natural History of the Fishes of Massachusetts, Embracing a Practical Essay on Angling.* New York: Freshet Press, 1970.

Trout Unlimited, Southeastern Massachusetts Chapter. "Quashnet River Restoration." November 1970.

CHAPTER 4

Teal, John and Mildred. *The Life and Death of a Salt Marsh.* Boston, Mass.: Little, Brown, 1969.

CHAPTERS 6 AND 7

Anaconda Corp. "Proposed Reclamation Plan for the Jackpile-Paguate Mine." 1980.

Bitler, John R., and Robert J. Evans. "Coal Surface Mining Reclamation Costs—Appalachian and Midwestern Coal Supply Districts." In *Third Symposium on Surface Mining and Reclamation.* Vol. II. National Coal Association, 1975.

Cairns, John, Jr. *The Recovery Process in Damaged Ecosystems.* Ann Arbor, Mich.: Ann Arbor Science Publishers, Inc., 1980.

Fung, R. *Surface Coal Mining Technology: Engineering and Environmental Aspects.* Park Ridge, N.J.: Noyes Data Corporation, 1981.

President's Council on Environmental Quality. *Environmental Quality 1981*, 12th Annual Report of the Council on Environmental Quality. Washington, D.C.: U.S. Government Printing Office, 1982.

"Reclamation Guidebook." *Coal Age* 82 (July 1977): 43–130.

Robinson, Paul. "Can Anaconda Reclaim Jackpile?" *Mine Talk* 1 (July–August 1981). Available from Southwest Research and Information Center, P.O. Box 4524, Albuquerque, N.M.

U.S. Department of the Interior, U.S. Geological Survey, Bureau of Indian Affairs. "Request for Public Comment, Jackpile-Paguate Reclamation Environmental Impact Statement, Laguna Indian Reservation, Valencia County, New Mexico." February 1981.

U.S. Department of the Interior, Office of Surface Mining Reclamation and Enforcement. *Implementation of Program Policies for Federal, State, and Indian Abandoned Mine Land Reclamation Under Title IV of the Surface Mining Control and Reclamation Act of 1977, Final Environmental Statement OSM–EIS–2,* Washington, D.C.: U.S. Government Printing Office, 1980.

Wells, Stephen G., and Devone E. Rose. "Applications of Geomorphology to Surface Coal-Mining Reclamation, Northwestern New Mexico." New Mexico Geological Society Special Publication No. 10 (1981): 69–83.

Wiener, Daniel Philip. *Reclaiming the West: The Coal Industry and Surface-Mined Lands.* New York: INFORM, 1980.

CHAPTERS 8 AND 9

Anderson, Roger. "The Prairies." *Outdoor Illinois* (February 1972).

Catlin, George. Cited in *Guide to the Arboretum Prairies.* Madison, Wisc.: Friends of the Arboretum, 1971.

Leopold, Nina. "Leopold at the Arboretum: A Daughter Remembers." *Arboretum News and Friends Newsletter,* University of Wisconsin Arboretum, Madison (Fall 1982).

Morrison, Daniel G. "Use of Prairie Vegetation on Disturbed Sites," Transportation Research Record 822, Transportation Research Board, Commission on Sociotechnical Systems, National Research Council. Washington, D.C.: National Academy of Sciences, 1981.

Skinner, Robert M. "Grassland Use Patterns and Prairie Bird Populations in Missouri." In *Prairie: A Multiple View,* edited by Mohan K. Wali. Grand Forks, N.D.: The University of North Dakota Press, 1975.

CHAPTER 10

Belliveau, Michael. "Hazardous Wastes—A Guide to Citizen Action." *CBE Environmental Review* (July / August 1982).

Brown, Michael O. *Laying Waste.* New York: Washington Square Press, 1979.

Cartwright, Keros. "Factors in Design, Location, and Integrity of

Landfills." *Great Lakes Waste and Pollution Review Magazine* 1 (April 1983).

CAS Registry Number 77–47–4, Chemical Evaluation Search and Retrieval System, NIH / EPA User Support, Computer Sciences Corporation, Falls Church, Virginia.

Committee on Disposal of Hazardous Industrial Wastes, National Materials Advisory Board, Commission on Engineering and Technical Systems, National Research Council. *Management of Hazardous Industrial Waste, Research and Development Needs,* NMAB–398. Washington, D.C.: National Academy Press, 1983.

Comptroller General. *Waste Disposal Practices—A Threat to the Health and the Nation's Water Supply.* Report to the Congress of the United States, U.S. General Accounting Office, CED–78–120, June 16, 1978. Washington, D.C.: U.S. Government Printing Office, 1978.

"Congress Ready to Move on Waste Law." *National News Report,* August 31, 1983.

Epstein, Samuel P., Lester O. Brown, and Carl Pope. *Hazardous Waste in America.* San Francisco: Sierra Club Books, 1982.

"Following U.S., Europe Awakens to the Dangers of Toxic Wastes." *New York Times,* February 20, 1983.

Gessner, G. Hawley. *The Condensed Chemical Dictionary,* 8th ed., rev. New York: Van Nostrand Reinhold, 1971.

Maugh, Thomas H. II. "Toxic Waste Disposal, A Growing Problem." *Science* 204 (May 25, 1979).

Nader, Ralph, Ronald Brownstein, and John Richard, eds. *Who's Poisoning America.* San Francisco: Sierra Club Books, 1981.

President's Council on Environmental Quality. *Contamination of Ground Water by Toxic Organic Chemicals.* Washington, D.C.: U.S. Government Printing Office, 1981.

Shabecoff, Philip. "418 Toxic Dumps Listed in Cleanup." *New York Times,* December 21, 1982.

———. "U.S. Efforts Grow to Protect Water." *New York Times,* July 26, 1983.

———. "Hazardous Waste Exceeds Estimates." *New York Times,* August 31, 1983.

"The Toxic Waste Crisis." *Newsweek,* March 7, 1983.

Trost, Cathy. "The Poisoning of Montague, Michigan," parts I and II. *Detroit Free Press,* July 19 and 26, 1981.

U.S. Office of Technology Assessment. *Technologies and Manage-*

ment Strategies for Hazardous Waste Control, Summary, OTA–M–197. Washington, D.C.: U.S. Government Printing Office, March 1983.

Williams, Winston. "Saving Face and Cleaning Up." *New York Times,* March 13, 1983.

CHAPTER 11

Burnham, W. A., J. Craig, J. H. Enderson, and W. R. Heinrich. "Artificial Increase in Reproduction of Wild Peregrine Falcons." *Journal of Wildlife Management* 42 (1978): 626–28.

Cade, Tom J. "Falcon Farming." *Animal Kingdom* 78 (1975): 3–9.

———. *Falcons of the World.* Sausalito, Calif.: Comstock Editions Inc., 1982.

———. "Manipulating the Nesting Biology of Endangered Birds." In *Endangered Birds,* edited by S. A. Temple. Madison: University of Wisconsin Press, 1978.

Cade, Tom J., and P. R. Dague. "Peregrine Falcon Recovery." *Delaware Conservationist* 22 (1978): 22–24.

Cade, Tom J., and Richard Fyfe. "The North American Peregrine Survey, 1970." *Canadian Field Naturalist* 84 (1970): 231–45.

———. "What Makes Peregrine Falcons Breed in Captivity?" In *Endangered Birds,* edited by S. A. Temple. Madison: University of Wisconsin Press, 1978.

Cade, Tom J., Jeffrey L. Lincer, Clayton M. White, David G. Rosenau, and L. G. Swartz. "DDE Residues and Eggshell Changes in Alaskan Falcons and Hawks." *Science* 171 (1971): 955–57.

Cade, Tom J., and Clayton M. White. "Alaska's Falcons: The Issue of Survival." *The Living Wilderness* 39 (1976): 35–47.

Cade, Tom J., Clayton M. White, and John R. Haugh. "Peregrines and Pesticides in Alaska." *Condor* 70 (1968): 83–87.

Enderson, James H. "A Breeding and Migration Survey of the Peregrine Falcon." *Wilson Bull.* 77 (1965): 327–39.

Fyfe, Richard W., Stanley A. Temple, and Tom J. Cade. "The 1975 North American Peregrine Falcon Survey." *Canadian Field Naturalist* 90 (1976).

Grossman, Mary Louise, and John Hamlet. *Birds of Prey of the World.* New York: Clarkson N. Potter, 1964.

Hickey, Joseph J. "Eastern Populations of the Duck Hawk." *Auk* 59 (1942): 176–204.

Hickey, Joseph J., ed. *Peregrine Falcon Populations*. Milwaukee: University of Wisconsin Press, 1969.

Hickey, Joseph J., and D. W. Anderson. "Chlorinated Hydrocarbons and Eggshell Changes in Raptorial and Fisheating Birds." *Science* 162 (1968): 271–73.

Jackson, Donald D. "Fighting Beak and Claw." *Sports Illustrated*, May 16, 1977.

Kaufmann, John. "Soaring Free Again," *National Wildlife* (February–March 1976).

Kaufmann, John, and Heinz Meng. *Falcons Return, Restoring an Endangered Species*. New York: William Morrow, 1975.

Nelson, R. Wayne. "Observations on the Decline and Survival of the Peregrine Falcon." *Canadian Field Naturalist* 84:313–19.

Piddock, Charles. "Falcons Rescued from Extinction." *Current Science* 62 (1977): 4–5.

Schick, Alice. *The Peregrine Falcons*. New York: The Dial Press, 1975.

Sherrod, S. K., and T. J. Cade. "Release of Peregrine Falcons by Hacking." In *Birds of Prey Management Techniques*, edited by T. A. Geer. British Falconers Club, 1978.

Wood, Peter. "To the Aid of Rare Birds." *Time-Life Nature / Science Annual*, 1977.

Zimmerman, David R. *To Save a Bird in Peril*. New York: Coward, McCann and Geoghegan, 1975.

———. "That the Peregrine Shall Live." *Audubon* 177 (1975): 38–49.

CHAPTER 12

Corbett, Michael N. *A Better Way to Live*. Emmaus, Penn.: Rodale Press, 1981.

Currie, Lauchlin. *Taming the Megalopolis*. Oxford: Pergamon Press, 1976.

Dickey, John Wagner. "Innovations in Transportation Systems for New Towns." In *Innovations for New Towns*, edited by Gideon Golani. New York: Praeger Publishers, 1976.

Gibson, J. E. *Designing the City: A Systemic Approach*. New York: John Wiley & Sons, 1977.

Kaiser, Edward J., Karl Elfers, Sidney Cohn, et al. *Promoting Environmental Quality Through Urban Planning and Controls*. Center for Urban and Regional Studies, University of North Carolina at Chapel Hill, for Environmental Studies Division, Washington Environmental Research Center, Office of Research and Development, U.S. Environmental Protection Agency, Grant R801376, June 1983.

Leckie, Jim, et al. *More Other Homes and Garbage*. San Francisco: Sierra Club Books, 1981.

MacCorkle, Stuart A. *Cities from Scratch*. San Antonio: Naylor, 1974.

Meier, Richard L. *Planning for an Urban World*. Cambridge: MIT Press, 1974.

Miller, Brown, Neil J. Pinney, and William S. Saslow. *Innovation in New Communities*. Cambridge: MIT Press, 1971.

Morris, David. *Self-Reliant Cities*. San Francisco: Sierra Club, 1982.

Morris, David, and Karl Hess. *Neighborhood Power*. Boston: Beacon Press, 1975.

Todd, John, and Nancy Jack Todd. *Tomorrow Is Our Permanent Address*. New York: Harper & Row, 1980.

———. *The Village as Solar Ecology*. East Falmouth, Mass.: The New Alchemy Institute, 1980.

CHAPTER 13

Becker, William S. "The Making of a Solar Village, A Case Study of a Solar Downtown Development Project at Soldiers Grove, Wisconsin." Wisconsin Energy Extension Service, undated. (Available from Lorian Press, Elgin, Illinois.)

———. "Come Rain, Come Shine, A Case Study of a Floodplain Relocation Project at Soldiers Grove, Wisconsin." Madison: Bureau of Water Regulation and Zoning, Wisconsin Department of Natural Resources, undated.

David, Elizabeth, and Judith Mayer. "Comparing Costs of Alternative Flood Hazard Mitigation Plans, The Case of Soldiers Grove, Wisconsin." *APA Journal* (Winter 1984).

GENERAL REFERENCES

Bradshaw, A. D., and M. J. Chadwick. *The Restoration of Land: The Ecology and Reclamation of Derelict and Degraded Land*. Berkeley and Los Angeles: University of California Press, 1980.

Cairns, J., Jr. *The Recovery Process in Damaged Ecosystems.* Ann Arbor: Ann Arbor Science Publishers, 1980.

Cairns, J., Jr., K. L. Dickson, and E. E. Herricks. *Recovery and Restoration of Damaged Ecosystems.* Charlottesville: University Press of Virginia, 1975.

Chadwick, M. J., and G. T. Goodman. *The Ecology of Resource Degradation and Renewal.* New York: John Wiley & Sons, 1975.

Council on Environmental Quality. *Global Future: Time to Act,* Report to the President on Global Resources, Environment and Population. Washington, D.C.: U.S. Government Printing Office, 1981.

Holdgate, M. W., and M. J. Woodman. *The Breakdown and Restoration of Ecosystems.* New York: Plenum Press, 1978.

Schiechtl, Hugo. *Bioengineering for Land Reclamation and Conservation.* Edmonton, Alberta: University of Alberta Press, 1980.

Tandy, Cliff. *Landscape of Industry.* London: Leonard Hill Books, International Textbook, 1975.

Thomas, William L., et al. *Man's Role in Changing the Face of the Earth.* Chicago and London: University of Chicago Press, 1956.

JOURNALS

Reclamation and Revegetation Research. Elsevier Science Publishers, Box 330, 1000 AH Amsterdam, The Netherlands.

Restoration and Management Notes. The University of Wisconsin–Madison Arboretum, 1207 Seminole Highway, Madison, Wisconsin 53711.

NEWSLETTER

Regeneration (quarterly newsletter). The Regeneration Project, Rodale Press, Inc., 33 East Minor Street, Emmaus, Pennsylvania 18049.

Index

Abnaki Indians, 26
acid mine drainage, 81–3, 85, 91, 92–3
aeration, 29
agricultural benefits, of prairie restoration, 125–6
agricultural pollution, 42–3; of Lake Annabessacook, 33–4; pesticide damage to peregrine eggs, 159–60, 165, 170–1; of salt marshes, 55
Agricultural Stabilization and Conservation Service, 34
air pollution, 4; C-56 fumes, 136–43, 147
Albany Felt Company, 28
algal growth, 35–6, 42, 56; in Lake Annabessacook, 27–9, 31, 37, 41
alum treatment (of Annabessacook), 37–41

American Indians, 9, 26, 70, 72, 112, 113, 131; mining damage to, 95, 99, 103–5; see also specific tribes
Anaconda Copper Company, 102–5
anatum, see peregrine falcon
Annabessacook, Lake, 26–43; and agricultural pollution, 33–4; alum treatment, 37–41; federal funds for restoration, 33–4, 41–2; nutrient levels of water, 28–9, 32–3, 35–8, 40, 41; treatment plant, 28–9
aquatic plants (in sewage treatment), 64–5
arsenic, 29
Assateague Island National Seashore, 58
Augusta, Me., 27, 28, 29

Soldiers Grove, relocation of, 184–95; expenses and fund sources, 190–2; solar design, 192–4
Southern Kennebec Valley Regional Planning Commission (SKVRPC), 29–30
Sperry, Theodore, 109–10, 111
Squannacook Wildlife Management Area, 22
Stefanon, Robert, 80–1
Stoddart, Marion R., 10–25
Stolzenburg, Kurt, 155–7, 171
stratification, of lake waters, 35
streams, mining pollution of, 81, 85, 87, 88, 89, 93, 104; *see also* rivers
suburban solar housing developments, 175–83
sulfides, 81
Sunbeam Coal Company, 87, 88
Surface Mine Control and Reclamation Act of 1977, 84, 97–8, 213–14
surface mining, *see* mined land reclamation

tax incentives, for restoration, 216
Tax Incremental Financing (TIF) district, 192
teratogens, 132
tern, 62
textile industry (Annabessacook area), 28
timber industry, 131; damage to forests, 70–1, 73–4, 78
To Save a Bird in Peril (Zimmerman), 159
tourism, harmed by pollution, 27

toxic chemical pollution, 25, 130–152; C-56, 132–52; cleanup of, 145–6; legal settlement of cases, 144–8; national statistics on, 142; of White Lake industrial site, 130–52
transportation, in imaginary future urban restoration, 207–10
treatment plants: for Annabessacook restoration, 28–9; aquatic plants used in, 64–5; in imaginary future urban restoration, 204; for Nashua River restoration, 17–19, 23–5; for White Lake toxic waste site, 148–9
trout, 27, 87; brook, 44–54
trout stream restoration, 44–54
Trout Unlimited, 46–54
tundra peregrine, 157, 161
turbidity, of river, 25
typhoid, 10

Udall, Stewart, 14
Ulishney, Fred, 79–84
United Mine Workers, 86
U.S. Army Corps of Engineers, 11
U.S. Bureau of Mines, 91, 92
U.S. Congress, 16, 42, 185, 215
U.S. Department of Labor, 21
U.S. environmental policy, 213–14; on flood disaster, 185–6, 190–2, 194; future restoration programs, 214–16; on mine reclamation, 84–5, 86–7, 90–2, 97–8; of Reagan administration, 42, 215; on water pollution, 16, 19, 21, 25, 33–4, 41–2; *see also* Environmental Protection Agency; federal funding

A Note on the Type

This book was set in a digitized version of Janson, a re-cutting made direct from type cast from matrices long thought to have been made by the Dutchman Anton Janson, who was a practicing type founder in Leipzig during the years 1668–1687. However, it has been conclusively demonstrated that these types are actually the work of Nicholas Kis (1650–1702), a Hungarian, who most probably learned his trade from the master Dutch type founder Dirk Voskens. The type is an excellent example of the influential and sturdy Dutch types that prevailed in England up to the time William Caslon (1692–1766) developed his own incomparable designs from them.

Composed by American–Stratford Graphic Services, Inc., Brattleboro, Vermont

Printed and bound by The Haddon Craftsmen, Inc., Scranton, Pennsylvania

Designed by Cecily Dunham